To Jean Piaget
To whom many books have been dedicated
but to whom no other author owes so much.

Child Development
and Experience

Child Development
and Education

A PIAGETIAN PERSPECTIVE

DAVID ELKIND

New York
OXFORD UNIVERSITY PRESS

Grateful acknowledgment is made to the University of Nebraska Press, to *Human Behavior*, and to Learning Systems Company for permission to reprint material which originally appeared in their publications.

0 9

PREFACE

The preface to a book should, I suppose, do several things. One of these is to introduce the reader to the author and to permit the author to give his reasons, or at least his justifications, for adding still another book to the library catalogues. Secondly, a preface should say a little bit about the book itself, what it covers and what it does not cover, who the audience is, and what the reader might expect in the way of return for reading the book. Last, but certainly not least, a preface should give credit where credit is due. For this writer, and I suspect for most others, there is a whole group of people, his family, his friends, his coworkers who—in a variety of ways—enable him to get the work done. This coterie of accomplices never gets mentioned on the title page but at least some recognition can be given in the preface. Accordingly, in this preface I will say something about myself, something about the book, and something about the people who helped make it possible.

First, something about the author and his reasons for writing this book. I am a child psychologist fortunate enough to have been introduced early in my career to Piaget's work. I had been trained in traditional learning theory and received my doctorate for a dissertation on the motivation of rats. I was also trained as a clinician and received a heavy dose of psychoanalytically oriented clinical psychology while serving a postdoctoral year as David Rapaport's research assistant at the Austen Riggs Center in Stockbridge, Massachusetts. But when I was introduced to Piaget's writings, I knew that at last I had found a psychology that was sufficiently broad to satisfy my philosophical preoccupations, my clinical interests, and my scientific conscience.

One of the unforeseen consequences of becoming a Piagetian psychologist was that at meetings of various sorts, educators were always asking me to say something about children that might be of interest or use to teachers. When I first started publishing Piaget-oriented research, in the early 1960's, Piaget was already well known in some educational circles. And by some process of intellectual contagion, I surmise, those working in the Piagetian tradition were expected to know something about children that was of value to school people.

Looking back on those early years I dread to think of some of the pronouncements I may have made regarding matters educational. My ignorance was brought home to me quickly enough by teachers bold enough to ask difficult questions and gutsy enough not to be satisfied with evasive and pedantic answers. By the mid-sixties I had realized, at last, that if I was going to talk meaningfully about education I ought to know a lot more about it than I did. My education in matters educational is rather long and drawn out, and it involved not only extensive reading, visiting schools, and observing in classrooms but also some more direct—hands on—experience as well. A few of these more practical experiences might be of interest to the reader.

In the spring of 1967 for a full semester I taught several second grade classes reading. It was in an inner city school and it was my first exposure to classroom teaching at the elementary school level. The next year, and every year since, we have brought children to our building from local schools to be tutored by undergraduates under my supervision. Over the years the program has grown and we now have groups of students in several different public schools and have started our own full day school, about which more will be said later. In the seminars we talk about observational skills, about assessment, about curriculum materials, about learning problems, and much more. The students in this program must commit themselves to a full year and must spend at least a day a week in the schools.

In 1970, Irene Athey and I were encouraged to apply for an Office of Education Grant to train early childhood specialists. The grant was awarded and we spent the next three years training teachers of teachers in early childhood education. It was a most valuable experience for me because many of the people in the program were very highly trained teachers and administrators and I learned a great deal about education from them. I am not sure how much they learned about children from me!

One of the dreams that grew out of our work with inner city children bused to our child development building was that someday we could open a full-day, full-time school for children who were of average ability but who were achieving below the academic norm. These were the children we had been working with over the years and I suspected that they were perhaps the most, or at least the most easily, salvageable. Thanks to a generous grant from a private foundation, we were able to open the doors of the Mt. Hope School in the fall of 1974.

It is a small school with no more than twenty children, two teachers, and a group of selected undergraduates who serve as tutors. Our building is a converted stone carriage house on an acre of land about a half-mile from the university. The children come from three middle city schools, and are bused to our building. We follow the public school curriculum and work closely with city school people. Our aim is to keep the children for a year and to return them to the city schools with self-confidence refurbished and tool skills improved. We are following our graduates up to see how they do when back in the public schools.

I will not say much more about the Mt. Hope School here, but it will come up repeatedly in later discussions. Many of the examples are, in fact, drawn from children who are attending or have attended our school. As headmaster of a school, I have learned a lot about the everyday workings of a school that I hadn't fully appreciated before. In addition, the school has allowed me to test at first hand some of the ideas and concepts I had been developing about learning, motivation, assessment, curriculum analysis, and about the running of classrooms. I feel more comfortable writing about these matters now that they have been tried out at the Mt. Hope School. This book, then, is an attempt to put down in one place some of the ideas about education that I have been developing over the years from my standpoint as a Piagetian. What I have tried to do is present a systematic approach to education from a child development point of view.

In the first section of the book, background information about the American social science scene, about Piaget's conceptual forerunners, and about Piaget's life and work is presented. Some readers may want to skip the first two chapters and go directly to the third. Indeed, the first two chapters can be read last by those who are relatively unacquainted with Piaget. For those who have some knowledge of his work, the first two chapters will, it is hoped, deepen their conceptual understanding of the context of Piaget's psychology.

The second section of the book is concerned with foundation material. In the chapter on understanding the child, some of Piaget's most important insights about children, including the stages of cognitive development, are presented. In the next chapter I have detailed three modes of learning that are either explicit or implicit in Piaget's writings. In addition I have tried to iterate several principles of learning that derive from developmental considerations and that might prove useful in the implementation of these three modes of learning in the classroom. The last chapter in this section concerns motivation and is again my attempt to build on Piaget's work and extend it to matters not covered by Piaget himself. So, while the matter of cognitive growth cycles is quite Piagetian, the motivational dynamisms described in the second part of the chapter are my own attempt to answer the question of what sort of motivation takes over when the developmental dynamics are at an end.

In the third section I have attempted to speak more directly to

classroom applications. The assessment chapter provides teachers
with an array of methods for determining children's levels of
cognitive development. The next chapter offers many examples
of how to analyze curriculum materials from a cognitive developmental point of view. My hope is that this chapter will sensitize
teachers, and curriculum builders as well, to the intricate problems
involved in creating child-appropriate curricula. The last chapter,
The Active Classroom, tries to detail how a teacher who has
absorbed what was presented in the previous chapters might
actually run a classroom.

Now that I have said what I have put into the book, it might be
well to say what I have left out. The book is written from a
Piagetian perspective and I have not tried to incorporate other
approaches, philosophies, or alternative models. In other words this
is not a comprehensive text in educational psychology. Nor have I
tried to summarize all of the voluminous literature related to topics
touched on in the book. Rather, I have tried to present basic
concepts and to illustrate them with anecdotal examples more
frequently than with experiments. Frankly, I believe that much of
the research in educational psychology is too far removed from
classroom realities to be of much help to teachers. I believe we need
much more natural history in the science of education before we
are entitled to become an experimental discipline.

I should probably say, too, that many of the subjects, topics, and
concepts discussed here could well be developed further and given
more substantial treatment. But while the temptation to make this a
really "big" book was great, I resisted it. A developmental approach
to education is not a finished system but a living, growing one that
is still young. To present such an approach elaboratedly would be
deceptive and suggest that it is farther along than it really is. My
hope is that the book will stimulate others not only to try these
ideas out in the classroom, but also to test them out by experiment.
I hope, then, that the book will be read not only by teachers in

training and teachers already in the field, but also by psychologists who are interested in educational research.

It is fitting to close by thanking the many people who made it possible for me to finish this book. My wife and children were gracious and understanding about my many physical and mental absences from the usual activities of family life. Miss Nancy Popoff, my secretary, has helped in many different ways; by typing the manuscript (and dealing with my atrocious handwriting), by her attention to style when I ignored it, and by her endless patience with my endless rewriting. Mrs. Sue Bank, the Mt. Hope School secretary, also helped with typing the manuscript among her many other chores. Mrs. Nancy Lyke and Miss JoAnn Deblinger, the teachers at the Mt. Hope School, taught me about classroom teaching and provided me with many classroom examples. Dr. Chari Briggs read an early draft of the manuscript and made many helpful comments. Kathy Paget and Donna Hetzel read parts of the book and made useful suggestions. A special thanks is due Leona Capeless for her gentle but thorough editing. And finally, Bill Halpin, my editor at Oxford, provided continual support and encouragement.

I could not close this preface without thanking the many teachers and administrators around the country whom I have had the pleasure of working with at educational meetings and conferences. Their comments, their questions, and their insights regarding children were a very important stimulus to my thinking. Much of what I learned from them is embodied in *Child Development and Education: A Piagetian Perspective.*

Rochester, New York   D.E.
January 1976

CONTENTS

BACKGROUND

THE SOCIAL SCIENCE CONTEXT

Just because truth is greater than man, do we have to look for it back among the Protozoa, the termites or the Chimpanzees?   J. PIAGET

Although Jean Piaget began publishing in the 1920s and experienced a brief popularity at that time, he did not become a major figure on the American scene until the 1960s. This delayed recognition of Piaget's work is probably due to a complex of interrelated factors. Like those of many men of genius, Piaget's ideas were ahead of his time. Many themes present in Piaget's earliest writing are only now coming to the fore in American social science. Contributing to Piaget's current acceptance are the attitudinal changes that have occurred in American education and psychology over the last fifteen years as the result of many different social forces. In this chapter, I want to review some of the themes basic to Piaget's work which are now becoming part of contemporary social science. I also intend to summarize some of the changes in American education and psychology that have contributed to Piaget's recent acceptance in America.

SOME PIAGETIAN THEMES

THE PSYCHOLOGICAL IMAGINATION

Piaget's psychological imagination, his broad view of human intelligence as the common denominator of all the sciences, was far ahead of that of most of his contemporaries. When Piaget began writing, in the 1920s, the social sciences were adamant in espousing

3

their independence of one another and of philosophy, from which they had just separated themselves. Anthropology was concerned with the study of cultures, with the mores and artifacts that made one culture different from another. And sociology studied social institutions, man in the aggregate. Psychology, in its turn, had to do with the study of individual human behavior. Each discipline had its own methods, its own theories and concepts, its own neatly carved-out empirical domain.

The need of the social sciences to differentiate themselves from one another and from philosophy was understandable when they were in the process of establishing themselves in their own right. But Piaget recognized that this was but a stage in social science (much as it is in the development of the child) and that these disciplines would not long abide by their arbitrary definitions and would begin to merge and to combine in various ways. The true scientific spirit cannot be limited by fixed boundaries or rigid conventions of methodology. What is most important in science is not the respective disciplines themselves but rather the problems, the questions that once asked need to be answered by scientific means.

In his own work Piaget crossed disciplines from the very start. Trained as a biologist, he combined methods of clinical psychology with naturalistic observation to answer questions about concepts proper to mathematics and physics as well as anthropology and sociology. The discipline that Piaget created, genetic epistemology, was a kind of experimental philosophy dedicated to the study of the role of human intelligence in the construction of all human knowledge. Piaget hoped to rejoin the social sciences by grounding the parent of them all, philosophy, in research. That is to say, philosophy, which gave birth to all of the experimental disciplines, had been rejected by them as being unscientific. Piaget, by creating an experimental philosophy, removed the main reason for the rejection of philosophy and provided a new discipline that could serve in the reunification of the sciences.

Although the reunification of the sciences suggested by Piaget's work has a long way to go for its full realization, much progress has been made in this regard. In contemporary social science, while the boundaries still exist for some investigators, they have been leaped over by many others. There is, for example, the work in "psychobiology" (1966), which related physiological changes in the organism to corresponding changes in behavior. In this discipline the workers combine the methods and concepts of the experimental biologist with the methods and concepts of the behavioral psychologist. While purists in both fields may object to such crossing over, the quality of work resulting from these efforts must be the final criterion of their worth.

Some other contemporary examples of such discipline crossings can be cited. The current movement in "psychohistory" originated by Erik Erikson (1950) is devoted to the utilization of both psychological and historical methodologies to provide a broader and deeper picture of men and women and of their times than is possible with either methodology alone. And there is "psycholinguistics," a thriving new field in which individuals trained in both child development and in linguistics use their knowledge in both domains to provide a comprehensive picture of the evolution of language in the child (e.g. Slobin, 1971).

The crossing of interdisciplinary boundaries is not limited to psychologists. In a recent book entitled *Sociobiology: The New Synthesis*, Edward Wilson (1975) describes another new interdisciplinary field which looks at the biological basis of social behavior in every type of organism including man. Likewise, in his work Erving Goffman (1963) combines anthropological field methods with sociological concepts and psychological insights to provide a "microsociological" picture of contemporary American behavior in public places. These examples could be multiplied, and they illustrate how many contemporary social scientists are combining methods and approaches as they concentrate on problems rather than upon disciplines.

This emerging perspective of social science as an overlapping set of methodologies, perspectives, and problems was set forth most dramatically by the late C. Wright Mills in his renowned book *The Sociological Imagination* (1959). He wrote:

> The social scientist seeks to understand the human variety in an orderly way, but considering the range and depth of this variety, he might well be asked: Is this really possible? Is not the confusion of the social sciences an inevitable reflection of what their practitioners are trying to study? My answer is that perhaps the variety is not as disorderly as the mere listing of a small part of it makes it seem; perhaps not even as disorderly as it is often made to seem by courses of study offered by colleges and universities. Order as well as disorder is relative to a viewpoint, to come to an orderly understanding of men and societies requires a set of viewpoints that are simple enough to permit us to include in our views the range and depth of the human variety. The struggle for such viewpoints is the first and continuing struggle of social science [p. 133].

The viewpoints of psychobiology, psychohistory, psycholinguistics, sociobiology, and microsociology, all reflect the kinds of perspective that Mills was calling for. These new viewpoints allow us to encompass, from a relatively simple perspective, a broad panorama of human depth and variety. Piaget's genetic epistemology is even more comprehensive than these interdisciplinary perspectives and speaks to a higher-order perspective that will encompass the disciplines themselves as part of the human variety. In this regard, Piaget's simple viewpoint of the human intelligence that underlies all of the sciences is still much in advance of contemporary interdisciplinary efforts. But these interdisciplinary efforts make Piaget's broader psychological imagination comprehensible, and hence have abetted Piaget's acceptance by American social scientists.

Piaget's psychological imagination, his vision of a reunification of the sciences grounded in a psychology of human intelligence, has important educational implications. Indeed, that is why so much emphasis is placed upon it here. If the disciplines are actually much less separate than they appear, if there are overlapping viewpoints, conceptions, and methodologies, then this clearly has implications for instructing children in these disciplines. Perhaps, for example, children ought first to be presented with problems and methods and only later with disciplines. Rather than starting children with "social studies" or with "science" labeled as such, perhaps they could begin with concrete problems such as describing the operation of an ant colony. In this way they might learn a general scientific method: observation, as well as some elementary facts about social organizations, without prejudging where the methods or the observations belong.

To be sure, the differentiation of the sciences provides a necessary division of labor and will continue to be useful. But new divisions of labor, new disciplines, have emerged and will continue to emerge. Consequently, in the education of children we must not insist too strongly on boundaries that may no longer exist when the child matures. Focusing upon problems and methods rather than upon disciplines is one way in which education can prepare children for the ever changing matrix of scientific disciplines and for a mature conception of the unity of the sciences.

STRUCTURALISM

Another contemporary theme which Piaget anticipated early in his own work is that of *structuralism*. Structuralism is a little hard to define because it is not a subject matter. Basically it is methodology, a way of looking at and organizing a realm of diverse phenomena that would otherwise seem unrelated. Although Piaget was a structuralist from the start of his career this methodology is only beginning to appear in contemporary scientific writing.

According to Piaget, the structuralist method of attacking phenomena is comprised of "three key ideas, the idea of wholeness, the idea of transformation, and the idea of self-regulation" (Piaget,

1970c). These are key ideas in the sense that they can be used to organize and to describe biological, physical, and social phenomena. Thus in contemporary science there are structuralists in anthropology, in linguistics, in mathematics, and in sociology. What marks a theory or conception as structuralist is, in every case, the method of approach, the manner of looking at and analyzing the subject matter in question.

Some examples of structuralist conceptions in different domains may help to make this methodology a little more concrete. In biology, to illustrate, the concept of an organism is a structuralist concept. An organism is a whole which is greater than the sum of its parts, it is a functioning totality whose parts enter into its wholeness but which cannot explain it. An organism is characterized also by rules of transformation, such as the ingestion of nutriments and their transformation into cells, energy, and wastes. Finally, the organism is also governed by principles of self-regulation such as homeostasis. Organisms function so as to keep body temperatures within certain limits, and to slough off through rest and sleep harmful byproducts of activity.

A society is another example of a phenomenon that can be described from a structuralist standpoint. Every society is greater than the sum of the individuals who make it up. Social institutions such as the family cannot be reduced to the individual members who make it up. Rather, it is the relationships between the individuals that constitute the institution in particular and the society in general. Within the society there are also rules of transformation by which individuals move from the estate of childhood into adulthood, from single to married, and so on. And finally, each society has principles of self-regulation, moral codes, laws, taboos, and religious values which serve both to control behavior and to correct it when it goes awry. This is not the place to go into the fine points of structuralism, or to argue the controversial aspects such as the priority of wholes and the breakdown of self-regulatory processes. All I wish to do here is to illustrate the basic concepts of structuralism and how they can be used to organize, at a very general level, many diverse types of phenomena.

One of the fields wherein structuralism surfaced early was that of information-processing and "cybernetics" (Wiener, 1948). With the rapid evolution of computers after World War II, new sets of concepts and ways of thinking about phenomena were introduced. Concepts such as "feedback" came into wide circulation, and familiar terms such as "program" and "memory" and "storage" took on new meaning. From a structuralist point of view, a computer program can also be regarded as a structural whole which is greater than the sum of the operations involved. It also contains a set of transformation rules regarding how information is to be processed. Finally, the program is self-regulating in the sense that the successive operations control one another, and determine what is to happen next. Computer programs help to organize phenomena in many different domains, from bank accounts to space flights.

Structuralist approaches have come to the fore in other domains as well, most notably in linguistics and in anthropology. Noam Chomsky's (1957) transformational grammars present a structuralist approach to language. According to Chomsky, each language constitutes a whole which cannot be reduced to the sum of its linguistic constructions, which are almost infinite. A set of transformational rules operates within the language to generate a variety of sentences from a few basic components. And finally, the operation of the transformational rules is self-regulatory in the sense that the sentences which are constructed stay within the rules of the system despite their novelty. Again, I am not arguing for the validity of Chomsky's analysis of grammar, which is currently being challenged, but only pointing out that the form of analysis is structural.

Within anthropology, the most noted exponent of structuralism is Claude Lévi-Strauss. He has argued (1969) that beneath many different social forms, such as kinship systems, there is a characteristic logic common to all societies. This logic, like Chomsky's grammar, generates a variety of cultural forms or wholes which are not reducible to the components. A kinship system is a set of relationships that cannot be reduced to the participating individuals. One and the same individual can be father, uncle, cousin, brother, and so on. The transformation rules of the system allow individuals to change their relations without leaving the system, for example, a sister becomes an aunt on the birth of a nephew or niece. And the system is self-regulational in that there are mores and taboos against such things as incest which would produce relations not allowable in the system, e.g. a woman being a wife to her father.

It should be said that, although Chomsky and Lévi-Strauss employ a structuralist methodology, Piaget is not in complete agreement with their conclusions. Both of these men assume that the underlying structures are innate, whereas Piaget regards them as developing and changing. Here is what Lévi-Strauss (1963) says about the structures that underlie cultural forms:

> If, as we believe to be the case, the unconscious activity of the mind consists in imposing forms upon content, and if these forms are fundamentally the same for all minds—ancient or modern, primitive or civilized (as the study of the symbolic function, as expressed in language, so strikingly indicates)—it is necessary and sufficient to grasp the unconscious structure underlying each institution and each custom in order to obtain a principle of interpretation valid for other institutions and other customs, provided of course, that the analysis is carried far enough [p. 21].

Piaget argues that both Chomsky and Lévi-Strauss fail to distinguish between structures that are formed by societal institutions and those that are constructed by the individual in the course of development. Kinship systems and languages are products of collective intelligence and are not the products of individual minds. The two cannot, therefore, be regarded as comparable, as Chomsky and Lévi-Strauss assume. Rather, what is needed is an analysis of how individual minds cope with collective structures. Much of

Piaget's research on concepts of space (1956), time (1970a), and causality (1974) deals with how children learn structures that have been elaborated by society.

Although Piaget's theme of structuralism may seem tangential to the topic of the present book, namely, psychology and education, it is not really so at all. Much of what we call the curriculum is in fact a product or embodiment of collective intelligence. History, social studies, science, language arts are all products of the collective intelligence of mankind, a structured whole if you like, which is not reducible to the contribution of the individual mind. These disciplines necessarily embody a logic, but it is not the same logic as that utilized by the child. The failure to distinguish between the logic (the structure) of the discipline and that of the child is a perennial source of curriculum problems. One of the major mistakes of the "new math" was that it was taught according to the structure of the discipline (in which the concept of sets is fundamental) rather than according to the structure of the child (in whom the unit concept is the fundament of quantitative thinking). Piaget is quite explicit in this regard. He writes (1970c):

> The logic or the pre-logic of the members of a given society cannot be adequately gauged by already crystallized cultural products: the real problem is to make out how the ensemble of these collective instruments is utilized in the everyday reasoning of each individual [p. 117].

In later chapters in this book, particularly the chapter on curriculum analysis (Chapter VIII), the difficulties presented to children by a confusion of the logic of the discipline with the logic of the child will be highlighted. Structuralism provides an analytic tool for examining the curriculum as well as for observing the development of intelligence, making it possible to evaluate the curriculum in relation to the mental capacities of the child. Structuralism, then, is an orientation which has particular relevance for education.

INTERACTIONISM

A third theme of Piaget's work which is echoed in contemporary social science is interactionism. What Piaget has maintained throughout his long career is that human intelligence is always a joint product of maturation, of social and physical experience, and of an overriding dynamic principle, equilibration. From Piaget's perspective, the nature-nurture problem is not one of either/or, but rather one of perpetual sequence. Experience gives rise to new mental structures which expand the child's range of potential experience that in turn gives rise to new mental structures. Interactionism means that one can never assign a human ability, trait, or behavior to heredity or environment alone but only to their sequential transactions.

When Piaget first began publishing, his interactionism ran head on against American environmentalism. In part this environmentalism was a product of our British empiricist heritage, in part a reaction to German nativism (particularly after World War I), and in part a reflection of values that were uniquely American. This American value system, a combination of the frontier and Puritan mentalities, placed great emphasis upon work and divine guidance as the prime necessities to success in life. Ours was a society opposed to aristocracy, to status based upon birth rather than upon accomplishment. And it was a society that refused to set limits on what it could accomplish. "The difficult we do today, the impossible will take a little longer." It is in the context of boundless faith in what any man could achieve, if he was industrious and God-fearing enough, that environmentalism in American social science has to be understood. In many ways American social science tried to demonstrate what the cultural value system already dictated, namely, that the environment was in a large part responsible for what we call "human nature."

In anthropology many different investigators demonstrated the environmental origin of human nature. Whether a society was aggressive and hostile, or kind and giving, was determined by its particular cultural constraints. The field studies of Ruth Benedict were among many which sought to demonstrate how large a part culture played in the shaping of human behavior. In her book *Patterns of Culture* (1934) Benedict recounts the story of a native infant who was reared by French missionaries. The child came from a tribe in Patagonia that was thought to be one of the most primitive in the world. Abandoned by the tribe in its chaotic rush to escape the missionaries, the child was adopted and reared by two of the missionaries who subsequently returned to Europe. By the time the child reached maturity she spoke two European languages, had Western habits, and was Catholic by religion. She had also attained a bachelor's degree in biology. Benedict used the example to illustrate the impact that culture can have on human character and personality.

In sociology too the emphasis was upon the environmental molding of self and personality. The so-called Chicago School of Sociology, the School of Mead (1934) and Burgess (1929) emphasized, among other things, the role of other persons in the construction of the self. The self grew out of the "reflected appraisal" of other persons in the course of social interaction. How we come to think about ourselves is a consequence of how others have reacted to us in the course of early experience. This was a far cry from the European emphasis upon inborn personality and character "types."

In psychology, environmentalism was also dominant. Its original and leading exponent was John Watson (1928). It was Watson who launched behaviorism and gave us the now well-known statement that, given an infant, he could, with proper conditioning, transform the child "into butcher, baker, beggarman, king." The concentration upon learning—defined as the modification of behavior as a result of experience—as the dominant problem of psychology reflected this environmental basis. The fact that learning was the dominant topic in psychology for three decades bears dumb witness to the prevalence of environmentalist thinking in this discipline.

It should be said that along with contradictions in the American value system (racism, for example, suggests that the environment has nothing to do with the plight of the blacks in America), there were contradictions in the disciplines. In psychology, for example, the field of intelligence testing grew up side by side with the growth of learning theory. And the same textbook that recounted the wonders to be wrought by the environment to people in different circumstances also proclaimed the doctrine of IQ constancy—the notion that the IQ is relatively impervious to environmental events. On the other hand, writers like Arnold Gesell (1948), who emphasized the role of maturation, seldom got mentioned in the textbooks on child psychology. There were contradictions aplenty in American psychology's environmentalism.

Social science attitudes have changed dramatically in the past twenty years as a result of many varied and complex social forces. One of these is the change in the American value system. With the disappearance of the frontier, the great depression of the 1930s and the decline of religion as a major force in American life, there was a significant shift away from individualism and toward social responsibility for the disadvantaged. This new sense of social responsibility, which had its origins in the welfare and social security legislation of the 1930s, erupted in full force in the 1960s with the civil rights movement. The exercise of social responsibility was called for by many disfranchised groups, including women, who demanded equal opportunities in our society.

Implicit in this shift from individualism to social responsibility was the recognition that in a complex and pluralistic society individuals are not always responsible for their own fate. It came to be recognized that forces beyond their control could determine people's fortunes in life. But if individuals are vulnerable to social forces, they are vulnerable to genetic factors as well, to physical and mental limitations that no amount of will power, hard work, or divine guidance is able to overcome. Hence the shift from individualism to social responsibility carried with it a new respect for the genetic factors in human behavior, and a greater recognition of human limitations imposed from within as well as from without.

This new awareness of individual limitations was aided and abetted by the dramatic rise of experimental biology and physiology during the same period. It is hard to appreciate fully how far we have come in these disciplines within the short space of several decades. The breaking of the DNA code was but one in a series of dramatic leaps forward in our understanding of genetic transmission. Moreover, the fields of psychobiology and sociobiology have demonstrated the close links between individual and social behavior and biological processes and substances. Once it was recognized that behavior could be determined by gene complexes and not single genes, it became clear that even complex behaviors could be genetically programmed.

The change in the American value system away from individualism toward social responsibility and the growth spurt in the biological disciplines were probably jointly responsible for a shift in social science away from a rigid environmentalism toward a more balanced view regarding the respective roles of nature and nurture. Unfortunately, a middle-ground, interactionist position is not always easy to maintain, and some contemporary theorists have swung almost entirely to more extreme positions. In the preceding discussion the nativistic positions of Lévi-Strauss and of Chomsky were described. And the genetic position of Jensen (1969) with respect to the intelligence of blacks is well known. Apparently it is easier to take an extreme position than it is to hold the middle ground.

Despite the emotional atmosphere generated by the recognition of the role of genetics in the determination of human behavior, recognition of this role did help make Piaget more acceptable to American social science. Nonetheless, Piaget was often (and still is) misread as a maturationist who argues for a fixed timetable of mental development. Nothing could be farther from the truth. What Piaget does argue is that there is a fixed sequence of development that must be gone through, but that the rate at which children progress through the stages will depend upon many different factors, including the nature of the physical and social environment in which they are reared.

Piaget's interactionist position again has important implications for education that will be emphasized in various places in this book. As I will discuss in more detail in the chapter on the active classroom (Chapter IX), the Piagetian position on education means that when instructing children both freedom (nature) and structure (nurture) must have a place. The teacher provides structure in the materials offered in the classroom, but provides freedom in the opportunities children have to explore and elaborate them. And, more generally, structure and freedom in the classroom are in constant alternation with one another, so that neither one nor the other dominates the educational scene. So freedom and structure, development and experience, are always involved in an educational program consistent with the Piagetian position. On the other hand, neither the entirely teacher-dominated nor the entirely child-dominated classroom is consistent with a true interactionist position.

CHANGES IN EDUCATION

Over the past several decades there have been changes in American education in some ways as dramatic as those that occurred in social science generally. Two of these changes are of particular importance for the present discussion in that they helped bring about the recognition of Piaget's work in education. One of these was the civil rights movement which brought about a new willingness on the part of educators to consider alternatives to existing educational approaches and formats. The second major change in education of relevance to the present discussion was the curriculum reform movement, which emerged at the demise of progressive education. It was the curriculum reformers who were among the most instrumental in "rediscovering" Piaget for education. Each of these changes now needs to be expounded in a little more detail.

THE CIVIL RIGHTS MOVEMENT

It is not necessary here to go into the whys and the wherefores of the civil rights movement that became so prominent in the 1960s. What is important from our present perspective is the effects this movement had upon the educational establishment. One consequence of the movement was that the poor academic achievement of many inner city children and the substandard quality of the education that they were receiving were brought to the attention of the general public. Among the many reactions to this public revelation was the effort to prepare young children for school by giving them a"head start" in government-sponsored early childhood programs. Another reaction was the search for new and different educational approaches that might suit the needs of minority children to a greater extent than the traditional school which was geared to the middle-class child.

The search for new alternatives in education led to the discovery, among others, of the informal education approach that had developed in some British primary schools (Featherstone, 1971; Silberman, 1970). In these child-centered schools the work of Piaget was well known (largely through the writings of Nathan Issacs (1959)) and his theory of child development was the conceptual rationale for much informal educational practice. Hence the discovery of the British informal educational methods had, as one result, a recognition of the implications of Piaget's writings for classroom practice. It was not only Piaget who was rediscovered as a consequence of education's new openness to alternatives. Montessori (1964) was rediscovered as well. There had been a short flurry of interest in Montessori in America early in this century, but that died after a critical attack by a student of John Dewey's (Kilpatrick, 1914). With the new emphasis on early childhood education brought about by the civil rights movement, and the new openness associated with it, however, Montessori schools took root all over the country. Such schools, which numbered only in the dozens in 1960, now number close to a thousand. The rediscovery of Montessori had reciprocal effects with regard to the rediscovery of Piaget. In both cases recognition of the one made recognition of the other European "educator" more acceptable.

As part of this snowballing effect of openness and search for alternatives, critics of American education also began to look to Piaget for support of their arguments. Educational innovators such as Holt (1964), Herndon (1968), and Kohl (1967) found intellectual affinities with Piaget's work and often used his writings to substantiate their demands for changes in the educational system. So Piaget was imported into American education through diverse routes, through informal British primary education, through the rediscovery of European educators generally, and through the writings of critics of American education who used Piaget to bolster their arguments.

THE DEMISE OF PROGRESSIVE EDUCATION,
AND THE CURRICULUM REFORM MOVEMENT

The new openness in American education in the 1960s owed something to the demise of the progressive education movement in the 1950s (Cremin, 1961). Progressivism in education, as fostered by John Dewey, argued that the central aim of American schools was to teach children to live productively in our society. To this end, the curriculum stressed American history and geography as well as politics and literature. In the progressive tradition, the classics and the history and culture of other countries were always regarded as secondary to the study of American life and culture. Not surprisingly, science played a small part in a curriculum designed to adapt children to the social life of the community.

Although only a small number of American schools were actually organized according to the ideals that Dewey advocated (e.g., 1956), the progressive philosophy did dominate the choice of curriculum materials for American education as a whole. In the 1950s this progressive philosophy came under a many-sided attack which reached the magnitude of a *Blitzkrieg* with the launching of the Russian Sputnik in 1957. Although the onslaughts came from noneducators, such as Admiral Rickover, as well as professional pedagogues, they all challenged the progressive conception that the principal aim of education was to teach children to adapt to society. The critics pointed to the inadequate achievements of children not only in science but in the tool subjects as well. The academic achievement of schoolchildren became a national debate.

These attacks on progressivism, in concert with many other historical factors described in detail by Cremin (1961), ended the reign of the progressive philosophy as a dominant force in American education. In its stead, a new philosophy of education, which held that the aim of education was to help children develop their mental abilities, to teach them how to think, came into prominence. One consequence of this new educational philosophy was the launching of a curriculum-reform movement that was supported by government agencies, most notably the National Science Foundation. Scholars of distinction in their own disciplines were recruited to write curricula for the schools. The late Max Beeberman at the University of Illinois became the leader in the writing of the "new math." At Berkeley, Robert Karplus began his work on science curricula, the Science Curriculum Improvement Study, an effort that has continued until the present day. Zacharias, at M.I.T., was another academic builder of science curricula for children. Jerome Bruner, then at Harvard, became involved in creating new social studies curricula, namely, *Man: A Course of*

Study. These were but some of many notable curriculum efforts that were the leading edge of educational reform in the 1960s.

The curriculum reforms of the 1960s opened still another route for the discovery and appreciation of Piaget's work. When the curriculum builders looked to American child psychology for child-development principles that might guide their efforts, they found precious little that was of use. Data on learning gleaned largely from experiments with rats, or with children but using concepts and apparatus designed for animals, had little to offer those who wanted to teach children mathematics, science, and social studies. The curriculum builders were forced to look beyond American shores for guidance, and when they did so they found an extensive body of information about how children come to understand number, space, time, causality, and much more. They also discovered a general theory of intellectual development that served to integrate these diverse findings and which also provided a general guide for curriculum instruction. The curriculum reformers, Beeberman, Karplus, Bruner, and others, have all acknowledged their large debt to Piaget.

In education, therefore, the search for new educational alternatives and the need to build new curricula adapted to the thinking of children led to the rediscovery of Piaget in the 1950s and early 1960s. Since that time his influence in education has grown steadily, so that today there is not a single recent textbook in educational psychology which does not devote a considerable portion of its pages to the research and theory of Jean Piaget.

CHANGES IN PSYCHOLOGY

Over the past several decades remarkable changes have occurred in American psychology as well as in American education. Not all of these changes can be detailed here, nor is this the place for a full historical accounting of why, when, and how many of the changes took place. Again, for our purposes it will suffice to review briefly those changes which were particularly relevant to making Piaget more acceptable to the American psychological establishment. These changes were the dethronement of learning theory, the emergence of ego psychology, and the advent of computers and information-processing concepts and theories in psychology. Each of these changes will now be discussed in a little more detail.

THE DETHRONEMENT OF LEARNING THEORY

It is really hard to appreciate, in the context of contemporary American psychology, the hammer-hold which learning theory had on the discipline during the period from the 1930s to the 1950s. Nor is it possible to comprehend how involved and intense were the studies and theorizing centered on a rat's behavior at a choice point in a maze. The maze-learning paradigm colored the whole of psychological research, including child psychology. I still recall one of the first psychological conventions I attended. In one session an investigator had built a life-size maze through which children were run with different weights hung upon their backs. The question had to do with the effect of effort on maze running. Much of the research on children was, and in some cases still is, modeled upon research first conducted with rats.

Interestingly enough, one of the most potent voices against the sterility of the maze-learning research was himself an animal investigator. It is odd but true that the publication of B. F. Skinner's *The Behavior of Organisms* (1938) was one of the more important events that paved the way for the eventual recognition and acceptance of Piaget's work by American psychology. What Skinner accomplished, and only someone within the system could have carried it off, was to challenge psychology's vain attachment to physics as a model of psychological science. Skinner argued that the kind of data we have in psychology, at least at this stage in our discipline, does not warrant elaborate experimentation and mathematical theorizing. Observing and counting, he argued, are more appropriate to our discipline than delicate experimental manipulations. Skinner, more than any other psychologist, helped to make a naturalistic psychology more acceptable in this country.

Obviously there were other factors beside Skinner's work that led to the dethronement of traditional learning-theory research. The social upheavals of the late 1950s and early 1960s made society look to psychology for help in providing better education for blacks, a better understanding of the psychology of persons who could assassinate a President, and better understanding of youth who were alienated and alienating. To these demands upon psychology, traditional learning theory had precious little to offer. Psychology was suddenly confronted with a concept it had not had to face before, namely, relevance. And it found that its encapsulated concern with rats could not be justified when society demanded a viable psychology of human behavior.

THE EMERGENCE OF EGO PSYCHOLOGY

Another significant development that helped make possible Piaget's acceptance in the 1960s was the advent of ego psychology. Although Freud alluded to ego processes early in his writings, he did not devote major attention to the ego until the latter part of his career (1927). For Freud, ego functions, cognitive processes as we would call them today, arose from a failure of the primary processes, such as fantasy, to satisfy basic needs. We come to test reality and to elaborate cognitive processes because hallucinations and fantasies, however elaborate they may be, cannot satisfy real physical hungers.

In the 1940s a group of psychoanalysts led by Heinz Hartmann (1951) introduced the notion of the "conflict-free ego sphere," the idea that some ego processes were present from the start of life and were not derived solely from the failure of primary-process thinking. This development in psychoanalytic theory lent new value and prestige to ego functioning. It prompted psychologists such as David Rapaport (1951), George Klein (1967), and Roy Schafer (1967) to explore phenomena such as ego autonomy, cognitive style, and the ego ideal from a cognitive as well as a dynamic point of view. And last but not least, it lent weight to the study of cognitive processes in children. David Rapaport (1951) was one of the first psychologists to recognize the significance of Piaget's work for ego psychology as well as for psychology generally, and it is not surprising that one of his students, to whom he introduced Piaget, is the author of the present book.

THE ADVENT OF COMPUTERS AND INFORMATION PROCESSING

A more general development that helped make Piaget acceptable in psychology was the advent of the computer and of information-processing technology and concepts. Computers provided a new and fascinating model for mental functioning that went far beyond the simple switchboard or chemical analogies utilized heretofore. When computers were programmed to play records, to play tic-tac-toe and chess, there was a beginning understanding of how complex, intricate, and magnificent the human brain really is. Terms like *feedback, storage, encoding, decoding, programs,* and *memory load* were at first used metaphorically and then descriptively with regard to human thinking. Attempts at computer simulation of cognitive processes also helped legitimize the study of human cognitive processes as complex mental abilities not reducible to simple associative linkages.

There were many other changes in psychology that contributed to a heightened recognition of Piaget's work. The growth of psycholinguistics, for example, made naturalistic research methods, such as those employed by Piaget, more acceptable. The rapid growth of clinical psychology brought into the discipline many people who were concerned with thought processes and who began to look to Piaget for guidance in this domain. And the rapid growth of developmental psychology as a sub-specialty was in part a consequence of Piaget's fame and influence, and in part contributed to it and to his acceptance in American psychology as a whole.

In contemporary psychology there are indications that Piagetian themes are surfacing in many different fields. In learning theory, for example, the notion of association by contiguity first gave way to the notion of mediation (by learned inner responses), which in turn has given way to the notion that learning is "assimilation of information about the environment" (Bolles, 1975). In addition it is argued that instead of universal laws of learning we may have to accept the fact that there are "species specific constraints on the kind of information that can be assimilated" (Bolles, 1975). In social psychology there has been a recent spurt of interest in "attribution" theory dealing with the conditions under which one person attributes certain characteristics to another (e.g. Livesley and Bromley, 1973). And in clinical psychology there is much current interest in Rotter's (1954) conception of locus of control—whether the individual believes he is master of his fate or that he is at the mercy of forces outside his control.

So, in a variety of ways, contemporary psychology is moving towards a transactional view of human behavior. Such a view sees the individual and the environment as in constant interplay so that it becomes irrelevant to talk about nature *or* nurture because nurture is always a product of nature and vice versa (Sameroff and Chandler, 1975). This transactional view of human learning and behavior is just what Piaget has been advocating from the very start of his professional career.

II
CONCEPTUAL FORERUNNERS

"The great man who at any time seems to be launching some new line of thought is simply the intersection or synthesis of ideas which have been elaborated by a continuous process of cooperation."   J. PIAGET

It is clear from Piaget's own expressions of indebtedness that his thinking was stimulated by the writings of leading scholars from such diverse fields as philosophy, physics, biology, sociology, and logic as well as by innovators in psychology and education. A comprehensive discussion of Piaget's intellectual heritage would constitute a large work in its own right. Only a glimpse of Piaget's conceptual heritage can be given here, but I believe it is important to acknowledge at least some of Piaget's intellectual forebears—if for no reason other than to make clear that Piaget's work did not emerge out of nothing. Accordingly, the first section of the present chapter will deal briefly with some of the Piagetian themes and concepts that have their origin in philosophy, biology, and psychology. The second section will review some of the themes and concepts that foreshadowed Piaget's own approach to educational matters.

PHILOSOPHICAL FORERUNNERS

Piaget thinks of himself as, first and foremost, a philosopher, but a philosopher of a very special kind. He has rejected both the speculative systems of traditional philosophy and the applied systems of the more recent philosophies of science. Rather, he has created his own philosophy, genetic epistemology, which seeks to answer philosophical questions by means of empirical investigation. Put differently, Piaget seeks to answer some of the questions about knowing that philosophers answered by means of "armchair analysis" by looking at how children come to know the world.

Although Piaget's approach to philosophy is extraordinarily innovative, it nonetheless contains a number of themes that were present in the thinking of many different philosophers from Aristotle to Hegel. While it is not possible to trace Piaget's philosophical heritage at length, some of his major intellectual forerunners can be briefly mentioned, particularly in relation to the themes for which they are best known and which are reflected in Piaget's own work.

ARISTOTLE

There are two different Aristotelian themes present in Piaget's work. One of these is taken from Aristotle's metaphysics, the other from his ethics. Although both themes are considerably modified in Piaget's psychology, they reflect the influence of Aristotle's writings.

The first theme has to do with the importance of reason as the highest of man's functions. Aristotle believed, according to Russell (1945): "insofar as men are rational they partake of the divine, which is immortal" (p. 172). Reason is present in both man and nature and so provides for the unity of biological and physical. Reason offers insight into physics, ethics, morality, politics, and so on. It is this Aristotelian belief in human intelligence as providing the underlying unity of the sciences that constitutes Piaget's "psychological imagination," described in Chapter I.

A second theme derived from Aristotle is that of the "golden mean," which is a principle of Aristotelian ethics. According to Aristotle, every virtue is a balance between two extremes which are, in themselves, vices. Courage, a virtue, is the mean between

cowardice and rashness. Likewise, justifiable pride is the mean
between vanity and humility. Of course there are many virtues that
do not seem to fit readily into this scheme. Truthfulness, for
example, which Aristotle says is the mean between boasting and
false modesty, applies to other domains than the self. When a
politician tells the truth about a proposed piece of legislation, this
honesty is in simple opposition to dishonesty. Some virtues would
appear to be two-valued.

However that may be, the notion that extremes are of somewhat
lesser value than a balanced middle ground is one that appears in
Piaget's work in many different guises. In Piaget's view, for
example, human intelligence lies between play (which is entirely
personal) and imitation (which is entirely social). Human intelligence is a healthy balance of the two and is at once personal *and*
social. Many other instances of this "golden mean" idea are present
in Piaget's writings. The concept of probability is midway between
the ideas of accident and determinism (Piaget, 1951), and the idea of
number is between the concepts of relation and of classification
(Piaget and Szeminska, 1952). As we shall see, the concept of the
golden mean appears in a very different way in Hegel's writing,
which also influenced Piaget. But, in my opinion, Aristotle's notion
of a golden mean has influenced Piaget every bit as much as Hegel's
dialectic.

KANT

Another major philosophical influence on Piaget came from the
writings of Immanuel Kant. By many philosophers Kant is regarded
as the most important thinker since Aristotle (a gap of two
thousand years!). It is clearly not possible to give a detailed
discussion of Piaget's relation to Kant here, but some of the Kantian
themes present in Piaget's work can be briefly described.

Perhaps as important as anything else was Kant's methodology.
In contrast to the ancient philosophers, such as Aristotle, who tried

to systematize knowledge, or to the empiricists, such as Locke, who tried to reduce it to its elementary components, Kant critiqued knowledge itself. That is to say, Kant assumed that you could understand the structures of human knowing by a critical analysis of human knowledge. Previous philosophers tried to understand the nature of human knowledge by describing the mental processes involved in acquiring knowledge. In a very real sense Kant was the first structuralist, in that he assumed a commonality between the structure of knowledge and the structure of human intelligence. As we saw in the preceding chapter, the structuralist theme is a fundamental one in Piaget's work, wherein the analysis of knowledge (concepts of all sorts) goes hand-in-hand with the analysis of mental structures.

A second Kantian theme reflects his major contribution to modern thought. Kant set himself the task of answering the question which might be phrased: How can we arrive at valid information about reality on the basis of reason alone? His answer, and one that created a Copernican revolution in philosophy (Kant himself said it would), was that reason was not "pure." Reason contained certain *a priori* categories of knowing which served to organize experience but which were not derived from it. Space, time, and causality are intellectual constructions which are elicited by experience but are not reducible to it. Raw experience, the environment in of itself (*Ding am Selbst*), is never known to us. All we know are our reconstructions of it. Although, in his day, this constructionist concept was well known with respect to color perception, Kant made the monumental leap to the constructionist view of *all* knowledge. There is no knowledge without mental activity, and no knowledge is a simple reading of environmental givens.

This constructionist view of human knowledge is clearly shared by Piaget. What Piaget has added to the Kantian position is that the categories of knowing are not static in the sense of remaining unchanged throughout the whole life cycle. Rather, Piaget has demonstrated that the child's conceptions of space, time, and causality, change with age and mental development. Piaget is thus a neo-Kantian in the sense that he accepts the proposition that all knowledge involves intellectual construction. But, in contrast to Kant, for whom the categories are primary and the process of construction is secondary, just the reverse is true for Piaget. For Piaget it is the constructive activity itself which gives rise *both* to knowledge on the one hand and to human intelligence (the structures of knowing) on the other.

HEGEL

One consequence of Kant's work was the devaluation of "pure reason," the traditional philosopher's stock in trade. Instead Kant argued for the importance of synthetic reasoning which was elicited by, but not limited to, experience. Hegel, who followed Kant, attempted to bring pure reason back into philosophy as a valid instrument. Hegel did, however, follow Kant in regarding human knowledge, and in Hegel's case human history as well, as the starting point of philosophical analysis. Hegel's philosophy is extraordinarily complex, and only two of his themes, which seem to have influenced Piaget, will be described here. One of the themes is wholeness, the other, dialectics.

A problem that has plagued philosophers from the beginning has been the problem of relations. "Left" and "right" are not properties of things in the way that color and form are. One and the same object can be both on the left and on the right of other objects, which—from a strict logical standpoint—is contradictory. In traditional logic there is a single subject and predicate, but in relations there are two subjects, "A is to the left of B" and hence, according to traditional logic, there can be no such proposition. One solution, the one adopted by Hegel, is to say that the proposition is itself a whole, a unity or a subject. Higher-order wholes can thus encompass lower-order contradictions.

It is not necessary here to go into Hegel's notions about wholes and reality. What is important is to note that Piaget's emphasis on wholes, as noted in the discussion of his structuralism, is a Hegelian emphasis. So, too, is the notion of wholes as complex systems, which are the higher-order wholes in Hegel's system. The wholes talked about in Gestalt psychology, the whole as greater than the sum of its parts, is also Hegelian. Piaget's relation to the Gestalt conception of wholes will be described later in the chapter.

The second Hegelian theme that appears in Piaget's work is the dialectic, Hegel's form of logic. He starts from the assumption that a predicate cannot be used to describe the whole of reality. You can say an apple is red, but if you say the universe is red you get into trouble. There are other colors besides red, so red cannot be the color of the universe conceived as the whole of reality. The dialectic is essentially a way of getting out of these logical dilemmas (first posed by Kant as antimonies).

The dialectic consists of a thesis, an antithesis, and a synthesis. Suppose we start with the thesis "reality is red." But this assumes that there are other colors such as blue which reality is not. Since nothing exists beyond the universal or absolute, we have to state the antithesis—"the absolute is blue." But again there are other colors besides blue. Hence we are forced into the synthesis "the absolute is red and blue." But there are other colors besides red and blue so that the process has to be undertaken all over again. Hegel applied this dialectical approach to many different issues, including intelligence. He assumed that intelligence begins with the senses, with a single awareness of objects. Then there is a criticism of the senses, as intelligence becomes subjective. A final stage is reached when there is a criticism of thought as well as of the senses, a true self-knowledge. Such self-consciousness, of what comes from without as well as of what comes from within, is the highest kind of knowledge.

The notion of a dialectic is very evident in Piaget's conception of development. For example, his concepts of assimilation, accommodation, and equilibration (about which much more will be said later) can be regarded as equivalent to thesis, antithesis, and synthesis. At each stage of intellectual development they take on different contents, but the basic process is the same. Logical contradiction was an anathema to Hegel which his dialectic resolved. For Piaget, logical contradiction becomes a basic dynamic of intellectual growth, the dynamic of an ongoing dialectic process between the child's reason and experience.

Much more could be said about Piaget's forerunners in philosophy and his debts to Bergson and Brunschvicg, among others. But the foregoing illustrations may suffice to place Piaget's work in the philosophical traditions that provided themes and problems which he proceeded to attack in his own way and with his own methodology.

FORERUNNERS IN BIOLOGY

Piaget's initial training as a scientist was in the field of biology. As a youth he gathered mollusks, classified them, and conducted naturalistic experiments with these crustaceans. Not surprisingly, biological conceptions and naturalistic methods have played a very great part in Piaget's research and in his theory. Again, it is not possible here to expound in depth Piaget's intellectual debt to leading thinkers in biology. Just a few men will be described whose thinking has had particular importance for Piaget's developmental psychology of intelligence.

Before proceeding to the discussion of individual investigators, it might be well to pose the question to which these workers addressed themselves, namely, the origin of the species. This question has puzzled mankind from the beginning of recorded history. One answer is recorded in the Biblical book of Genesis, in which the species are described as God's creation. Somewhat different explanations were offered by the Greeks, who anticipated modern notions of evolution. Andromache said there was a watery primordial matter that was the basis for all evolution. Heraclitus suggested that evolution might involve conflict and a struggle for survival. Aristotle's contribution was to classify animals and to insert some order into nature's variety. It is in the context of the abiding question regarding the origin of the species and the early answers given to these questions that later contributions must be understood.

LAMARCK

One of the truly influential writers on evolution in the modern period was Lamarck. His conceptions of evolution are summarized as four laws (Dowdeswell, 1962):

i. Nature tends to increase the size of living individuals to a predetermined limit.
ii. The production of a new organ results from a new need.
iii. The development reached by a new organ is directly proportional to the extent to which it is used.
iv. Everything acquired by an individual is transmitted to its offspring.

Lamarck answered the question of how desirable traits were retained and undesirable ones lost, by his theory of "the inheritance of the effects of use and disuse." From this point of view a snake lost its limbs when it took to crawling, and an elephant got its trunk by using its snout to grasp and squirt. Like Erasmus Darwin (Charles Darwin's grandfather), Lamarck believed that characteristics acquired as a result of interaction with the environment could be inherited. In contemporary language, Lamarck was proposing that what an individual learns, permanently affects his genes, i.e., causes a mutation.

Piaget is clearly not a Lamarckian but he does believe that the environment can produce changes that may eventually be inherited. In his early work on mollusks (1920–21) he discovered that when a ridged mollusk from the lakeshore was removed to a pond, the ridges did not appear in subsequent generations, which were smooth shelled. What this demonstrates, that an organism's genetic potential will be differently realized in different environments, has come to be called the "norm of reaction."

Perhaps a more familiar example will help to make this concept concrete. Suppose an individual grew up in Arizona and never experienced allergies. When, however, the individual moves to the Northeast he develops a host of allergic reactions to various pollens. Hence, whether or not an individual will show a genetic potential for allergies depends upon the environment in which he lives. And if he and his offspring remain in the new environment the latent potential for allergies will continue to be manifest. So Piaget is a sort of neo-Lamarckian in the sense that he believes that different environments can bring out different latent, genetic potentials. It is in this sense, of the environment bringing out latent genetic potentials (rather than producing a genetic mutation), that one can speak of the inheritance of environmentally realized characteristics.

DARWIN

It is probably fair to say that the single most important conceptual influence on Piaget came from the writings of Charles Darwin (1956; first pub., 1859), whose theory of evolution involved the concepts of *adaptation, natural selection,* and *variation.* With regard to adaptation, Darwin argued that those species which could best survive in any given environment were best adapted to it. This was not an entirely circular argument because Darwin had collected enormous amounts of evidence to show, in detail, how species varied with different locales. For example, giant tortoises from different islands could be distinguished by characteristic variations in shape.

Darwin's concept of *natural selection* (which Alfred Russell Wallace arrived at independently and at about the same time) held that species which were best adapted to the environment were likely to breed and dominate resources at the expense of those species less suited to the environment. Natural selection, however, could only operate if there was considerable *natural variation* in a species to select from. And selected characteristics had to be transmitted. Although Darwin's theory of genetic transmission (Pangenesis) is not widely accepted, it revealed his awareness of the necessity of postulating genetic mechanisms for reproducing the products of selection and for producing variations.

The concept of adaptation is at the very heart of Piaget's work. From Piaget's standpoint, human intelligence is an extension of biological adaptation and amounts to adaptive thinking and action. However, while Darwin was concerned with the evolution of the species, Piaget has been concerned with the development of the individual. For Piaget, therefore, the principal modes of adaptation are *assimilation* and *accommodation*, by which an individual adapts to his world. For Darwin the modes of adaptation were variation and natural selection, by which a species adapts to its environment.

Perhaps Piaget's debt to Darwin is as much attitudinal as it is conceptual. Darwin's work made possible the conception of a developmental psychology of intelligence. If the species can evolve progressively, adapting itself to the environment, this must be the means by which the individual evolves as well. So Piaget's conception of individual intelligence as the progressive adaptation of thought and action to the environment is a direct analogue of Darwin's theory regarding the origin of the species. I do not believe it is accidental that one of Piaget's most important studies is entitled *The Origins of Intelligence in Children* (1952b).

FORERUNNERS IN PSYCHOLOGY

The psychological work going on during the early decades of the century also had an impact upon Piaget, but in a somewhat different way than did the work of his forerunners in biology and philosophy. For one thing, Piaget was a contemporary of the first full-fledged psychologists and matured during the formative years of the discipline. So the impact of psychologists on Piaget was more personal and direct. Although the psychological ideas of other psychologists influenced Piaget, the personal contacts, support, and criticism were probably of equal or greater value in his development. In a full-scale biography these personal influences will have to loom large, but here they can only be alluded to.

Of particular interest to Piaget was the work of the Gestalt psychologists, Köhler (1947), Koffka (1935), Wertheimer (1945), and Lewin (1936). These psychologists took physics as their scientific paradigm and were concerned to show that human behavior could be described by concepts and models analogous to those which had proved useful in explaining physical phenomena, namely, field theory. In addition, there was in the background of Gestalt theory a Hegelian influence. The emphasis of Gestalt theorists upon wholes as systems, irreducible to the sum of their parts, is a Hegelian conception.

It was the Gestalt psychologists' concern with wholes, rather than their concern with physical models, which interested Piaget. When the Gestalt psychologists tried to describe perceptual organizations in terms of rules—good form, continuity, closure, and so on—they were employing a structuralist methodology. But the Gestalt psychologists, while stressing wholes which involved some rules of transformation and self-regulation, made two errors from Piaget's point of view. One of these was the reliance on electrochemical models of brain physiology to explain the operation of wholes, and the other was the claim that the principles of organization were innate.

At the time the Gestalt psychologists were writing, Piaget believed that the available models of brain functioning were not sufficiently advanced to serve as analogues to intellectual functioning. And the notion that the principles of mental organization were innate was, he believed, contrary to what his observations suggested regarding the persistent interaction of nature and nurture. But among the many psychologies emerging at the time Piaget found Gestalt psychology among the most congenial. Its leaders were literate, widely read, and had broad cultural as well as scientific interests. And, among the psychologists, only the Gestalt psychologists had some appreciation for the structuralist methodology inherent in Piaget's work.

In addition to the Gestalt psychologists there were many other early workers in the field who had an impact upon Piaget. James Mark Baldwin was a developmental psychologist who appreciated the epistemological significance of child study; that is, he understood that such study had relevance for the general question of "how we know" reality. Indeed Baldwin's (1906) "genetic logic" is a kind of predecessor to Piaget's genetic epistemology. Piaget is indebted to Baldwin in more particular ways as well. To illustrate, he credits Baldwin for the concept of "circular reaction," which plays an important part in Piaget's description of the evolution of the child's construction of reality.

G. Stanley Hall and his questionnaire studies of children's conceptions affected Piaget in a less direct way. Although the information regarding the "contents of children's minds" (1891) was of limited value because of the uncontrolled nature of the questionnaire studies, it was suggestive. Hall's notion that the child "recapitulated the development of knowledge in the race" contained the notion that children have world views different from adults'. This was in contrast to the then accepted notion that the child's mind was simply "emptier." Piaget, too, emphasizes the child's conception of the world as being different from the adult's rather than less, although he does not accept the recapitulation hypothesis.

Another important influence on Piaget was the work of Alfred Binet. Although Binet is best known for the development of the intelligence test, he also did important work on individual differences in personality. His book, *L'Étude expérimentale de l'intelligence*

(1903) based upon studies of his two daughters is an unheralded classic investigation of personality types. Many of the "little experiments" that Binet employed with his two daughters, such as comparing quantities that were the same in amount but different in appearance, are suggestive of Piaget's more elaborate conservation experiments. Moreoever, Piaget began his child psychology by giving intelligence tests in Binet's old laboratory school, and Piaget's own semi-clinical interview is, in part, a derivative of Binet's psychometric testing procedures.

Piaget also worked with and was influenced by Edouard Claparède and Pierre Bovet, both of whom had held Piaget's chair in Geneva before Piaget. Claparède's (1906) interest in education and the relation of child development research to education sensitized Piaget to this issue, and he has for many years held administrative positions with International Education Associations. Some of Claparède's notions, such as prise de conscience, the "coming to consciousness" during the learning process, stimulated several of Piaget's research studies. But Claparède had a personal influence as well and appeared to be a professional "father figure" to Piaget, whom he very much admired. It was a mutual admiration, and Piaget always writes warmly about Claparède.

Pierre Bovet is perhaps best known for his work in the development of the religious conceptions of children (1928). He described the young child's conception of adults as God-like figures who were all-knowing and powerful. According to Bovet, this situation changes as the result of particular experiences. When the child discovers a fault in parental knowledge or reasoning, there is a dethroning of the parent in the child's eyes and a subsequent search for new God-like figures. Eventually the young person discovers that all human heroes have feet of clay and is led to the notion of a transcendental God. Again, some of Bovet's concepts and findings were background for some of Piaget's own work, particularly for his early writings on the child's conception of the world.

Perhaps the single most continuing psychological influence upon Piaget came from the work of Henri Wallon, who, though older than Piaget, was contemporaneous with him. The two men were good friends, but they disagreed at many points about the course of mental growth. Wallon was a Marxist and a dialectician. He was particularly concerned with how children moved from one stage to another, and of the role of emotions in this transition. He tried to integrate the cognitive and the affective in an ongoing dialect of development.

Wallon (1947), too, collected interview material with children, but it was less systematic than that collected by Piaget, and the interpretations were more questionable because of the lack of depth in the data. Here is a sample of a Wallon interview in which the "couple," two ideas that are closely related in the child's mind, is clearly revealed:

> C: "The moon, what is it?" "There is light in the moon." "Can you see the moon now (it is daytime)?" "No." "Why?" "Because it is raining." "How does the rain block the light of the moon?" "Because the moon is for nice weather." "If it was not raining now, could you see the moon?" "Yes." [p. 79]

Here the "couple" has to do with the association of moon and "light" on the one hand and the association of moon and "night" on the other. The above dialogue shows the child struggling with these contradictory "couples." Wallon's work was a constant stimulus and challenge to Piaget's, and the two men often attacked the same areas in succession. It was a very productive friendship and professional interaction.

FORERUNNERS IN EDUCATION

The heritage of Piaget's educational ideas dates back at least as far as Rousseau, and that is about as far back as we will go. Indeed, in reading Rousseau one finds many ideas that might have grown out of Piaget's psychology as well. Piaget's connection to other educational innovators is more open to conjecture, but that he had read the classic writers in the field, such as Pestalozzi, Froebel, and Montessori, is clear from his allusions to their work (Piaget, 1970b). In this section some of the major themes of each of these writers and those of John Dewey will be briefly presented in relation to ideas shared by Piaget.

ROUSSEAU

An influential forerunner of contemporary education and Piaget was Jean-Jacques Rousseau. In his classic description of the rearing of a young aristocrat, *Émile* (1956), Rousseau put forth a theory of knowledge and learning that continues to be advocated in some sectors of society today. Rousseau was an exponent of the "noble savage" theory in regard to the primitive peoples who were being discovered by European explorers in the New World and in Africa. According to the "noble savage" theory, "all that comes from nature is pure and unsullied, all that comes from society is dirty and corrupt."

Émile was as much a critique of educational methods of the time as it was a prescription for education. Rousseau argued that we know little of childhood and yet presume we do and thus make serious mistakes. He also pointed out that what is learned in school is but a small part of the total learning the child is engaged in. What is learned in school is given special social status not because of its importance, but because of the circumstance under which it is acquired. To remedy the situation we need to give equal status to skills and accomplishments acquired outside of school.

Rousseau (1956) was one of the first to recognize the importance of child-centered education, of teaching the child that which is of use to him rather than that which is of use to adults.

> A man must indeed know many things which seem useless to a child. Must the child learn, can he learn, all that the man

must know? Try to teach a child what is of use to him as a child and you find that it takes all of his time. Why urge him to the studies of an age he may never reach, to the neglect of those studies which meet his present needs? But, you ask, will it not be too late to learn what he ought to know when the time comes to use it? I cannot tell. But this I know, it is impossible to teach it sooner, for our real teachers are experience and emotion, and adult man will never learn what befits him except under his own conditions. A child knows he must become a man; all the ideas he may have as to man's estate are so many opportunities for his instruction, but he should remain in complete ignorance of those ideas that are beyond his grasp. My whole book is one continued argument in support of this fundamental principle of education.

The principle of teaching children that which they are capable of understanding at their level is a clear-cut implication of Piaget's work. Indeed, his findings provide the tools for a better understanding of what children are capable of comprehending at any particular stage of development. A corollary to the idea of teaching at the child's level is teaching children that which is of use and interest to them at the time, without concern for the long-range value of the material. Rousseau argues that it is better to nourish the child's appetite for learning with tasty material of transparent worth than to kill this appetite with tasteless, heavy material of considerable cultural value. Again this is a theme implicit in Piaget and described in more detail in the chapter on motivation (Chapter VI).

Another Rousseauian principle that is echoed in Piaget's educational psychology is the willingness to lose time:

Hold childhood in reverence and do not be in a hurry to judge it for good or ill. Give nature time to work before you take upon yourself her business, lest you interfere with her dealings. You assert you know the value of time and are afraid to waste it, you fail to perceive that it is a greater waste of time to use it ill than to do nothing and that a child ill taught is further from excellence than a child who has learned nothing at all.

The impatience of the adult for children to be grown up ignores the fact that the child is a growing organism and as such follows a timetable that cannot be rushed.

> Nature would have children be children before they are men. If we try to invert this order, we shall produce a forced fruit, immature and flavorless, fruit that rots before it can ripen. Childhood has its own ways of thinking, seeing and feeling.

Piaget's emphasis upon the fact that there is an "optimal time" for the growth of certain abilities echoes Rousseau's insistence upon the fact that growth takes time and cannot be hurried.

Piagetian and Rousseauian views are parallel in still another respect. One of Rousseau's insights was the importance of the coordination of perceptual *and* motor activity in the learning process. In Rousseau's time, and too often today, learning is regarded as primarily a matter of perceptual input. Indeed, contemporary information-processing theories of learning sometimes emphasize the role of perception to the exclusion of the motor system. Rousseau recognized that it is the coordination of perception and motor action that is important to learning. Piaget's emphasis upon sensorimotor coordination and the abstraction from action (based on perception of actions) again emphasizes that motor as well as perceptual activity is crucial in discovering and learning about the world.

A final parallel between Piaget and Rousseau has to do with Rousseau's emphasis upon the difficulty of learning. He recognized how easy it was for children to acquire verbal terms without understanding, and how deceptive this was: "The apparent ease with which children learn is their ruin. We fail to see that this very ease proves that they are not learning. Their shining, polished brain merely reflects, as in a mirror, the things we show them." True learning involves struggle and difficulty. A personal example highlights this point. One of my sons said to me, "I don't understand, you go out and come back on a sailboat like you do on a motorboat, so why not go on the motorboat since it is faster?" He was puzzled and struggling to learn, to make sense out of his world. That struggle cannot, indeed should not, be avoided. As Piaget writes (1964), "The aim of education is to teach children to think for themselves and not to accept the first idea that comes to them."

It has to be emphasized that these parallels between the educational concepts of Rousseau and Piaget are just that—parallels. Rousseau arrived at his insights regarding learning and education by means of keen observation and intuition. Piaget gleaned his insights through ingenious experiments and theoretical analysis. The parallels do not suggest that Piaget borrowed from Rousseau so much as they indicate that "great minds run together" when they are dealing with the same subject matter even when they approach this subject matter with different tools and from different historical perspectives.

Other writers in education also foretold some aspects of Piaget's educational psychology. Rousseau was primarily a theorist rather than a practitioner. Dewey has said, in fact, that had Émile been a real child he would have been a "prig." But the writers we turn to now were practitioners, and their ideas about education derived from actual work in the classroom. Their efforts changed not only the ways in which people thought about children but also the ways in which children were actually taught. If nothing else, their ideas helped to prepare a social climate amenable to the writings of a Jean Piaget.

PESTALOZZI

For a small country, Switzerland has produced more than its share of outstanding psychologists, psychiatrists, theologians, and educators. Even Rousseau, though not a native Swiss, resided for a long time in Geneva. So it is really not surprising to find that the modern era in elementary education was ushered in by yet another Swiss, Heinrich Pestalozzi, who was born in Zurich in 1746. It was Pestalozzi who tried to put Rousseau's Enlightenment ideas about children and education into practice.

The spirit of the Enlightenment was the admonition not to accept ideas on the basis of authority but rather to test them against experience. The traditional scholarship had used authority, such as Aristotle, as the basis of all learning. Bacon's *Novum Organum*, published in 1620, was the most notable expression of this revolt against authority as the basis of all knowledge. (The contemporary revolt against classical psychoanalysis which used Freud rather than experience as the basis for advances in theory is a modern-day version of the Enlightenment.) Rousseau extended the Enlightenment to education and challenged traditional, authoritative approaches to education. Experience, not authority, was to be the bedrock of education. Pestalozzi was the first to put this experience-based education into practice.

It is not really possible here to go into a detailed account of Pestalozzi's life and work, and a summary is to be found in Green (1914). Pestalozzi started several schools for what today would be called disadvantaged children, none of which lasted very long or was very successful. But out of his concrete experience Pestalozzi devised a pedagogy published in many books, perhaps the most famous of which was *Gertrude Teaches Her Children*. In the "letters" contained in this book, Pestalozzi described exercises concerned with developing the child's inner powers or faculties rather than with giving him what was needed for social situations, the catechism, etc. This was one of the reasons that Pestalozzi was under constant attack and could not establish a successful (i.e., state- and parent-approved) school. What he wanted children to learn was not what parents expected their children to acquire.

Pestalozzi was a son of the Enlightenment in that he stressed the education of the intellect rather than the learning of rote lessons.

He was particularly concerned that children acquire "definite" ideas. According to Pestalozzi one moves toward definite ideas by the following steps (Letter VI).

I. A. Separating the objects, thereby removing the confusion in sense impressions.

   B. Bringing together again in representations the objects which are alike, thereby making them clear.

   C. Raising these perfectly clear ideas to definite conceptions.

These steps are to be attained by:

II. A. Presenting confused sense conceptions separately.

   B. Changing the conditions under which the observations are separately made.

   C. Bringing them finally into connection with the remaining content of our knowledge.

Thus knowledge grows:

III. A. From vagueness to distinctness.

    B. From distinctness to clearness.

    C. From clearness to definiteness.

More explicitly knowledge grows as:

IV. A. Through the consciousness of the unit, form, and name of an object we attain *distinct* knowledge.

   B. Through the gradual extension of our knowledge to all its remaining qualities it becomes *clear*.

   C. Through the knowledge of the connection of its distinguishing ideas it becomes *definite*.

Progress in all three elementary subjects (reading, writing, and arithmetic) advances from:

V. A. Vague to distinct observation.

   B. Distinct observation to clear representation.

   C. Clear representation to definite conception.

[Green (1914), pp. 90–91]

Pestalozzi thus believed *actual sensory experience carefully organized and systematically worked out* to be the only sound basis of instruction.

This was the major principle of Pestalozzi's philosophy which he reiterated in many different ways throughout his various writings.

> . . . the man who in his youth has not caught butterflies, nor wandered over hill and dale hunting for plants, etc., in spite of all desk work, will not get far in his subject. He will always be exposed to blunders he would not otherwise have made.

What the child knows, he should know thoroughly and at first hand.

Unfortunately, despite his theoretical emphasis upon the importance of direct experience, Pestalozzi did not always practice what he preached. His children learned empty formalisms with the aim of training them in special powers.

> I was not so much concerned that my children should learn to spell, to read, and to write, as I was anxious that their mental powers should develop through these exercises in as all-around and effective way as possible. To that end I made them spell words by heart before they knew the alphabet and the whole room could spell the hardest words before they knew a single letter.

What happened was that Pestalozzi became enamored with the view that language awakens "the very impressions which these tones have always produced in the race" and hence language learning could substitute for experience. In Pestalozzi's later work, emphasis upon language learning, particularly in young children, eclipsed the principle of learning from direct sensory experience.

Pestalozzi's writing ushered in the modern era of education. His concern with the organization and presentation of curriculum materials stimulated a whole educational literature that has continued up to the "programmed materials" of today. The organizational format of Pestalozzi's schools, in which children learned through participation in community activities, was the forerunner of a theme that reappeared in progressive education, in British informal education, and in contemporary alternate schools. Pestalozzi's emphasis upon experience (regardless of his practice), his concern with the organization of materials, and his view that education is coextensive rather than separate from everyday life are modern notions he shares with Piaget.

One of Pestalozzi's most influential followers was a German, Friedrich Froebel. Like Pestalozzi, Froebel began by starting his own schools and developed his ideas about education from direct observation of children. Froebel was a deeply religious man who believed in the essential goodness of children. His educational program was moral and philosophical as well as instructional. The aim of education was to create individuals who could realize themselves fully and totally. Evil and badness did not exist separately but were manifestations of incomplete, interrupted, or stunted development. Education had to provide for the child's moral, aesthetic, and physical growth as well as for his or her intellectual development.

In practice Froebel tried always to find the universal in the particular, to start with something simple like a coin or a simple geometric form and move from that to more general ideas about man and the world. Froebel's treatment of the crystal (1893) is a case in point. The formation of crystals provides insight into diverse forms and into the concept of force:

> We meet this effect of force, henceforth, at every step of the study of crystal forms; indeed, the operation of crystallogenic force seems to be limited to this, and all crystals seem to owe their characteristics exclusively to this tendency. Indeed, this must be so; it is the first general manifestation of the great natural laws and tendencies to represent each thing in unity, individuality, and diversity; to generalize the most particular, and to represent the most general in the most particular; and lastly, to make the internal external, the external internal and to represent both in harmony and union.

From a Froebelian point of view, a ball represents not only a sphere, but the earth, the universe, and the unity and diversity of man. The most sophisticated concepts can be derived from objects in the everyday world that surrounds us.*

Another Froebelian contribution was the conception of the child's developmental stages and their relation to learning. Pestalozzi was concerned with the general principles of learning regardless of the child's developmental level. But Froebel recognized that children learned differently at successive stages of development. Although his stages were primitive by todays standards, they foreshadowed some contemporary ideas. For example, Froebel suggested that the preschool child seeks to make his internal world external through language, whereas the elementary school child seeks to make the external world internal, to incorporate cultural knowledge. This distinction between preschool and elementary education is echoed in contemporary arguments against formal education in early childhood programs (Elkind, 1969).

Perhaps Froebel's greatest contributions were his humanism and his holism. He regarded all children as valuable regardless of their social status or background, and he thought that all children had the potential to live rich, creative, and productive lives. Second, he was opposed to the compartmentalism and drill of Pestalozzi and argued instead for the development of the child as an integrated whole. Education should provide for a full life with opportunities for work and play, for leisure and recreation, for art and spiritual renewal. Childhood should be regarded not as mere preparation for life, but as an important period of life valuable in and for itself.

The work of Froebel and Pestalozzi created considerable educational ferment in both Europe and in America. In part at least, their work contributed to much educational reform and to the provision of publicly supported education for all children. The "enlightened"

---

* Bruner's (1961) famous dictum that a child can be taught any subject matter at any age in an intellectually honest way, is a latter-day version of this Froebelian theme.

view of childhood which they presented also contributed to reforms in dealing with retarded and defective children. Although individual workers like Itard (1962; orig. pub., 1806) and Seguin (1907) had worked with such children on a small scale, it was only toward the end of the nineteenth century that the special educational needs of the retarded and defective child came to be fully appreciated. The work of Alfred Binet, and of Maria Montessori was closely connected with provisions for exceptional children. We have already spoken briefly of Binet, and Montessori remains to be considered.

MONTESSORI

Maria Montessori was an exceptional person in many respects. She was the first woman to attain an M.D. degree in Italy and did so under personally trying conditions. Her early work was with retarded children and she leaned heavily for her inspiration upon the writings of Itard and Seguin. Later she was commissioned to begin educational programs for disadvantaged children living in apartment buildings in Rome. In setting up these little schools, *casa dei bambini,* she adapted many of the principles that she had learned in working with exceptional children.

Like Pestalozzi and Froebel, Montessori was more of a practitioner than she was a theorist. She often borrowed contemporary theoretical concepts to describe and account for her practice, and these did not always quite fit. As a practitioner, however, she was a superb teacher and clinician. Her contributions on the practical plane, particularly to early childhood education, were enormous. It was Montessori (1964), for example, who recognized that little children need a world scaled to their dimensions and had her schoolrooms furnished with child-sized chairs and tables.

Montessori (1964) also recognized the importance of classroom organization and introduced the concept of the "prepared environment." In the Montessori classroom, shelves around the walls and in center cupboards are filled with materials that are ready for the child to take out and start working with. In such a classroom different children can work with different materials for varying lengths of time. Such a prepared environment allows the child to make choices and take responsibility for his own learning. It also provides opportunities for learning to share and to take turns (when two or more children want to use the same materials at once).

Montessori is perhaps best known for the various instructional materials she constructed. Many of these materials have to do with basic sensory impressions and conceptions. The pink tower is a series of size-graded blocks which children can use to build a pyramid-like tower. Skeins of colored yarn of different hues and of different saturation of the same hue are used to help children with color discrimination. Metal modules of different sizes, fit within a wooden form, provide experience in size-weight relationships. Lines of ten beads that can be joined with other lines are used to teach basic number concepts. Many of the materials were "autodidactic" in the sense that children could detect their own "errors" when working with them.

In her approach to the education of young children, Montessori combined some of the ideas of Pestalozzi and Froebel. Her materials are such as to help the child separate and then combine sensory impressions, much as Pestalozzi advocated but did not practice. And, in her use of materials to teach not only sensory concepts but also ways of dealing with the self and other children, she followed Froebel's emphasis upon the unity of all educational materials and practices. That is to say, the child who works with the Montessori materials was learning general social, as well as particular cognitive, skills.

In her theorizing Montessori borrowed from the biology of her time and came to speak of "sensitive periods." For Montessori, sensitive periods were those times in the child's life when she was most open to particular forms of sensory training. In the course of development there are times when a child is "ready" to acquire

certain skills and abilities. During this period the child spontaneously seeks out the nourishment required for growth and spontaneously practices that ability at great length. During this period repetition is a sign of mental abilities unfolding. (This is discussed at greater length in the chapter on motivation, Chapter VI.)

While it is not possible to review here all Montessori's contributions, one other has to be mentioned. Montessori was a staunch
advocate of the position that teachers must be, first and foremost,
close observers of children. She believed that teachers have to
watch how children use materials for clues as to how the materials
should be best presented. It is important to emphasize this point,
because some of Montessori's followers have rigidified her teaching
practices to the point where children are allowed to use materials
only in prescribed ways. This is contrary to the spirit of Montessori
teaching, which is to allow children to experiment on their own and
to take clues for teaching practice from children's spontaneous
explorations. This does not mean that children should not be given
direction, but only that there must be awareness that direction
should sometimes come from the child. In her emphasis on the
teacher as an observer who can learn from children, Montessori
shares an important component of Piaget's educational psychology.

JOHN DEWEY

The last figure to be dealt with in this background sketch of
educational forerunners is John Dewey. In some ways Dewey was
like Rousseau. Dewey was a philosopher of first rank who
concerned himself with many philosophical areas other than
education. But in other ways Dewey was like Pestalozzi, Froebel,
and Montessori, who were primarily practitioners. From 1896 to
1903 he directed, with the assistance of his wife, a laboratory school
at the University of Chicago, where he and his colleagues were able
to test out some of his educational ideas.

In his early writings Dewey reflected the influence of Hegel and argued for the importance of universal truths for education. But he later came under the influence of William James, who converted him to pragmatism. The basic tenet of pragmatic philosophy is that all thinking, all concepts, have to be tested against their consequences in the real world and not against universal truths. A rather vulgar way of expressing this philosophy is to say "that if it works it is good." Not only should children be taught within a pragmatic framework, they should learn to be pragmatic in their own personal orientation toward life.

The kind of educational program associated with Dewey was called "progressive," and an excellent history of that movement is provided by Cremin (1961). For our purposes it is enough to say that Dewey, in his description of educationally valuable schools, quoted heavily from the works of Rousseau, Pestalozzi, Froebel, and Montessori. In the book he wrote with his daughter Evelyn Dewey, entitled *Schools of Tomorrow* (1962), various schools around the United States that followed the principles of progressivism were described.

According to William Brockman in his introduction to the Deweys' *Schools of Tomorrow*, progressive schools have the following characteristics:

> 1. A living school building, where pupils have contacts with several teachers in various types of activity each day; 2. community life with democratic interaction and cooperation under the guidance of teachers; 3. a longer school day with fewer and shorter occasions; 4. the discontinuance of traditional subject matter as such; 5. encouragement of each child towards the highest standards of achievement and a policy of continuous promotion; 6. discipline is intrinsic, not imposed by the teacher; 7. wholesome play as an integral part of the school program, and 8. wholesome, informal living in place of the rigid traditional education.

Although the education advocated by Dewey was experience-based, rather than authority- or discipline-based, he did not believe all experiences were of equal educational value. In his book *Experience and Education* (1938) Dewey made it clear that experiences could be mis-educative as well as educative.

> Any experience is mis-educative that has the effect of arresting or distorting the growth of further experience. An experience may be such as to engender callousness; it may produce lack of sensitivity and of responsiveness. Then the possibilities of having richer experience in the future are restricted. Again, a given experience may increase a person's automatic skill in a particular direction and yet tend to land him in a grove or rut; the effect again is to narrow the field of future experience. . . . Each experience may be lively, vivid, and "interesting" and yet their disconnectedness may artificially generate dispersive, disintegrated, centrifugal habits. The consequence of formation of such habits is inability to control future experiences.

Dewey challenged not only the idea that all experience is "good" or educative, but also the idea that all growth is beneficial. The young person who is becoming a criminal as a consequence of his or her associates is a case in point. Growth which is too rapid or too slow, too narrow or too broad, could also be detrimental to the individual. In the instance of growth, as in the instance of experience, a more detailed analysis of the practical import of these terms is required before they can be wholeheartedly advocated.

Dewey said that the educative value of experience could be assessed according to two principles, *continuity* and *interaction*. In talking about continuity, Dewey had in mind more than "preparation" for later subjects by training in earlier ones; rather, for Dewey preparation "means that a person, young or old, gets out of his present experience all that there is in it for him at the time which he has it" (p. 49). Here Dewey suggests that the present be exploited to the full and not sacrificed to some long-distant future goal. In fact, Dewey said, utilization of the present experience to the full is the best preparation for the future. Experiences of all sorts interact in ways that cannot always be predicted, but it is this interaction that makes fully enjoyed experience so beneficial. Continuity and interaction are made optimally possible when given experience is dealt with as fully and broadly as possible.

As often happens, many of Dewey's ideas were misinterpreted and distorted. He was often blamed for the excesses of some progressive schools despite the fact that the practices in such schools violated the very principles of education that Dewey espoused. Yet Dewey's work carried forward the ideas of his predecessors (Rousseau, Pestalozzi, Froebel, and Montessori), refined and articulated them, and put them in the popular idiom of his age. His work set the stage for the contemporary informal education movement.

Dewey's contributions to educational theory were enormous. In contrast to his predecessors, Dewey looked closely at terms that had come to be romanticized as all good, such as "experience" or "activity" or "freedom." Dewey analyzed these concepts and demonstrated that they were too general to be of much practical use in education. His refinements of the concepts of experience and activity helped to distinguish between positive and negative experience, directed and aimless activity. In the best tradition of the evolution of knowledge, Dewey helped us to improve our understanding of basic educational concepts by analysis and differentiation.

Piaget has followed in Dewey's footsteps to the extent that he has further differentiated concepts such as experience and thinking. In his description of the construction of reality, Piaget has given a very detailed analysis of the way in which experience is organized in the child's activities and how it is related to the child's level of intellectual development. While Dewey described thinking in general pragmatic terms, Piaget described it in developmental terms that highlighted the strengths and weaknesses of the child's mental abilities at successive age levels. Piaget's psychology is consistent with the progressive, experience-based, thrust of Dewey's educational philosophy and has furthered it by differentiating and documenting the concepts that Dewey himself challenged and analyzed.

III

PRÉCIS OF PIAGET'S LIFE AND WORK

"Raised in Protestantism by a devout mother and the son of an unbelieving father, I experienced early in life, and in a very lively manner, the conflict between science and religion." J. PIAGET

It is probably fair to say that Jean Piaget is the single most influential psychologist writing today. His work is cited in every major textbook in psychology, education, linguistics, sociology, psychiatry, and other disciplines as well. There is now a Jean Piaget Society, which each year draws thousands of members to its meetings. And there are many smaller conferences both here and abroad that focus upon one or another aspect of Piaget's work. It is simply a fact that no psychologist, psychiatrist, or educator today can deem himself fully educated without having had some exposure to Piaget's work.

The man who has made this tremendous impact upon social science is now in his eightieth year and shows no signs of letting up his prodigious pace of research, writing, and lecturing. In the last few years he has published more than half a dozen books, has traveled and lectured extensively (he delivered the keynote address to the Piaget Society in June 1975 in Philadelphia), and continues to lead a year-long seminar attended by interdisciplinary scholars from around the world. The seminar is held in Geneva at Piaget's Center for Genetic Epistemology, which he founded more than fifteen years ago.

Each year Piaget invites scholars from all over the world to attend the Center for a year. Perhaps the greatest thrill of my life was the personal invitation from Piaget to spend a year at the Center in 1964–65. It was at the Center that I became acquainted with Piaget personally, and we have remained good friends over the years. I recall meeting Piaget about two years ago in New York when he came to America to receive the First International Kittay Award for scientific achievement. The ceremony was held at the Harvard Club, and Piaget presented a paper in the afternoon and a brief acceptance speech at the formal dinner that evening. The affair was attended by a small group of invited guests, many of whom, like myself, had worked with or been associated with Piaget in some way.

When Piaget appeared he wore his familiar dark suit and vest with the remarkable sweater that somehow keeps appearing and disappearing as you watch him. Piaget is of average height, solid in build, and looks a little like Albert Einstein, an impression heightened by the fringe of long white hair that surrounds his head and by the scorched meerschaum that is inevitably in his hand or in his mouth. Up close, Piaget's most striking feature are his eyes, which somehow give the impression that they see with great depth and insight. My fantasy has always been that Freud's eyes must have looked something like that. (Piaget's eyes are remarkably keen as well, despite his glasses. A year before the Kittay ceremony I visited him in Geneva and we took a walk together. As we climbed the small mountain in the back of his home, he pointed out wild pigeons, and flora and fauna toward the top which I could not see at all!)

On the afternoon of the Kittay Award ceremony, Piaget talked about his research on conscious-awareness. As one has come to expect from him and his coworkers, the studies were most original. In one investigation he asked children to walk upon all fours and then to describe the actions they had taken, for example, "I put my left foot out, then my right hand." What he found was that young children had great difficulty in describing their actions and that it was not until middle childhood that they could describe their actions with any exactness. Piaget also said (but was most probably joking) that he also asked some psychologists and logicians to perform the task. The psychologists did very well, but the logicians, at least according to Piaget, constructed beautiful models of crawling that had nothing to do with the real patterning of their actions!

At the dinner meeting that evening Piaget showed another facet of his personality. In the talk he gave when receiving the award he related his fantasy of the committee meeting at which it was decided that the award should go to him. He said that he imagined that the physicians on the committee were reluctant to give the award to a neurologist or physiologist who in turn were reluctant to see it go to a neurochemist or molecular biologist. Piaget appeared as the compromise candidate because he belonged to no particular discipline (except to the one he himself had created, although he did not say this) and was, therefore, the only candidate that everyone could agree upon. The speaker who gave Piaget the award assured him that, while his fantasy was most amusing, it had no basis in fact and that Piaget had been the first person nominated and was unanimously chosen by the selection committee.

There was not much chance to talk to Piaget after the dinner, but it was probably just as well. He does not really like to engage in "small talk," and at close quarters it is often difficult to find things to say to him other than about research. And yet such discussions seem rather inappropriate at dinner parties. His difficulty with small talk does not seem to extend to women, however, and with them he can be most charming in any setting and is not above even clowning a bit. It should be said, too, that on formal social occasions, when he is officiating or performing some titular function, he is most gracious and appropriate. It is the small interpersonal encounters, such as occur at the dinner table, that seem most awkward for him. Perhaps his total commitment to his work has produced this social hiatus, but it is certainly a small price to pay for all that he has accomplished.

Despite his achievements, Piaget's very great impact upon contemporary social science is surprising for several reasons. For one thing, it has been phenomenally rapid and recent. Although Piaget began writing in the early decades of this century, his work did not become widely known in this country until the early 1960s. It is only in the past ten years that Piaget's influence has grown in geometric progression to his previous recognition. For another, he writes and speaks only in French, so all of his works have had to be translated. Third, his naturalistic research methodology and avoidance of statistics are such that many of his studies would not be acceptable for publication in American journals of psychology. Most surprising of all is the fact that Piaget is advocating a revolutionary doctrine regarding the nature of human knowing that, if fully appreciated, effectively undermines the assumptions of much of contemporary psychology and education.

What, then, is it about Piaget's work and theory that has made him so influential despite his controversial ideas and his unacceptable (at least to a goodly portion of the academic community) research methodology? His influence comes from the fact that, theory and method aside, his descriptions of how children come to know and think about the world ring true to everyone's ear. When Piaget says that children believe that the moon follows them when they go for a walk at night, that the name of the sun is in the sun, and that dreams come in through the window at night, it sounds strange and is yet somehow in accord with our intuitions. In fact, it was in trying to account for these strange ideas (which are not innate because they are given up as children grow older and are not acquired because the ideas are not taught by adults) that Piaget arrived at his revolutionary theory of knowing.

In the past, two kinds of theories have been proposed to account for the acquisition of knowledge. One theory, that might be called the *camera* or *copy theory*, suggests that the mind operates in much the same way as a camera does when it takes a picture. This theory assumes that there is a reality that exists outside our heads and that is completely independent of our knowing processes. Like a camera, the child's mind takes pictures of this external reality, which it then stores up in memory. Differences between the world of adults and the world of children can then be explained by the fact that the adult has more pictures stored in his memory than does the child. Individual differences in intelligence can also be explained in terms of the quality of the camera, speed of the film, and so on. In this analogy, dull children would have less precise cameras and less sensitive film than bright children.

A second, less popular, theory of knowing asserts that the mind operates not like a camera but rather like a projector. According to this view, the infant comes into the world with a built-in film library that is part of his natural endowment. Learning about the world amounts to running these films through a projector (the mind) that displays the film on a blank screen that is the world. This theory asserts that we never learn anything new, that nothing really exists outside our heads, and that the whole world is a product of our own mental processes. Differences between the world of adults and the world of children can be explained by arguing that adults have projected a great many more films than have children. And individual differences can be explained in terms of the quality of the projection equipment or the nature and content of the films.

The projector theory of knowing has never been very popular because it seems to defy common sense. Bishop Berkeley, an advocate of this position, was once told that he would be convinced that the world was not all in his head if, when walking about the streets of London, the contents of a slop bucket chanced to hit him on the head. The value of the projector theory, sometimes called the *idealistic* or *Platonic* theory of knowing, has been to challenge the copy theorists and to force them to take account of the part which the human imagination plays in constructing the reality that seems to exist so independently of the operations of the human mind.

In contrast to these ideas, Piaget has offered a nonmechanical, creative, or *constructionist* conception of the process of human knowing. According to Piaget, the child constructs reality out of his experiences with the environment in much the same way that an artist paints a picture out of his immediate impressions. A painting is never a simple copy of the artist's perceptions, and even a portrait is "larger" than life. The artist's construction involves her experience, but only as it has been transformed by her own imagination. A painting is always a unique combination of what the artist has taken from experience and what she has added to it from her own scheme of the world.

In the child's construction of reality the same holds true. What the child understands reality to be is never simply a copy of what he has received by his *sense* impressions; it is always transformed by the child's own ways of knowing. For example, the writer happened to observe the child of a friend playing at what seemed to be "ice cream wagon." He dutifully asked customers what ice cream flavor they desired and then scooped it into make-believe cones. When I suggested that he was the ice cream man, however, he disagreed. When I asked what he was doing, he replied, "I am going to college." It turned out his father had told him that he had worked his way through college by selling Good Humor ice cream from a wagon. Here is but one example of how a child re-created his own reality from material offered by the environment. From Piaget's standpoint, we can never really know the environment, but only our reconstructions of it. Reality is always a reconstruction of the environment and never a copy of it.

Looked at from this standpoint, the discrepancies between child and adult thought appear in a much different light than they do for the camera and projector theories. Those theories assume that there are only quantitative differences between the child and adult views of the world, that the child is a "miniature adult" in mind as well as in appearance. In fact, of course, the child is not even a miniature adult physically, because the proportions are all wrong. A young child's head is about a fourth of his or her body size, while it is only one-seventh the body size of an adult. And, intellectually, his reality is qualitatively different than the adult's, because his means for constructing reality out of his experiences with the environment are less adequate. For Piaget, the child progressively constructs and reconstructs reality until it approximates that of adults.

To be sure, Piaget recognizes the pragmatic value of the copy theory of knowing and does not insist that we go about asserting the role of our own knowing processes in the construction of reality. He does contend that the constructionist theory of knowing has to be taken into account in education. Traditional education is based on a copy theory of knowing and assumes that if the child is given the words he will acquire the ideas that they represent. A constructionist theory of knowing asserts just the reverse, that the child must attain the concepts before the words have meaning. Thus Piaget stresses that the child must be active in learning, that he must have concrete experiences from which to construct reality, and that only in consequence of his mental operations on the environment will he have the concepts that will give meaning to the words he hears and reads. This approach to education is not new and has been advocated by such workers as Pestalozzi, Froebel, Montessori, and Dewey. Piaget has, however, provided an extensive empirical and theoretical basis for an educational program in which children are allowed to construct reality through active engagements with the environment.

Piaget's concern with the educational implications of his work comes naturally, because he has, for the whole of his career, been associated with the Institute de Rousseau, which is essentially a training school for teachers. And Rousseau, himself, made explicit a theme that has permeated Piaget's work, namely, that child psychology is the science of education. The union of child development theory and educational practice is thus quite natural in Switzerland, particularly in Geneva, where Rousseau once lived and worked. Indeed, Piaget's Swiss heritage, while it does not explain his genius, was certainly an important factor in determining the directions toward which his genius turned.

Switzerland is a small country that is exceptional in many different respects. It is, first of all, extraordinarily beautiful, a land of deep valleys, craggy mountains, and broad lakes from which the mountains rise up sharply and majestically. The houses, with their steep red tile roofs, carved wooden porches, and overflowing flower boxes, add extra charm to a landscape that is already heart-stoppingly beautiful.

Perhaps the most extraordinary thing about Switzerland is the number of outstanding psychologists and psychiatrists it has produced in relation to the modest size of its population (2,000,000 people). One thinks of Claparède, who preceded Piaget at the Institute de Rousseau in Geneva; of Carl Gustav Jung, the great analytic psychologist; of Hermann Rorschach, who created the famed Rorschach inkblock test; and of Friderich Binswanger, the existential psychiatrist. And then, of course, there is Jean Piaget. There appears to be something in the Swiss milieu that is conducive to producing more than its share of exceptional social scientists.

Piaget himself was born in a small village outside Lausanne. His father, a professor of history at the University of Lausanne, was particularly well known for his gracious literary style. Piaget's mother was an ardently religious woman who was often at odds with her husband's free thinking and lack of piety. Growing up in this rather conflictual environment, Piaget turned to intellectual pursuits, in part because of his natural genius, but perhaps also as an escape from a difficult and uncomfortable life situation.

As often happens in the case of true genius, Piaget showed his promise early. When he was ten he observed an albino sparrow and wrote a note about it which was published in a scientific journal. Thus was launched a career of publications that has had few equals in any science. When Piaget was a young adolescent he spent a great deal of time in a local museum helping the curator, who had a

fine collection of mollusks. This work stimulated Piaget to undertake his own collection and to make systematic observations of
mollusks on the shores of lakes and ponds. Piaget began reporting
his observations in a series of articles that were published in Swiss
journals of biology. As a result, Piaget won an international
reputation as a mollusciologist, and on the basis of his work he was
offered, sight unseen, the curatorship of a museum in Geneva. He
had to turn the offer down, however, because he was only sixteen
and had not yet completed high school.

Although Piaget had a natural bent for biological observation, he
was not inclined to experimental biology. The reason, according to
Piaget, was that he was *maladroit* or not well coordinated enough to
perform the delicate manipulations required for experimental
biology. Piaget's observations on mollusks was only one of his
many intellectual pursuits. He was very interested in philosophy,
particularly in Aristotle and Bergson, who speculated about biological and natural science. Piaget was initially much impressed by the
Bergonian dualism between life forces (*élan vital*) and physical
forces, but eventually found this dualism unacceptable. More to his
liking was the Aristotelian position which saw logic and reason as
the unifying force in both animate and inanimate nature. What
living and nonliving things have in common is that they obey
rational laws. Not surprisingly, Piaget came to regard human
intelligence, man's rational function, as providing the unifying
principle of all the sciences, including the social, biological, and
natural disciplines. It was a point of view that was to guide him
during his entire career.

In 1914 Piaget had intended to go to England for a year to learn
English as many young Europeans did, but the war intervened.
Consequently, despite many rumors to the contrary, Piaget does
not speak or understand spoken English very well, although he has
a fair command of written English.

At the University of Lausanne, Piaget majored in biology and, not
surprisingly, conducted his dissertation on mollusks. Early in his

college career, he took what Erik Erikson (1950) might call a "moratorium"—a period away from his studies and his family. Piaget's moratorium was in a Swiss mountain spa. During this moratorium he wrote a novel (1918) which described the plan of research he intended to pursue during his entire professional career. To a remarkable degree, Piaget has followed the plan he outlined in that book.

After obtaining his doctorate Piaget explored a number of traditional disciplines, looking for one which would allow him to combine his philosophical interest in epistemology (the branch of philosophy concerned with the question of how we know reality) and his interest in biology and natural science. He spent a brief period of time at the Burgholzli Psychiatric Clinic in Zurich where Carl Gustav Jung had once worked. In those years, Piaget was much impressed by Freudian theory and even gave a paper on children's dreams in which Freud showed some interest. But he never had any desire to be a clinician and left the Burgholzli after less than a year.

From Zurich Piaget traveled to Paris, where he worked in the school that had once been used as an experimental laboratory by Alfred Binet. Piaget was given the chore of standardizing some of Sir Cyril Burt's reasoning tests on French children. Although the test administration was boring for the most part, one aspect of the work did capture his interest. Children when responding to an item often came up with unusual or unexpected replies. Although these replies were "wrong" or "errors" for test purposes, they fascinated Piaget. In addition, when children came up with the wrong answer to questions such as "Helen is darker than Rose and Rose is darker than Joyce; who is the fairest of the three?" Piaget was curious about the processes by which the "wrong" response was arrived at. It seemed to him that the contents of the children's errors and the means by which they arrived at wrong solutions were not fortuitous but systematic and indicative of underlying mental structures which generated them.

These observations suggested to Piaget that the study of children's thinking might provide some of the answers he sought on the philosophical plane; he planned to investigate them; then move on to other problems. Instead, the study of children's thinking became his life-long preoccupation. After Paris, Piaget moved permanently to Geneva and began his investigations of children's thinking at the Rousseau Institute. The publication of his first studies in the field, *The Language and Thought of the Child* (1952a), and later, *The Judgment and Reasoning of the Child* (1951b), *The Child's Conception of the World* (1951a), *The Moral Judgment of the Child* (1948), gained international recognition and made Piaget a world-re-nowned psychologist before he was thirty. Unfortunately these books, which Piaget regarded as preliminary investigations, were often debated as finished and final works.

When Claparède retired from his post as Director of the Institute of Educational Science at the University of Geneva, Piaget was the unanimous choice to succeed him. Piaget held this post, as well as his professorship at that university, until his recent retirement. As Piaget's work became better known, many students came to work with him and collaborated in his research efforts. One of these students was Valentine Châtenay, whom Piaget proceeded to court and to wed. In due course they had three children, Jacqueline, Laurent, and Monique. These children, grown now, have been immortalized by Piaget in three books that are already regarded as classics in the child development literature, *The Origins of Intelligence in the Child* (1952b), *The Construction of Reality in the Child* (1954), and *Play Dreams and Imitation in Childhood* (1951c).

The books came about in this way: After Piaget's initial studies of children's conceptions of the world, he turned to the question of how these notions came to be given up and how children arrive at veridical notions about the world. What Piaget was groping for was a general theory of mental development that would allow him to explain both the "erroneous" ideas he had discovered in his early works and the obviously valid notions arrived at by older children and adults. It seemed clear to him that the mental abilities by which children reconstruct reality have to be sought in the earliest moments of psychic existence, hence the study of infants.

In his study of infants Piaget, like other investigators such as Milicent Shinn (1900) and Wilhelm Preyer (1887), employed his own children. Piaget's infant studies were, however, novel in several respects. Perhaps the most novel aspect had to do with Piaget's perspective. Piaget did not assume that there was an external reality for the infant to simply copy and become acquainted with. Rather, Piaget saw the construction of reality as being the basic task of the infant. This way of looking at infant behavior allowed Piaget to observe and to study aspects of the infants' reactions that had previously been ignored or whose significance had not been fully appreciated. Piaget noted, for example, that infants do not search after desired objects which disappear from view until about the end of the first year of life. To Piaget this meant that the young infant has not yet constructed a notion of objects that continue to exist when they are no longer present to his senses.

Traditional psychology has been very harsh toward any hint in psychological writings ascribing feelings and thoughts to others without full justification. Piaget wanted to conjecture what the infant's experience of the world was, but he also wanted to do this in a scientifically acceptable and testable way. His solution to this difficult problem is another testament to his genius.

In one book, *The Origins of Intelligence in Children* (1952b), Piaget describes the evolution of children's mental operations from the outside, as it were. In this book he introduced some of the basic concepts of his theory of intelligence, including *accommodation* (changing the action to fit the environment) and *assimilation* (changing the environment to fit the action). Piaget could demonstrate these concepts by detailed accounts of infant behavior. When the infant changed the conformation of his lips to fit the nipple, this provided one of many examples of accommodation. And when the infant tried to suck upon every object which brushed his lips, this was but one of many examples of assimilation.

Other important theoretical concepts were also introduced. One of these was the *schema*. A schema is essentially a structured system of assimilations and accommodations, a behavior pattern. Sucking, for example, as it becomes elaborated, involves both assimilation and accommodation and the pattern gets extended and generalized as well as coordinated with other action patterns. When the infant begins to look at what he sucks and to suck at what he sees, there is a coordination of the looking schema and the sucking schema. Objects are constructed by the laborious coordination of many different schemata.

In the *Origins* book Piaget thus emphasized description and concepts that, at every point, could be tied to behavioral observations. They are extremely careful and detailed and reflect Piaget's early biological training. I once had the opportunity to see his notebooks, and they were filled, page after page, with very neat notations written in a very small hand. Here is an example of one of Piaget's observations (1952b).

> Laurent lifts a cushion in order to look for a cigar case. When the object is entirely hidden the child lifts the screen with hesitation, but when one end of the case appears Laurent removes the cushion with one hand and with the other tries to extricate the objective. The act of lifting the screen is, therefore, entirely separate from that of grasping the desired object and constitutes an autonomous "means" no doubt derived from earlier and analogous acts [p. 222].

In the book *The Construction of Reality in the Child* (1954) Piaget concerned himself more with the content of the infant's thought than with the mental processes. He employed many of the same observations but from the perspective of the child's-eye-view of the world. These inferences were, however, always tied to concrete observations and were checked in a variety of different ways. In this book Piaget talked about the infant's sense of space, of time, and of causality, but at each point buttressed the discussion with many illustrative examples and little experiments such as the following:

> At 0:3 (13) Laurent, already accustomed for several hours to shake a hanging rattle by pulling the chain attached to it . . . is attracted by the sound of the rattle (which I have just shaken) and looks simultaneously at the rattle and at the hanging chain. Then while staring at the rattle (R) he drops from his right hand a sheet he was sucking, in order to reach with the same hand for the lower end of the hanging chain (C). As soon as he touches the chain, he grasps it and pulls it, thus reconstructing the series R-C [p. 330].

This example was used by Piaget to demonstrate the infant's construction of a notion of practical time, i.e., the series R-C.

One of Piaget's important conclusions from the work presented in the *Reality* book is that for the young infant (less than three months), objects are not regarded as permanent, as existing outside the infant's immediate experience. If, for example, an infant drops one object she was playing with she merely looks at the place where the toy fell and does not actively search for it. To the young infant, an object is but an image that appears and disappears at certain places. By the end of the first year, however, the infant actively searches for toys she had dropped. The one-year-old has constructed, via the coordination of looking, touching, etc., schemata, a world of objects which she regards as existing outside of her immediate experience and which she can respond to in their absence.

Piaget's book *Play, Dreams and Imitation in Childhood* (1951c) is the third work in the infant trilogy and argues that the symbols with which we represent reality are as much constructions as the reality itself. Piaget found that symbols derive from both imitation (a child opens its mouth in imitation of a matchbox opening) and play (a child holds up a potato chip and says, "Look, a butterfly"). In Piaget's view, therefore, symbolic activities derive from the same developmental processes that underlie the rest of mental growth and are not separate from, but part of, intellectual development. Piaget also found that the development of symbolic process does not usually appear much before the age of two. This coincides with the everyday observation that children do not usually report dreams or "night terrors" until after the second year. It is not until that age that most children have the mental ability necessary to create dream symbols.

Piaget's studies on infants were conducted during the 1930s, at which time he was also teaching, following new lines of research, and writing theoretical articles on logic and epistemology. Piaget's fame attracted many gifted students to Geneva. One of these was Alina Szeminska, a Polish mathematician who did some fine work in mathematics and geometry. The book *The Child's Conception of Number* (1952) was one fruit of their collaboration. Another gifted graduate student was Bärbel Inhelder, whose thesis on the conservation and the intellectual assessment of retarded children (1943) was a landmark in the extension of Piagetian conceptions to practical problems of assessment and evaluation. Bärbel Inhelder, who became Piaget's permanent collaborator, has worked with him since her student days. When Piaget retired, his university chair was given to Inhelder—a significant fact in a country where women still do not have the right to vote!

During the 1930s, Piaget's life-long academic affiliations and work patterns became fully established and solidified. Although Piaget had a university appointment from the start of his career, the Rousseau Institute did not become an official part of the University of Geneva until the 1940s. Piaget worked hard to ensure that it was an interdisciplinary institute, so that it would not be saddled with the stigma usually associated with schools of education at universities.

Largely due to Piaget's influence, teacher training is heavily weighted in the direction of child-development theory and research. In addition to the courses on child development offered by Piaget and his staff, students must participate in child-development research. With the aid of his undergraduate students, it was possible for Piaget and his graduate students to examine large numbers of children of all ages when they were conducting a particular research investigation. The assertion, which is sometimes made, that Piaget's studies were based on very few subjects, is true only for his infancy investigations. In all of his other explorations Piaget usually employed hundreds of subjects.

Piaget's general mode of working is to set a problem for a year or for several years and then to pursue it intensely and without distraction. Indeed, when he is working, say, on "causality," he does not want to talk about or deal with research problems he has dealt with in the past. Once he has completed a body of work he loses interest in it and all of his energies are devoted to the task at hand. Generally Piaget holds a meeting with his colleagues and graduate students once a week at which the possible ways of exploring the problem are discussed and data from ongoing studies are presented. These are lively, exciting sessions in which new insights and ideas constantly emerge and serve as stimuli for still further innovation.

In contrast, at the meetings of the center for visiting scholars the students tend to be quiet while the visitors do most of the talking. I have one rather vivid memory of a particular seminar meeting. Piaget had been talking about some of the research and I interjected that I was taking the part of the devil, but why did he insist upon using the words "assimilation" and "accommodation"? After all, would not the American terms "stimulus" and "response" serve equally well? The question brought instant silence to the group, most of whom were aghast and waiting for lightning to strike me where I sat. Piaget, however, was most amused and a lively twinkle came into his eye as he replied, "Well, Elkeend, you can use stimulus and response if you choose, but if you want to understand anything, I suggest that you use assimilation and accommodation."

At the end of the year Piaget gathers up all the data that have been collected and moves to a secret hideaway in the mountains.

There he takes long walks, cooks omelets, thinks about the work that has been done and integrates it into one or several books which he writes in longhand on square pieces of paper. Piaget has disciplined himself to write at least four publishable pages every day, usually very early in the morning. The remainder of his morning is spent teaching, meeting with students and staff, or with a continuation of his early morning writing. In the afternoon Piaget routinely takes a walk during which he sorts out the ideas he is working on and in this way prepares for the next day's writing. Piaget keeps to this routine to this day, as his health permits. As a consequence of keeping to this writing schedule throughout his career, it has been estimated, he has written the equivalent of more than fifty 500-page books.

Perhaps Piaget's major achievement of the 1930s and 1940s was the elaboration of his theory of intelligence into the four stages as we now know them. This theory was articulated in close connection with Piaget's conservation experiments that provided the data base for the theory's elaboration. The experiments, which resembled those on the permanence of objects in infants, enabled him to evaluate children's performance on somewhat comparable tasks at many different age levels.

As a result of numerous investigations of children's conceptions of space, time, number, quantity, speed, causality, geometry, and so on, Piaget arrived at a general conception of intellectual growth. He argues that intelligence, adaptive thinking and action, develops in a series of stages that are related to age. Although there is considerable variability among individual children as to when these stages appear, Piaget does argue that the sequence is a necessary one. This is true because each succeeding stage grows out of and builds upon the work of the preceding one. At each level of development the child is again confronted with the task of constructing or reconstructing reality out of his experiences with the world he put together during the previous stage. In addition, he must not only construct new notions of space, time, number, and so on, but also either discard his previous concepts or integrate them with the new ones. From a Piagetian standpoint, constructing reality never starts entirely from scratch and always involves dealing with old ideas as well as acquiring new ones. A summary of the stages is presented in the next chapter.

In the last few decades, Piaget has extended his researches into new areas (such as memory, imagery, consciousness, and causality) and has consolidated and refined his theoretical conceptions and related them to different disciplines. While it is not really possible to review all of this work here, some parts of it with significance for education should be mentioned. We will look first at some of the research and then at some of the theoretical contributions.

One of the major research contributions during this period was the study of memory from the standpoint of Piaget's developmental stages. The research was published in a book under the joint authorship of Piaget and Inhelder (1973). Like Sir Frederick Bartlett's (1932) book *Remembering,* this work by Piaget and Inhelder, *Memory and Intelligence,* has a good chance of becoming a classic in its field. As in the case of Bartlett's book, the Piaget and Inhelder work presents new data, new conceptualizations, and fresh and innovative research approaches. While *Memory and Intelligence* provides no final answers to questions about memory, it offers a richness of hypotheses and experimental techniques that will stimulate other researchers for years to come. Considering that this truly innovative book was written during Piaget's seventieth year, one can only marvel at his unabated creativity and productivity.

The argument of the book is straightforward enough. What is the nature of memory? Is it passive storage and retrieval or does it involve intelligence at the outset and all along the way? Piaget's answer is that memory, in the broadest sense, is a way of knowing which is concerned with discovering the past. Although symbols and images are involved in memory, they do not constitute its essence. Rather, intelligence has to be brought to bear to retrieve the past and hence, all "memories" show the imprint of the intellectual schemata used to reconstruct them. Intelligence leaves its mark not only on the memory itself, but even upon the original registration which can only be coded within the limits of the child's existing schemata.

All of this is not particularly new and could be derived from the work of Bartlett and other writers. What is new and what gives this book its special claim to being a classic is the repeated demonstration that the child's memory of a given past experience improves* with his level of intellectual development. A child, for example, who is shown a series of size-graded sticks before he can understand the relations involved, and who draws it poorly, may draw it correctly from memory six months later. The child's intellectual understanding of the series modified the memory of it in ways that are predictable from cognitive developmental theory. This transformation of memories as a result of cognitive growth is demonstrated in many different domains (with numerical correspondences, geometric figures, permutations, causality) and with consistently comparable results.

To be sure, there are many questions one can raise about the "experiments" themselves. Often the number of children involved is not very large and not all the children show the expected results. The procedures are not always clearly described and the results are presented in tables of percentage-passing and without the imprimatur of significance tests. This is simply Piaget's style. There is no point in being annoyed by it or in demanding that he become more rigorous. What he has provided is, in the end, much more valuable than tightly controlled experiments, namely, ideas that challenge the mind and open up whole new areas for experimental research.

The work on memory is only one of a series of areas to which

* Bartlett (1932) and Freud (1953b) emphasized the distortions of memory produced by the subject's activity, while Piaget and Inhelder (1973) have emphasized the improvements in memory brought about by the subject's maturing intelligence.

Piaget and his colleagues are applying this theory of intellectual development. In addition, works on imagery (1971), on consciousness (1974a), and causality (1974b) have all been completed and new projects are under way. Considering that much of this creative intellectual work has come during Piaget's eighth decade, one has to acknowledge that creative scientific work is not necessarily the province of the young.

In addition to the research, however, Piaget has also published a number of books that serve to summarize and integrate much of the work he has done over the past half century. These books include a general text (1969) in collaboration with Inhelder, on child development which introduces the Piagetian work for a general audience. A work on biology and knowledge (1971) relates the developmental findings regarding intelligence to more traditional biological conceptions and shows their underlying unity. A little gem of a book is *Structuralism* (1970c), which in a few brief chapters outlines clearly the central thrust of this methodology as it has been applied in many different disciplines.

Of particular relevance to education is Piaget's book *Science of Education and the Psychology of the Child* (1970b), which is essentially a critique of traditional education. The argument is that education is too concerned with the technology of teaching and too little concerned with understanding children. In Piaget's view, the overemphasis on the science of educating, rather than upon the science of the children being educated, leads to a sterile pedagogy wherein children learn by rote what adults have decided is valuable for them to learn. Basically, Piaget feels that teacher training and educational practice must have child development as their basic discipline. The psychology of the child should be the primary science of education.

These are but a few of the achievements of Piaget's fourth phase. The accolades continue to multiply as the extent of Piaget's achievement begins to be recognized. His most recent honorary degree was from the University of Chicago in the spring of 1974. He has been awarded the Distinguished Scientific Achievement award of the American Psychological Association and the G. Stanley Hall Award from Division Seven of the same association. These are but a few of the many ways in which the scholarly world has shown its recognition of, and respect for, the contributions of Jean Piaget.

FOUNDATIONS

IV
UNDERSTANDING CHILDREN

"Intelligence thus begins neither with knowledge of the self nor of things as such but with knowledge of their interaction and it is by orienting itself simultaneously towards the two poles of that interaction that intelligence organizes the world by organizing itself."   J. PIAGET

At the heart of Piaget's contribution to psychology and to education are the many insights his work has provided for understanding the thought and the behavior of children. Three of these insights will be described in the present chapter. The first has to do with externalization, the process which makes it difficult for us fully to appreciate when the reality of the child is different than our own. The second has to do with the stages of cognitive development, the progressively more complex systems of intellectual abilities and concepts that mark the evolution of mental life. A third insight has to do with egocentrism, aspects of children's thought and behavior that bring them into conflict with adults. Piaget's insights regarding egocentrism lead us into the affective domain and demonstrate that Piaget's work has relevance for understanding the child's emotional, as well as his cognitive, life.

THE PROBLEM OF EXTERNALIZATION

One insight that Piaget's work has provided and that has received relatively little attention has to do with *externalization*, the process by which we attribute to the external world the products of our own mental activity. A similar phenomenon is well known in clinical

Based on D. Elkind, *Cognitive Development* (Homewood, Ill.: Learning Systems Company, 1975 c.), pp. 1–13.

psychology, where it is called *projection*, and is regarded as a defense mechanism. In a clinical context, projection occurs when a person attributes his own thoughts or feelings to others. The paranoid patient, for example, who is very angry with the world believes that the world is angry *at him* and develops delusions of persecution.

While externalization has features in common with projection, it is not quite the same process. First of all, externalization is common to everyone. As beginning psychology students we learned that such experiences as color were in our heads and not in the objects in which they seemed to reside. An orange is not orange, it just happens to reflect that spectrum of light waves that excites certain cones in our retina which send signals to area 17 in the brain which we experience as color. Even with instruction and reflection, however, it is difficult to keep in mind that objects are not colored. This immediate and unconscious attribution of the products of our own mental activities to things is what is meant by externalization.

Externalization, however, is not limited to sensory and perceptual phenomena and happens at the conceptual level as well. The development of object permanence in the infant, to be discussed in more detail later in the chapter, provides a prototype of the operation of externalization at the conceptual level. Young infants deal with objects as if they had no permanence beyond their immediate presence. Piaget's (1954) three-month-old daughter Jacqueline several times looked at the place where her father had been, as if looking would reinstate his image. Through a progressive coordination of sensorimotor schemata, Jacqueline constructed a concept of her father as a person who existed outside of her immediate sense experience and independently of her own actions. When she was about one year of age she called for him when he was out of the room. For our purposes, the significance of this achievement (which will be described in more detail later) is that once Jacqueline had constructed the concept of her father she was not aware of her part in the process and saw him as existing apart from her own mental activity.

The same holds true for the conservation of quantity among school-age children. Conservation of liquid quantities (Piaget and Szeminska, 1952) is a familiar example. The child is presented with two glasses filled equally high with orange-colored water. After the child agrees that both glasses contain "the same amount to drink," the water from one glass is poured into a tall narrow glass so that the level is higher than in the other glass. The child is asked whether the amount to drink in the tall glass is the same as that in the lower, wider glass. Young children (age 4–5) tend to say that the tall glass has more while older children (age 5–6) tend to say that the amount to drink is the same. For the older children, quantity is now regarded as having an existence outside the immediate perceptual appearance and to be independent of their thought. The child externalizes her quantity concepts in much the same way that the infant externalizes the concept of the permanent object.

What holds true for concept formation in the child holds equally true for concept in the adult. In the process of constructing and reconstructing our world, we progressively externalize it to the point where it appears quite independent of our own mental activity. It is because of this externalization that we adults are so astounded to learn that children do not have conservation. Indeed, a whole literature of research studies has been produced, in part at least, to demonstrate that young children *do* have conservation (e.g. Brainerd and Allen, 1971; Gelman, 1967; Mehler and Bever, 1967). Thanks to externalization, which makes the world seem independent of our thought process, we are opaque to the conceptual world of the child when it is different from our own. While externalization is a very adaptive process in everyday life, it is not so when our concern is with the education of children.

The educational significance of this phenomenon of externalization appears, to me at least, to be quite profound. Effective teaching presupposes that the curriculum builder and teacher not only know *what* the pupil is to learn, but that they also understand some of the difficulties the pupil will encounter in attempting to learn the material. This is obvious in the teaching of motor skills, such as skiing, sailing, or golfing. Professional teachers closely observe the learner's difficulties and help the student to deal with "natural" tendencies (such as the reluctance to "follow through" with a stroke) which interfere with learning the right movements. Such teachers work at providing mental images and exercises that will enable the learner to acquire the correct coordinations.

In contrast to professional teachers, amateurs often try to teach by modeling the correct behavior. This is what I call the "watch me" school of instruction. The impetus to teach a complex skill by modeling it to the novice is a reflection of externalization. Once a skill (like a concept) is acquired, it is externalized, and the difficulties involved in acquiring it are lost from consciousness. The skilled skier, sailer, or golfer who is not a skilled teacher behaves as if the novice could learn the skill by observing, by looking hard enough. To the proficient individual, the skill is outside his mind and resides in his overt actions and not in the complex mental coordinations that make those actions possible. Unfortunately, it is next to impossible to learn a complex skill by observation alone.* One does not learn to play the violin by watching Heifitz or the piano by observing Rubenstein.

An illustration of a curriculum based on externalization may help to communicate the significance of this phenomenon for education generally. Because I have been particularly interested in the problem of beginning reading (e.g. Elkind, 1975), I will use it as an example. In America, most reading programs, regardless of their orientation, begin with letters and sounds. The printed letter is regarded as an environmental given that needs only to be looked at to be understood. From this standpoint learning to read is primarily a matter of learning to discriminate letters or "critical features" and to associate them with sounds (Gibson and Levin, 1975). Both of these skills can be learned by imitating the teacher's behavior.

* Observation can be important once a certain amount of proficiency in the skill is attained. A good tennis player can improve by watching an expert but a novice tennis player could not.

But the fallacy here is exactly the same as the fallacy involved in assuming that one can learn to play the piano by watching and copying Rubenstein, or that one can learn to swim by watching and copying Mark Spitz. A letter is a complex mental construction that most adults have conceptualized and externalized so that it seems more simple and external than it really is. In fact the concept of a letter is even more difficult to arrive at than the concept of a number. That is why it is usually easier for children to learn to read numbers than to learn to read letters and words. Because adults start teaching children to read where they should be ending, namely, with the conception of the letter, most children acquire the concept of a letter in spite of, rather than because of, reading instruction.

What is involved in constructing the concept of a letter is comparable to what the child has to do in constructing the concept of a number. Number, and quantity in general, presupposes a unit concept. A unit, say a number, is at once like every other number—in that it is a number—and different in its order of enumeration. The number 3 is like the number 1 and the number 5 in that all are numbers, but 3 is different from them in that it comes after 1 and before 5. A number expresses simultaneously a class and a relation, likeness and difference. It is clear from Piaget's work (Piaget and Szeminska, 1952) and from the many replications of it (e.g., Elkind, 1961, 1964) that the ability to coordinate sameness and difference is a function of concrete operations that appear at about the age of five or six.

If we now look at letters, they pose the same problems as number but more so. A letter, say E, is like every other letter in that it is a letter, but it is different in its order of enumeration. It comes after D and before F. In addition, it is sometimes associated with certain sounds, with other sounds at other times, and with no sound at still other times. A letter is thus a complex cognitive construction involving not only the coordination of likeness and difference but also the presence and absence of certain sounds. If concrete operations are required to construct numbers, they would seem to be even more essential in the construction of a letter.

This is not the place to go into a detailed discussion of beginning reading. Suffice it to say that despite the pervasiveness of the printed word in our environment, only about one in a hundred children reads before the age of six. Of these most are above average intelligence so that their mental age, if not their chronological age, is at the six-year level (Durkin, 1966; Briggs and Elkind, 1973; King and Friesen, 1972). If reading were simply a matter of discrimination and association, and not a matter of logical construction, many more children would read early, and the problem of reading instruction would not loom so large on the educational horizon.

Many other examples could be given of how externalization blocks adult understanding of the child's learning task, but the foregoing may suffice to illustrate the point. Piaget's work, by making us aware of the phenomenon of externalization, has opened new paths to the instruction of children. It suggests that the best way to learn how to instruct children in a subject is to watch children struggling to learn it on their own, to see the difficulties they encounter from their point of view. But it also suggests that the child's task can be made much easier by ensuring that the child is dealing with the subject matter at hand and not with convoluted instructions, inappropriate contents, or confusing illustrations. We shall return to this topic again in the chapter on curriculum analysis (Chapter VIII).

PIAGET'S STAGES OF COGNITIVE DEVELOPMENT

A convenient way of talking about cognitive development, and the one that is employed by Piaget, is to describe it in terms of "stages." It must be said that there is considerable disagreement about the concept of stages in psychology. Many psychologists would like to do away with the term altogether. And yet, when its meaning is clearly defined, it can be a useful descriptive term. Some of the ways the term "stage" has been employed, and the way it will be used here, can now be described.

Perhaps the most objectionable use of the term "stage" occurs in popular language, when it is said that a child is at the "walking stage" or the "talking stage." Implicit in such statements is that the term "stage" helps to explain the behavior in question. Clearly this is not the case; the term "stage" is redundant and adds nothing to the information conveyed by the statement "the child is talking" or "the child is walking." Most objections to the use of "stage" derive from this popular but improper use of the term.

There is another, and more acceptable, way in which the term "stage" is occasionally used. At certain times in development, environmental input of a particular kind may be more important than it is at a later time. Chicks at seventeen days will "attach" themselves to whatever is moving and alive in their vicinity. Thereafter, the chicks will follow the object to which they were attached as if it were their mother. The time when this attachment occurs is called a "critical period," and the term "stage" is sometimes used in the sense of a "critical period." When it is said that "she is at the independent stage" or "if he doesn't learn it now, he never will," "stage" is used in the sense of a "critical period."

A third way of using the stage concept occurs when certain behaviors follow one another in a necessary sequence. This is the sense in which the term "stage" is used in rocketry. To say that the "third stage" has fired means that a certain sequence of events has occurred and that another sequence has begun. In this sense, "stage" signals the fact that a necessary sequence of events is under way and that each successive event builds upon the preceding event and is also a necessary prerequisite to the following event. Crawling is a "stage" in the development of walking because it is a necessary antecedent to that action. Thus, whenever a necessary sequence of behaviors can be observed in development, it is appropriate to label the successive steps in the sequence as "stages."

In the study of cognitive development, the term "stage" is most often employed in the third sense, to designate one mode of behavior in a necessary sequence of behaviors that is related to, but not determined by, age. This is the sense in which Piaget uses the term, and it is the sense in which it will be employed in the present book.

INFANCY

For purposes of discussion we might say that the infancy period is one primarily concerned with construction of the *object world*. During the first few months of life the information the infant receives from the environment comes, as it were, in bits and pieces. This is true because the infant's ways of dealing with the sensory inputs, his sensorimotor *schemata*, are not coordinated one with the other. When the infant looks at an object, the visual image or schema of the object is not connected with the tactile schema of the object, so that he doesn't reach for it when he sees it, or look for it when he touches it. The young infant's world is a series of uncoordinated sense impressions that are not connected in any spatial or temporal framework.

One consequence of this lack of coordination of sense impressions is that the infant behaves as if he could create and destroy objects by bringing them into the range of his senses or by moving them out of his experience. He does not distinguish between the instance when his mother disappears from view because she leaves the room and the instance when he turns his head so that he can no longer see her, although she is still there. The game of "peek-a-boo," where the adult hides behind open hands and spreads fingers to look at the child, reflects the young child's difficulty in conceiving a face when it is not immediately present to his senses.

Closely related to the infant's behavior in relation to creating and destroying objects is his reaction to absent objects. Because he has no conception of objects as such, i.e., as a combination of properties, he behaves as if objects no longer present to his senses are, in fact, destroyed and nonexistent. When an adult plays with an infant of several months, the infant is likely to look up, laugh, and gurgle. Should the adult duck out of sight, the infant will continue to laugh and gurgle. The young infant acts as if the looking, laughing, gurgling will re-create the adult, and when it does not the infant continues as if the adult had never been there.

How do the coordinations that make the construction of an object world possible come about? In Piaget's view the basic process is the *circular reaction*. When an infant puts his thumb in his mouth and sucks, a circular reaction has been set going. Putting the thumb in the mouth sets off the sucking schema which reinforces the "putting thumb in mouth" schema. More elaborate secondary and tertiary circular reactions come about later when the infant introduces objects into the self-stimulation cycle. An infant who kicks a mobile so that he can watch it move is engaged in a secondary circular reaction in which the object plays a part in the cycle.

Through many and varied primary, secondary, and tertiary circular reactions the infant gradually coordinates his schemata into objects that have many properties at once. By the end of the first year of life the infant's object concepts are well elaborated and he knows that what can be seen can also be touched, heard, and tasted, and also that these objects continue to exist when they are no longer present to his senses. At the end of the first year of life, the youngster begins to cry when an adult who has been playing with the infant disappears. Out of sight is no longer out of mind, and the person is regarded as having a permanent existence outside the infant's experience. In Piaget's terminology, the object is *conserved*.

The construction or reconstruction of objects goes hand in hand with the elaboration of space, time, and causality concepts. As the infant elaborates objects, he also learns to deal with their spatial relations to one another and to himself. The earliest space awareness thus originates in sensorimotor coordinations and is limited to the space of the child's (momentary) actions and experience. Early time awareness involves simple temporal sequences such as X before Y. The understanding of causality is the understanding of specific temporal sequences anticipating what will happen to what.

By the end of the second year of life the child has further elaborated his object concepts as well as his budding space, time, and causality notions. For one thing, he can now look for objects that have been displaced several times. When an adult puts a ball behind a chair and then behind a couch, the child goes immediately to the couch. At a younger age he would have gone to the chair despite the fact that he had seen the ball moved again. Prior to the end of the second year the infant can find objects that are hidden from view but not when the hiding involves several displacements.

During the infancy period, therefore, the infant constructs permanent objects that continue to exist outside of experience and rudimentary notions of space, time, and causality. As the earlier discussion indicated, once the infant constructs these concepts he immediately *externalizes* them so that they appear to be part of the world and independent of his own mental activities. For the infant at the end of the second year of life, as for the adult, there is a world of objects about him which seems so objective, so "out there," that the role of mental activity in its construction is completely obliterated. While this externalization is an adaptive process, it has the negative consequence that it blinds adults to the difficulties children encounter in reconstructing their world out of their experiences with the environment.

THE PREOPERATIONAL PERIOD

Sometime during the second year of life, children begin to engage in a number of symbolic activities. One of the most prominent of these activities is the production of words. But there are other facets to this emerging "symbolic function" as well. For the first time children "create" symbols. A young child may hold up a potato chip and say "butterfly" or cross two ice cream sticks and call the result an "airplane." In such activities the child demonstrates that he is actively searching out, and creating referents for the words he has acquired.

The symbolic function is illustrated by other behaviors as well. By the time the child is three or four he engages in a variety of symbolic play. Preschool children who "pretend" they are mommies and daddies and clomp around in adult shoes and hats illustrate another mode of symbolizing their experience. The child's ability to imitate absent objects and activities also reflects his newly developed symbolic activities. A young child who sees his mother mixing a cake may, a few hours later, imitate her behavior. The ability to observe behavior, but delay copying it, is what Piaget calls *deferred imitation.*

As children become more and more capable of symbolizing their experience consciously, they also become capable of symbolizing it unconsciously. During this period children begin reporting dreams and night terrors. In addition, several characteristic "phobic" reactions often appear. Some children, during the preschool years, show an excessive fear of dogs, or of horses, or of particular people. Many times these fears cannot be traced to actual life experiences. Rather, the feared object seems to have become an unconscious symbol of some other fear. For example, if a boy is afraid of his father (but cannot deal with this fear because he loves the father as well), the fear may be represented symbolically in the fear of an animal.

The appearance of the symbolic function extends the range of the child's adaptive capacity. Symbols allow children to deal with reality that is once or twice removed from immediate experience. The advantages of this are fairly straightforward. Through symbolization the child is able to use past experience to deal with the present and the future. Symbolization thus brings anticipation and foreknowledge into the child's repertoire of adaptive functions.

Symbolization also allows the child to deal with places that are somewhat removed from experience and thus expands the "space" in which he can move in and about. The symbolic function allows the child to reconstruct a larger reality of past and future and of spatially removed settings that greatly enlarges and enriches his world.

If the world of the preschool child is much more elaborate than that of the infant, it is still relatively primitive by adult standards. For, although the preschool child now has the intellectual wherewithal to deal with the immediate practical world of the home, nursery, or day-care center, he lacks the broader, more abstract, and general concepts of space, time, and causality that characterize adult reality. In fact, by adult standards the child's view of the larger world outside the immediate one is quite vague and erroneous.

Young children, for example, have an *animistic* view of the larger world, and believe that trees and plants as well as moving clouds and rolling stones can have motives and intentions. The fearfulness of young children in strange places reflects this animism, and young children can see moving branches and shadows as evil forces. Motion pictures for children sometimes use such devices as menacing trees and plants that play into the child's animistic mode of thinking. Animism also accounts for the young child's occasional concern for an inanimate object such as a stone. The young child's solicitude stems from the fact that for her the stone is not inanimate at all, but animate.

Young children's sense of causality is also different from that of adults. The thinking of young children is characterized by what has been called *phenomenalistic causality*, the belief that when two events occur in succession the first one "causes" the second. If, for example, a young child raises the window shade in the morning and sees the sun coming up over the horizon, he may believe that raising the window shade causes the sun to rise. The young child's readiness to believe in magic wands, fairy godmothers, and the like rests in part upon phenomenalistic causality. In a world ruled by that sort of causality, there are no limits to what can lead to what.

Phenomenalistic causality has other consequences as well. It helps to explain why young children become so attached to blankets, teddy bears, and other "security" objects. What often happens is that the child is scared or unhappy and clings to the blanket or teddy bear for comfort, which it in fact provides through the child's sense of touch. Accordingly, because of phenomenalistic causality, the child believes that the blanket or teddy bear made him feel better. The next time he is troubled or upset, he returns to the object that provided comfort the last time. What the child doesn't realize is that any soft object will provide the same tactile stimulation. Once attached to a particular object, the young child is loathe to let it go.

Closely related to phenomenalistic causality is another mode of thinking in young children that has been called *nominal realism*. Young children have a special reverence for names and symbols of all sorts. Their new-found capacity to create symbols does not carry with it, at least immediately, the capacity to distinguish clearly between the symbol and the referent. Young children tend to think that the symbol partakes of the referent. The young child believes that the name of the moon is in the moon and that it was always called moon and that it is impossible to call it anything else. Names are not arbitrary designations for the young child, they are properties of the objects they represent.

Nominal realism helps to explain some aspects of young children's social behavior, particularly their difficulty in "sharing." To the young child, his toys and possessions are symbols of himself and are thus seen as part of himself. When a child is asked to share his toys, he is in effect being asked to share a part of himself. His resistance to sharing is thus understandable. One way to help children to share is to put the child's name, in large letters, on the toy to be shared. By placing his name on the toy, the child is assured that it is still his and still part of himself.

A couple of other facets of young children's thinking should be mentioned. One of these is *egocentrism*. In Piaget's psychology, egocentrism is not a pejorative term but, like mental realism and phenomenalistic causality, one that reflects a characteristic mode of thought. In general, young children are unable to take another person's point of view when it is different from their own. If you stand opposite a four- or five-year-old, and ask him to show you his right and left hands and then yours, egocentrism is easy to observe. A child who knows his own left and right hands does not recognize that, for a person standing opposite him, right and left will be reversed. Accordingly he assumes that your right and left hands will be on the same sides of his body as they are on yours. He is unable to put himself mentally in another person's place and so recognize the relativity of right and left.

The young child's egocentrism often gets him into trouble with adults. He is impervious to whatever activity the adult is engaged in, no matter how delicate or precarious. A child may shout in his mother's ear just as mother is about to thread a needle or just as father is about to sink a putt in his backyard putting green. Telling a young child to be still so that one can talk on the telephone is usually not sufficient to get him to lower the noise level. Again, it is the child's inability to take the adult's point of view that produces this behavior and not moral perverseness. In the preceding paragraphs egocentrism has been described in the narrow sense as a characteristic of young children's thinking. Later in the chapter it will be discussed in its broad sense as a phase of thinking at all age levels.

One more characteristic of young children's thinking should be mentioned. Much of our everyday behavior is conducted in a series of progressive "frames" that are more or less clearly articulated. We move from the "getting dressed" to the "breakfast" to the "going to work" frame, each of which has its own sets of rules, regulations, and prohibitions. Young children have trouble learning the general rules which make it possible for us to operate when some aspects of the frame are different. For example, we do the "getting up," "dressing," and "breakfast" frames at motels and at friends' homes while visiting without too much trouble, but young children have difficulty in learning frames and in adapting to old frames in new settings.

A familiar situation is the "gift giving" frame. In such a frame a relative or friend may decide to give the child a gift, usually money or a sweet. The child is supposed to appear a bit embarrassed, but to accept the gift and to thank the giver. But young children often "forget" to say thank you. In fact, the gift-giving frames are so different one from the other that the child lacks the ability to abstract and recognize their comparability. The same holds true for frames requiring "please" and "excuse me." This is not to say that the child should not be encouraged to say "thank you," "please," and "excuse me" but to indicate that the child's failures are more a matter of intellectual immaturity than of social insensitivity.

One type of frame transformation the child has particular difficulty in dealing with has to do with being treated as an individual and as a child. Young children are used to being at home and to being treated as individuals. But when they enter a nursery school or kindergarten they are sometimes treated as members of a group. This requires that the child shift frames, from thinking of himself as a unique individual to thinking of himself as a representative or member of a class of individuals. The difficulty young children have in making this shift is one reason that good early childhood education involves considerable individualized instruction.

Young children, then, have a view of reality quite different from that of older children and adults. While adults occasionally revert to child-like ways of thinking, such as phenomenalistic causality, animism, and nominal realism, these modes dominate the intelligence of the young child. Moreover, the child's egocentrism and his difficulty in learning rules and in switching frames make him a poor candidate for formal instruction. In many ways the cognitive task of the young child is to make his internal world external through symbolizations of all sorts, and he needs the freedom, within well-defined limits, to do so.

THE CONCRETE-OPERATIONAL PERIOD

Between the ages of about five and seven (usually) children develop what Piaget calls *concrete operations*. These operations are an internalized set of actions that allows the child to do in his head what before he had to do with his hands. When a young child is given an object assembly puzzle (one in which the pieces make a particular object), he begins to work on the puzzle immediately and tries to solve it by trial and error. The child with concrete operations, however, is likely to examine the pieces and to figure out what the object is before he begins assembling the parts. That is to say, he first puts the puzzle together in his head before he attempts to do so in fact. In the concrete-operational child, therefore, thought often precedes action, whereas in the preschool child action often precedes thought.

Concrete operations make possible a great many achievements not observable at the preoperational level. At the heart of these achievements is the child's ability to quantify his experience. Preschool children have some qualitative notions of quantity; they have no notions of "more" or "less" or "same," of "bigger" and "smaller," and so on. But these judgments reflect only *nominal* or *ordinal* scalings and do not reflect a true *interval* scale which is what is generally meant by "quantification."

A nominal scale occurs when the child calls a big block "Daddy," a medium size block "Mommy," and a tiny block "Baby." In such a scale, quantitative differences are dealt with as qualitative differences, as absolute properties of things rather than as dimensions. In ordinal scales there is a gradation but without a fixed unit. When a child groups blocks according to "biggest, next biggest, smallest" he is using an ordinal scale in which the difference between successive elements is not uniform.* Only when a child constructs a unit can he arrive at interval scales and be able truly to quantify his experience. It should be said that the construction of units is a pervasive cognitive task of the young child and underlies his understanding of diverse fields of reality, many of which are not quantitative in appearance. The understanding of classification, that a car can be a Ford and an automobile at the same time, is every bit as quantitative as 2 + 2 = 4.

Concrete operations make the quantification of reality possible, because they allow the child to coordinate apparently contradictory properties within the same person or object. Preschool children have no trouble in seeing that a ball is round, brown, and made of rubber. But they do have trouble as soon as they have to deal with these properties separately and apart from the object in which they inhere. When, to illustrate, a child is shown five white wooden beads and ten brown wooden beads, he can say which group has more beads (ordinal scale). But he cannot answer the question of whether there are more wooden or more brown beads. To do that he would have to think of beads as both brown and wooden and white and wooden and recognize that there are more wooden beads than brown ones. But when the young child thinks of the beads as brown, as being in a class, he tends to think of a class as a place and if the beads are in the "brown" place they cannot be in the "wooden" place. As soon as the child attempts to deal with properties apart from objects, he concretizes them and thinks of them as places (Piaget and Szeminska, 1952).

The young child's failure to distinguish men in general from "Daddy" reflects the same quantitative inadequacy. Mothers of young children are not infrequently embarrassed when their young children approach strangers whom they call "Daddy." This is the

* Judging pies or cakes at a fair is comparable. The cakes can be ranked but it is impossible to say that one is twice as good as another.

same difficulty children encounter in the bead problem, only in reverse. In the bead problem the child assumes that the one cannot be many, that a brown bead cannot be wooden. But in the "Daddy" problem the child assumes that the many cannot be one. Since there are many men, they must all be "daddys." The problems of quantification of the one and the many and of the all and the some are thus as much an issue in classification as they are in the understanding of physical dimensions and properties. What concrete operations do then is allow the child to grasp that an object or person can at the very same time be both alike and different from other objects and persons. Concrete operations allow the child to do this because they permit a "reversibility" of thought. A child who appreciates that two objects are the same in certain ways can proceed to examine their differences, but he can also return to their similarities. Once the child appreciates that one and the same element can be both like and different from others, he has the mental ability to construct a notion of a unit, and it is the unit that permits the true quantification of experience in all its many different domains.

Because the construction of units is so important, a few concrete examples may be in order to demonstrate their formation. The concept of number alluded to in an earlier discussion (cf. pp. 81–82) is perhaps the most straightforward example. Young children have a nominal concept of number and may use "one" or "two" or "three" correctly but mainly as a description of groupings. By the age of four or five, many children can arrange objects in a series according to size and thus have a beginning sense of ordinal scaling. But if the children have arranged a series of sticks in a row it is difficult for them to insert further elements. Their seriation was based on a pictorial image (say of a staircase), and they do not grasp how anything else can be fitted in. By the age of six or seven, children understand that one and the same element can be both larger and smaller than others and they can insert new size-graded elements into an existing series. Once a child realizes that an element can be the same as others (by being a member of the series) and different (in its order of enumeration), he has a true, or interval, number concept (Elkind, 1964; Piaget and Szeminska, 1952).

The quantification of thought made possible by concrete operations is most well known through Piaget's conservation experiments which were described briefly in an earlier discussion (cf. p. 79). Young children, who lack a true unit conception of quantity and think of it only in nominal or ordinal terms, believe that quantity changes with a change in appearance. That is to say, without a way of thinking in terms of units, the child has to judge quantity by its appearance or perceptual properties. In a typical conservation task, the child is shown the quantities (of liquid, or of clay, or of pennies in a row, or of sticks of equal length) and is asked to judge whether there is the same amount, number, or length in each quantity. Then one of the quantities is changed in appearance (liquid is poured into a differently shaped container, clay balls are rolled into a sausage, a row of pennies is spaced out or a stick is displaced ahead of the other) and again the child is asked if the two quantities are the same in amount, number, or length.

Young children before the age of five tend to make their judgments on the basis of the perceptual appearance of the quantity. A quantity of liquid in a tall, narrow container *looks* like more than the same quantity in a low, wide container. So long as the child has only a nominal or ordinal concept of quantity he can only judge it by its visible dimensions and thus makes errors. Once a child comes to think of quantity in terms of units, however, he recognizes that the number of units does not change with a change in appearance and, hence, that the quantity does not change. The child's discovery of the many different conservations—of mass, weight, number, length, space, and so on—all reflect the quantification of his thinking.

Still other achievements can be attributed to the quantification made possible by concrete operational thought. Learning of rules is a case in point. As suggested earlier, young children have great trouble in learning rules, whether the rules of a game like checkers or the social rules for saying "please" and "thank you." The young child's difficulty resides in seeing the relation between the one and the many, between the single instance in which a rule operates and the others where it does or does not apply. Once again the child is confronted with the problem of recognizing that social situations can be both alike and different at the same time. Different gift-taking situations are alike in that the child takes a gift for which he should say "thank you," but they are different with respect to the individuals and settings involved.

The same problem confronts a child who is, say, learning the rules of tic-tac-toe. What the child must recognize is that a line can be made in several directions, or that one and the same X can be used to make lines horizontally, vertically, and diagonally. In checkers the child must learn that every checker is alike in the sense that it is a checker, but different in the moves it can make depending upon its position. Looked at cognitively, rules have to do with how things can be the same and different simultaneously. "When two vowels go walking, the first one does the talking" suggests that two different vowels can have the same sound. And the rule "i before e except after c" says that while the sound of *ie* remains the same, the order in which they appear depends upon the preceding consonant.

More generally, rules permit us to move from the one to the many, from the general to the specific, precisely because they presuppose quantification. This syllogism, which comes to be understood (implicitly) by the elementary school child, illustrates this direction:

> All candy is sweet.
> This caramel is candy.
> Therefore: This caramel is sweet.

From a quantitative point of view, *all* X's are Y, that Z is an X, therefore, Z is a Y. Again, what is involved is the relation between the one and the many, between a caramel as a specific object and as a member of the class candy.

The rule-learning and rule-making propensities of the concrete-operational child give a particular quality to this age level much as symbolic propensities of the preschool child give a special expressive quality to that age period. What characterizes the culture of childhood proper is rules—rules for playing games and for not playing, for what to do when it rains or snows, when a siren blows, a black cat crosses your path, or you step on a crack. The language and lore of childhood provide a rich compendium of rules and regulations for guiding the child's behavior in almost all situations involving other children (cf. Opie and Opie, 1960).

The rule-learning and -making propensities of elementary school children are shown in their avocations as well. Children are devoted collectors of all sorts of things from rocks, to coins, to baseball cards. What characterizes a collection is that each element in the collection is alike in being a member of the class coins, rocks, or stamps, but is also unique in its condition and presence in the collection. Collections, like so much else in the lives of elementary school children, reflect the quantification of their thought.

Just a few additional points about the concrete-operational stage: A common misunderstanding about learning during this age period persists. Because the elementary school child can solve problems in his head by means of symbolic manipulation, it is often assumed that he no longer needs *things* to think or reason about. In many schools and homes, elementary school children are surrounded by books, by television, and by little else. Implicit in this environmental arrangement is the assumption that the child, like the adult, can now live comfortably in an abstract world of symbols. That is, however, a false assumption.

Concrete-operational children can indeed solve problems mentally, but the problems themselves have to be related to materials and not just symbols. Children think most effectively about things.

Consider the following situations. If a child is shown two sticks, A and B, one of which (A) is longer than the other (B), he can correctly judge the longer of the two. If the child is then shown B and C he can again judge that B is longer than C. He can also deduce, without comparing A and C directly, that A is longer than C. The same holds true for most conservation problems that require the child to reason about concrete materials and previous judgments.

But when a similar problem is presented entirely in the verbal mode, children have great difficulty. The following task is representative. If an elementary school child is asked, "If Mary is taller than Jane and Jane is taller than Alice, who is the tallest of the three?" he will not be able to solve the problem. The reason is that he has no external referents with which to tie up his mental symbols. Accordingly, while children do not need to manipulate materials manually in the way preschool children do, they still need materials to which they can attach their mental symbols. Classrooms for elementary school children, and homes as well, should be rich in materials for children to think about.

THE FORMAL-OPERATIONAL PERIOD

Adolescence is usually thought of in terms of the dramatic physical and emotional changes that mark this period. Equally dramatic, but less often attended to, are the cognitive changes coincident with the other metamorphoses undergone in the early teens. Intellectually, children acquire what Piaget calls *formal operations*. These formal operations underlie a whole new set of intellectual attainments that bring the adolescents' reality into close alignment with that of adults.

One way of thinking about formal operations is that they are second-order operations, operations on operations, as it were. Since the first-order operations are mental, it follows that formal operations deal with the operations of intelligence, rather than with objects in the world. This means that adolescents can now think about thinking—both their own and that of other people. Adolescents begin to use words such as "belief" and "intelligence" and "values," which are seldom heard in the conversations and discussions of children. These terms reflect conceptualizations of thought-process not real-world objects.

Formal operations also permit young people to think in terms of propositional logic. Such logic is a more abstract form of the logic the elementary school child performs upon real objects. A common adult word game illustrates what is involved in propositional logic. Each of the players selects a five-letter word which remains concealed from the other players. Then each player suggests to the adjacent player a five-letter word and asks how many of its letters are in the secret word. The adjacent player then tries to discover the secret word by determining which letters are in it from the list of words suggested. Looking at a list of words, such as "board," "bored," and "bound," he tries to figure out which letters in those words are in the secret word.

Logically, what is involved is keeping many variables in mind simultaneously, that is, b o d are present in all three words, but a is not. Formal-operational thinking is thus the kind of reasoning that is needed for scientific thinking and experimentation. The individual must keep many abstract variables in mind simultaneously. Concrete-operational children cannot play this game, but they can play chess, because in chess the operations are tied to concrete objects and moves.

The attainments made possible by formal operations are reflected in the school curriculum. Algebra is taught in junior high school and high school because it involves a higher-order symbol system. Algebraic symbols are symbols for numbers. Understanding algebra thus requires formal operations; the same is true of trigonometry and calculus. To be sure, children are sometimes taught algebraic-like symbols $(4 + x = 8)$, but in such cases the symbols are used in simple and concrete ways. It is not until adolescence that children can deal with simultaneous equations in two or three unknowns.

Formal operations also greatly expand young people's concepts of space and time. It is only during adolescence that young people grasp the true extent of geographical and celestial space and of historical time. The reason again has to do with the higher-order modes of thought. In the spatial realm, for example, "a thousand miles" is a complex concept and presupposes that the child has both a notion of how long a mile is and how long a mile multiplied by a thousand would be. But since a mile is a mental conception, multiplying it requires operating upon a mental operation. Similar considerations hold true for historical time. A century is a multiplication of years, and years are already a complex temporal concept. No wonder, then, that children still ask their parents if there were dinosaurs when they were children!

Other accomplishments made possible by formal operations should be mentioned. First, adolescents can begin to grasp and understand metaphor and simile. The problem here is the same as it was at the concrete-operational level, but on the plane of representation. The concrete-operational child had to learn that one and the same *object* could belong to two different classes, or participate in two different relationships. To understand metaphor and simile the young person must grasp that one and the same proposition or statement can have different meanings. To understand the proverb "a rolling stone gathers no moss" the young person must grasp the fact that the sentence can be interpreted in multiple ways. The ability to deal with metaphor and simile helps to explain why as a child one can read *Alice in Wonderland, Gulliver's Travels,* and biblical parables in one way, and in quite another way as an adolescent.

A very important contribution to adolescent thinking made possible by formal operations is the construction of ideals and possibilities—the adolescents' own metaphors, if you will. Adolescents can conceive of ideal countries, ideal religions, and ideal parents. They often compare these ideal constructions with their actual counterparts and find the counterparts sadly wanting. At least some of the "storm and stress" associated with adolescence is a consequence of this disaffection produced by the adolescent's unfavorable comparison of the actual with his ideal world.

Adolescent idealism is valuable, despite the discomfort it causes adults. What eventually happens is that, usually through engagement in meaningful work, the young person comes to discover that there is a difference between conceiving an ideal and attaining it. Young people move out of adolescence and become truly adult, not when they give up their ideals, but rather when they appreciate the need to *work* toward their attainment.

A few additional observations regarding cognitive development in adolescence are in order before closing this discussion of stages. When adolescents begin thinking about other people's thinking, they often assume that other people are thinking about them. They become, as a matter of fact, convinced that others are as concerned with them and their appearance as they are with themselves. Hence the "self-consciousness" so characteristic of young adolescents has to be attributed, in part at least, to the appearance of formal operations. While the physical and physiological transformations undergone by the adolescent play a part in this self-consciousness, its cognitive determination must also be recognized.

In a like manner, the severe depressions and occasional suicides among adolescents are to some degree also attributable to formal operations. Because children do not think about other people's thinking, they do not really see themselves as others do. Hence a child with a physical handicap or some other sort of "stigma" is not usually too troubled by it. When, however, that young person becomes an adolescent, the acute concern with what other people think and the belief that their evaluation is negative can lead to serious depression and unhappiness. Again, the point is not to deny that other factors play a role in adolescent depression, but rather to state that formal operations are a necessary though not a sufficient condition for such emotional states.

In closing this discussion of cognitive development, therefore, it is well to emphasize that cognition is not separate from the affective domain of feelings and emotions. There can be no feelings, no emotions that are not structured cognitively. What an individual experiences in the way of feelings and emotions depends in part upon the circumstances, in part on his level of development. It is simply a fact that some complex feelings, such as awe and reverence, may be impossible before the attainment of formal operations. A comprehensive discussion of cognitive growth should emphasize its consequences for emotional and social growth as well. A beginning attempt in this direction is the following conceptualization of egocentrism.

EGOCENTRISM IN CHILDREN AND ADOLESCENTS

In the preceding discussion the concept of egocentrism was used in the narrow sense as a characteristic of the preschool child's thinking. But there is also a broader sense in which the term egocentrism can be used. In this broader sense egocentrism refers to the fact that at each stage of development young people confuse what comes from without and what comes from within. There are characteristic confusions associated with each stage of mental development and these will be described below. It is an irony of intellectual growth that the new structures that appear at each stage of development free the child from the egocentrism of the previous stage yet, at the same time, ensnare him in a new form of egocentrism.

EGOCENTRIC STRUCTURES IN EARLY CHILDHOOD

Between the ages of three and six children acquire the symbolic function, the ability to create symbols and to learn signs that can represent their experience and their concepts. But the young child's ability to create symbols and to learn signs far outstrips his ability to comprehend them in socially accepted ways. Because this discrepancy pervades the young child's thinking, egocentrism is rampant during this stage. Egocentrism colors his attempts to discover all aspects of his world and justifies calling this stage one in which the child behaves according to *assumptive philosophies*, a global set of beliefs as to how the physical and social worlds operate.

Many assumptions of young children's philosophies were described earlier (pp. 86–92). One assumption is that the world is *purposive*, that everything has a purpose or cause, and that there is no possibility of chance or arbitrary events. Another assumption is that of *artificialism*, that everything in the world is made by and for man. Still another assumptive philosophy is *nominal realism*, the belief that names are essential components of the objects they designate and cannot be separated from them or changed. Finally, although it does not exhaust the list, there is the assumption of *animism*, the belief that nonbiological objects are alive.

Typical of the egocentric concepts of this and later stages is a fundamental confusion between what comes from within and what comes from without the child. Such confusion is to be expected if reality is truly constructed and is neither copied from some fixed and separate world, nor simply remembered as if it were an innate idea. But this epistemological confusion takes different forms at different age levels and reflects the level of conceptualization at those age levels.

At the preschool level, the confusion is between what the child knows concretely of himself—feelings, intentions, sensory experiences—and what he knows concretely of the world, namely, its tangibility and its objectivity. In effect, what the young child does is construct his psychic world on the model of the physical world and construct the physical world on the model of his psychic reality. Hence the young child believes that his dreams come in through the window at night, that other people can feel his toothache, and that the wind, moon, and sun are alive.

Some concrete examples may help to show how egocentric behavior can sometimes be misinterpreted by adults. One reason young children find it difficult to keep "secrets" is their belief that adults and other children know what they are thinking anyway. This belief that others know what they are thinking is also shown in young children's "referential communication" activities. When a four-year-old has to describe an object to another child, who cannot see it, he does not describe it in objective terms but in subjective ones useful to himself and not to others. But the young child believes that his idiosyncratic description (like the words he makes up) are immediately understood by others (Glucksberg, Krauss, and Higgins, 1975).

When young children deal with adults, another facet of egocentrism comes into play. A young mother has a headache and lies down in her room with the shades drawn. Her four-year-old son rushes in and tugs at her arm to come and see the fort he has built. She says she has a headache and asks to be left alone, but the child persists until the tone of his mother's voice tells him it would be more prudent to withdraw. It would be wrong to attribute the child's behavior to thoughtlessness and insensitivity rather than to what it is, namely, intellectual immaturity. He was, after all, quite incapable of putting himself in his mother's place and of grasping her need for quiet and rest. Learning to share and to take turns, to take the other person's point of view, to listen to the other person while he is talking are accomplishments that rest on the attainment of concrete operations. To attribute to moral or characterological deficits the child's failure to engage in these behaviors is not only an injustice, it also interferes with effective child rearing and education.

EGOCENTRIC STRUCTURES IN MIDDLE CHILDHOOD

At about the age of six or seven in Piaget's view, new mental abilities emerge which take the child far beyond what he was capable of doing at the preschool level (see above, pp. 92–98). These new mental abilities, concrete operations, resemble the operations of arithmetic in their mode of activity and function as a system rather than in isolation. Thus if a child knows that the class of children minus the class of boys equals the class of girls $(C - B = G)$, one can infer, with reasonable certainty, that he also knows that the class of children minus the class of girls equals the class of boys $(C - G = B)$. As discussed earlier, these operations also enable the child to grasp the notion of a unit which is both like every other unit in being a unit and different in order of enumeration or seriation.

The concrete operations that emerge around the age of six or seven enable the school-age child to progressively comprehend many of the verbal representations he acquired but understood only egocentrically at the preschool level. He begins to grasp, for example, that "right" and "left" are relations and not absolute properties of things. And he comes to appreciate that changes in the appearance of quantities does not mean a change in their amount. The concrete operations of middle childhood thus gradually overcome the egocentric notions found at the preschool level.

But concrete operations also engender new egocentric concepts in their own right. With his new mental abilities, the school-age child can now mentally represent various possible courses of action. The preschool child, in contrast, was able to represent only properties and things. The new ability to represent possible courses of action appears in many different ways. For example, when a preschool child is presented with a finger maze he proceeds by immediately putting his finger to the maze and succeeds, if he does, by trial and error efforts. A school-age child will, in contrast, survey the maze and mentally represent various paths until he discovers the right one. Only at that point will he put his finger to the maze.

In the maze situation the ability to represent actions internally works quite well because there is immediate and unequivocal feedback as to the correctness of the representation. But in many other situations, there is no mental way to test which of several possible courses of action will succeed. In such circumstances an experimental frame of mind is required that permits one to hold in thought several hypotheses while testing each in succession. The ability to do this is, however, only made possible by the formal operations of adolescent intelligence. Consequently, the school-age child is in the position of being able to conceptualize alternate paths of action but of not being able to test these alternate paths in systematic ways.

The school-age child is thus in the same position with respect to representing possible courses of action that the preschool child was with respect to representing classes, relations, and units. In both cases there is a lag between the ability to represent experience and the ability to test the social validity of the representations. In the school-age child, as in the preschool child, the result is the formation of egocentric conceptions. At this stage these egocentric conceptions deal with assumptions having to do with possible courses of action in the real world and might be called *assumptive realities*.

As in the assumptive philosophies of the preschool child, the assumptive realities of the school-age child reflect a confusion between the mental and the physical, between the reality of mind and the reality of matter. When the school-age child arrives at a possible course of action, a hypothesis or strategy which cannot be immediately tested, he often mistakes this *conceptual possibility* for a *material necessity*. Once he has adopted this egocentric position, he proceeds to make any disparate facts fit the hypothesis rather than the reverse. This mode of egocentric thought is not unfamiliar at the adult level and is epitomized in folk sayings such as "love is blind" or "no mother has a homely child."

The following examples illustrate the operation of assumptive realities. In one study Peel (1960) gave children and adolescents a text describing the rock formations at Stonehenge without revealing their supposed function. The subjects were asked to decide whether the formations were used as a fort or as a religious shrine. The children (nine years old) made their decisions on the basis of a few facts and, if given contrary information, rationalized this to fit in with their hypotheses. Adolescents, in contrast, based their hypotheses upon multiple facts and, if given sufficient contrary information changed their hypotheses.

In another experiment Weir (1964) had five- to seventeen-year-olds work on a probability task. The apparatus was a box with three knobs and a payoff chute. One knob was programmed to pay off (in M&M candies or tokens) none of the time, another was programmed to pay off one-third of the time, and a third was programmed to pay off two-thirds of the time. Subjects were instructed to find a pattern of response (knob pressing) that would produce the most rewards. The solution was to press only the two-thirds knob.

The results, plotted as number of trials to a successful solution, showed an inverted U curve with respect to age. The young children (four to five), who were getting M&Ms, did not waste time and quickly learned which knob gave them the most candy. Adolescents approached the task with many complex hypotheses and tried out a variety of patterns. In the process they discovered the fruitfulness of the two-thirds knob and eventually stuck to pressing it. But the children age seven to nine had great trouble. They adopted a "win, stick, lose, shift" strategy which they assumed was correct, and blamed the machine for being wrong. This is a good example of the assumptive realities of the seven- to nine-year-old child.

The assumptive realities of grade school children are often a source of conflict between these children and parents and adults. These conflicts often revolve around "stealing" and "lying." Children do not really understand stealing and lying in the same sense as adults do, as an issue of moral character. For them it is more often a game, a challenge to what one can get away with in outwitting an adult or another child. And when children take something or make up a story, they often take what they make up to be reality and change the facts to fit their made-up story. Such reasoning infuriates the adult who believes the child is adding insult to injury by his tall tales.

A not unusual example of this phenomenon occurred in a supermarket just before Halloween. A mother who had been shopping with her son noticed that he was eating a Milky-Way as they were leaving the store. When they were in the station-wagon heading for home she asked him where he had gotten the candy bar. Her son insisted that his friend Tom had given it to him several days before. His mother rejoined, "If he had given it to you days ago, you would have eaten it by now. Did you take it out of the bin by the counter?" To which her son replied, "No, Tom gave it to me." The mother now convinced of her son's guilt (her own assumptive reality) said, "I saw you take it, admit it." It is interesting how often we adults lie in order to get children to tell the truth! At her son's continued refusal to admit his guilt, his mother became more and more infuriated and visions of reform school began floating through her head. At last she brought out her big guns, "Tell me the truth and I won't hit you or tell your father."

The point is that the child was operating under an assumptive reality as to his own innocence and believed in it, whether or not he had really taken it from the store. If we recognize this, it makes the behavior a little easier to deal with. There is no need to drag the young man back to the store to make public apologies in front of a line of embarrassed shoppers. Rather, one can say, "Maybe that is the way you think it happened, but it might have happened in another way. In case it did, let's take a dime from your allowance and give it to the checker the next time we go to the store. If it turns out to have happened the way you say, I will pay you the dime back."

Among grade-school children, therefore, lying and stealing have a somewhat different meaning than they do for adults because of the pervasiveness of assumptive realities. Once we understand this we can attribute many of these behaviors to intellectual immaturity rather than to moral corruption. This relieves us as adults of considerable anger and permits us to deal with the situation in a rational and adult manner. Again it is important that children learn such things as not to steal candy bars from stores. But, in the long run, such learning is more long-lasting if the teaching is done in the spirit of understanding rather than in one of anger and punishment.

EGOCENTRIC STRUCTURES IN ADOLESCENCE

Roughly coincident with the onset of puberty is the appearance of the new mental structures that Piaget calls "formal operations" (cf. pp. 98–102). Like concrete operations, formal operations function as a system but extend the young person's intellectual powers far beyond what they were in childhood. This is true because formal operations allow the preadolescent to represent his own representations. Formal operations are to concrete operations as algebra is to arithmetic, a second-order, higher-level symbol system. While concrete operations make it possible for the child to conceive available courses of action in the real world, formal operations permit the adolescent to conceive of possible representations. Possible representations include theories, ideals, and metaphors. Formal operations also enable the young person to hold many hypotheses in mind while testing each one systematically. In a word, formal operations make possible experimental thinking.

Formal operations enable the child to be aware of his hypotheses as hypotheses, as mental constructions, and permit him to test these against the evidence. In this way, formal operations enable the child to overcome his egocentric assumptive realities. But these operations also make it possible for the adolescent to represent his own and other persons' feelings and thoughts. Although he has the mental ability to test out these assumptions, the young adolescent lacks the motivation to do so. He is so preoccupied with the changes in his physical appearance and his new feelings and emotions that he has little interest in testing his assumptions about what other people think and feel. For a few years, therefore, the young adolescent operates on the basis of *assumptive psychologies* about himself and other people.

As in the case of the assumptive philosophies of preschool children and assumptive realities of elementary school children, the assumptive psychologies of the young adolescent represent a confusion between the child and his world, now on a psychological plane. What happens is that the young adolescent takes what is unique to himself as being universal to mankind but also believes that what is universal to mankind is unique to himself. Such assumptive psychologies are sometimes gratifying and sometimes painful; it is often the painful ones that eventually cause young people to test these assumptions about how other people think and feel.

For example, an attractive young woman with a minor facial blemish at the early-adolescent stage is convinced: (a) that everyone notices and thinks about it; (b) that everyone regards it as horribly ugly and detestable; and (c) that it is the sole criterion by which people judge her as a person. Hence the conclusion, "Everybody thinks I am ugly. I must be ugly." In this instance, which is so familiar as to be commonplace, the young person mistakes a personal, idiosyncratic self-appraisal for one that is a uniform, consistent appraisal by mankind.

The reverse is also true, and young people believe that their feelings which are universal, or nearly so, are unique. A young man who has been saving up to buy a new car feels that no boy in the world has ever wanted a car so much as he. But boys growing up all over the world want horses, boats, or even bows and arrows as signs of their maturity. Far from being unique, the desire for a symbol of adult male status is probably universal in male adolescents. In the same way, a young woman who is in love for the first time believes that her feelings are unique and that no one has ever experienced the exquisite pain she is enduring—"Oh Mommy, you don't know how it feels"—and yet every woman, at one time or another, has felt the same way.

Like the assumptive philosophies of the preschool child and the assumptive realities of the elementary school child, the assumptive psychologies of the adolescent can be misinterpreted by adults. When an adolescent girl says that her mother could "never understand" how she feels, this can be interpreted as the child's insensitivity and a direct attack upon the parent's capacity to have any sympathetic understanding. But it is not a personal attack at all and reflects the adolescent's belief that no one, including the parent, can understand those feelings. This is but one example of the many possible instances in which intellectual immaturity on the part of the adolescent becomes transformed into statements that could be read as derogatory to parents and other adults when in fact they are not, or at least not in the way they might appear.

Far from being limited to contributing to our understanding of the intellectual development of children, Piaget's work also provides important insights in the affective domain. Many behaviors on the part of children and adolescents which heretofore seemed evidence of bad character turn out to be manifestations of intellectual immaturity. Piaget enables us to avoid irrational anger and thus helps us to deal with children from a position of sympathetic understanding rather than hostility.

V
THREE MODES OF LEARNING

"The object is known only so far as the subject achieves action on it, and this action is incompatible with the passive character which empiricism, at various degrees, attributes to knowledge."   J. PIAGET

Within American psychology, learning has generally been defined as the modification of thought and behavior as a consequence of experience. From a developmental point of view, however, this definition of learning is much too narrow. Not only is the child's thought and action changed by experience, but experience itself is changed as a direct result of the child's maturing mental operations and motor coordinations. To be sure, these maturing operations and coordinations are in part attributable to experience, but it is equally true that experience is in part attributable to them. In short, there is inevitably an interaction, and what a child learns is always a product of experience that is itself conditioned by her level of cognitive development.

If we recognize that all learning is at once assimilative and accommodative—involving, as it does, taking something from the environment into the self and putting something from the self into the environment—it is still possible to distinguish different modes of learning in which one or the other of these processes is more prominent. From this standpoint we can distinguish three modes of learning: one which emphasizes the assimilative process, another which emphasizes the accommodative process, and another which emphasizes the integration of the products of the other two learning modes. Each of these three modes of learning is important in its own right. The present chapter will be devoted to a description of these three modes of learning and of the principles which seem to best characterize their operation.

OPERATIVE LEARNING

In general, operative learning is in play whenever the child's intelligence is actively engaged by the materials she is interacting with. Such learning can be observed, for example, when a child repeats an action like seriating (ordering according to size) a set of sticks over and over again. This behavior is quite different from the rote repetition used in memorization of verbal materials. In repeating an action like seriation, what the child is doing is abstracting the *action* of seriation itself. Once the action is abstracted the child will be able to seriate in her head without having to do it in fact.

Operative learning also occurs when the child is confronted with logical conflicts and contradictions that encourage her to arrive at higher organizations. For example, most children acquire the conservations (of mass, weight, number, length, etc.) on their own because these materials are auto-didactic in the sense that they present intrinsic difficulties to conceptualization. A child comparing two pencils discovers that they are of equal length when they are side by side but that one appears longer when it is pushed ahead of the other. If she looks in the other direction she finds that the situation appears reversed and that the unmoved pencil extends beyond its partner and that *it* looks longer. These contradictions, inherent in judgments based on perception, emerge from the child's active manipulation of the materials. They force her to abstract from her own actions upon the pencils. Once she does this she can arrive at the equality of the length of the pencils on the basis of the reversible transformations (pushing one ahead of the other) that can be performed upon them. By abstracting her actions, the child can replace perceptual judgments for those based on reasoned, internalized actions.

Operative learning, in addition to facilitating the development of mental operations, also gives rise to *practical intelligence*. Practical intelligence consists of the operations and knowledge the child requires to get about in the everyday world. Much of it, thanks to externalization, is unconscious. A child who operates according to the conservation of liquid quantity does not get upset when her coke is served in a wider glass than that given to her sisters. She knows the amounts are the same. But she is not aware of *how* she knows that the quantities that come out of two coke bottles remain the same even if they end up in different sized containers. Although practical intelligence is common to most children who have attained concrete operations, there are individual differences. A child who is not very skilled in practical intelligence is often called "clumsy."

FIGURATIVE LEARNING

Some aspects of reality cannot be reconstructed or rediscovered to any great extent and must be largely copied. Language, for example, is partly acquired in this way. An infant's babbling contains most of the vowel and consonant sounds to be found in almost all of the world's languages. But, gradually, the child shapes his language in conformance with the language of those in her environment. Pronunciation, accent, and intonation are all more or less copied linguistic cues which are part of interpersonal communication. Many other aspects of the communicative process, such as facial expression, gesture, and distance from speaker to speaker, are culturally conditioned, which is to say, figuratively learned.

In general, figurative learning has to do with associative rather than with rational processes. Memorizing mathematical facts, telephone numbers, and poetry are all examples of figurative learning. Although figurative learning seems simpler than operative learning, it in fact builds on the constructions of operative intelligence. For example, in order for a child to remember something she must be able to record it in the first place. But if the operative structures do not permit such recording, the memory cannot take place. A child, for example, will not be able to "remember" viewing a size-graded seriation of sticks if she is not capable of constructing that series on her own. So figurative learning is not a throwback to the copy theory of knowing. Once the child constructs a bit of reality (unconsciously by concrete operations) she can learn about it figuratively and consciously.

The knowledge that results from figurative learning has sometimes been called *symbolic intelligence.* Symbolic intelligence has to do with systems of interpersonal communication. The symbolic world includes not only language but also other sign systems such as those of mathematics, symbolic logic, and the motor sign systems used by the deaf. The deaf are, therefore, not deficient in symbolic intelligence. Actually, deficiencies in symbolic intelligence are best illustrated by the aphasic disorders in which one or another aspect of the symbolic process is disrupted. Forgetting a name is a momentary aphasia, a temporary deficiency in the operation of symbolic intelligence.

CONNOTATIVE LEARNING

As described above, much of practical intelligence is unconscious. Symbolic intelligence, in contrast, is almost always conscious or potentially conscious. A child can recall a name with ease, but cannot put into words the means by which she discovered the conservation of number. The conscious conceptualization of one's own mental processes, what has been called *reflective intelligence,* does not usually appear until adolescence and the attainment of formal operations. It is only at that time that young people are capable of thinking about thinking.

Nonetheless, I believe that there is a kind of reflective intelligence that emerges as soon as the child acquires language and which mirrors the tension between unconscious practical intelligence and conscious symbolic intelligence. That is to say, children hear and acquire many words for which they have no concepts, and they have many concepts, thanks to the unconscious workings of practical intelligence, for which they have no words. Hence children try to relate their concepts to their verbal symbols, a process I propose to call *connotative learning*. Connotative learning is expressly concerned with the construction of meanings, with establishing connections between concepts and figurative symbols. It is no less than the child's efforts to make sense out of her world.

The motivation for connotative learning is at once intrinsic and social. It is play. Once a child masters a concept or a word, he or she wants to play with these accomplishments. (See Chapter VI.) To play with a concept is often to try out various verbal expressions for it, and to play with words is often to tie them to new concepts. When a child writes poetry or describes an excursion there is a kind of connotative learning going on. The child is trying, in an experimental way, to fit thought to language and vice versa. In a very real sense connotative learning involves the *re-presentation* of experience at the concrete operational level. It could be said, then, that there is a re-presentational intelligence at the concrete operational level which precedes reflective intelligence at the formal operational level.

The distinction among operative, figurative, and connotative learning modes needs to be qualified in certain respects. First, all three modes of learning are limited by the child's level of cognitive development and the cognitive structures that are present at that level. A concrete-operational child, for example, will not be able to learn about gravity operationally, because the concept involves the coordination of more variables than she is capable of bringing together at the same time (i.e., relative mass, acceleration, and so on). Likewise, a child at the concrete-operational level will not usually be able to repeat an "if . . . then" or "either . . . or" construction, because understanding these constructions requires formal operations. Finally, a child will not be able to give appropriate meanings to words that are beyond his or her conceptual level. A preoperational child could say "infinity" (learn it figuratively) but not understand it (learn it connotatively).

It must also be said that some types of tasks require one or more of these modes of learning simultaneously. Indeed, the more complex the task, the more likely this is to be the case. Reading is a good example. In beginning reading the child may learn the names of the letters and a number of sight words, all of which are figurative accomplishments. As soon as the child begins to learn phonics, however, operative learning comes into play. And, as soon as the child starts to read simple stories, connotative learning also comes into the picture. It is not surprising, then, that young children who are just learning to read may concentrate on one or another mode and neglect the others. When young children read out loud, they often concentrate so much on the decoding, the operative task, that they ignore the meaning of what it is they are reading. They ignore the connotative task.

The relation of these various learning modes to their products may also change in the course of development. What was once operative can become figurative. Learning to decode words, for example, becomes a figurative skill for the advanced reader for whom the connotative or comprehension task becomes the salient one. Likewise, a figurative accomplishment, such as the memorization of the lines for a play, can become connotative in the hands of a skilled actor who gives the lines added meaning through gesture, intonation, and expression.

Despite their obvious interactions and the fact that it may be difficult at times to determine whether one or another mode of learning is in play, the distinction among the operative, figurative, and connotative modes has heuristic value. Perhaps the most pervasive problem in contemporary education, a problem that will be discussed in detail in the chapters on curriculum analysis (Chapter VIII) and the active classroom (Chapter IX) is the failure really to comprehend these different modes of learning. Again and again one finds the curriculum makers saying that they are providing children with operative tasks when the material itself can only be learned figuratively. While all three types of learning are significant to the child and have an important place in education, it is a grave error to confuse them and to assume that children are learning concepts when they are only learning words.

I want now to describe some general principles which I believe hold for these different types of learning and which may serve as guides for implementing them. The principles are largely developmental and suggest what most often comes before what. In my view, the sequencing of tasks is all-important. Whether we are talking about operative, figurative, or connotative learning, the underlying cognitive structures must always be kept in mind. It is these logical substructures that dictate the sequence to be followed with any particular learning mode.

SOME PRINCIPLES OF LEARNING

PRINCIPLES OF OPERATIVE LEARNING

The qualitative precedes the quantitative. One of Piaget's greatest contributions to our understanding of learning is his demonstration that in children's operative learning the qualitative precedes the quantitative. Too often in education unit concepts are taken for granted and assumed to be self-evident rather than arrived at through a laborious process of construction.

A case in point is the concept of number to which we briefly referred earlier (p. 94–95). Piaget's research has demonstrated that the notion of a unit, basic to the understanding of all mathematics, is gradually constructed out of the child's active attempts at classification and seriation. Young children must practice sorting objects according to one or another dimension (color, size, form, weight, coarseness, etc.) as a prerequisite to forming a unit concept.

But they must also practice seriating objects, arranging them in an order from big to little, bright to dull, coarse to smooth.

As a consequence of his classifying activities, the child gradually develops a notion of *cardinality*, of the numerosity of a set of like objects which can be given a name. The notion of a "group of black buttons" is the natural forerunner to the cardinal assessment of the group "ten black buttons." In the same way, the seriation of objects that vary in a particular dimension is the qualitative analogue to ordinality. "This stick before that one" is the precursor of "seventh before eighth" and "eighth before ninth."

The child arrives at a notion of a numerical unit only as he combines his understanding of classification and seriation, of cardination and ordination. A true numerical unit is, in effect, at once both a cardinal and ordinal. That is to say, a true numerical unit (such as the number 9) is cardinal in that it is like every other number (or that it *is* a number and thus belongs to the class of numbers) and ordinal in that it is different from every other number (in its position within the series of numbers). The child arrives at a true unit concept only when he integrates his conceptions of classification and of seriation. These qualitative notions precede the quantitative in the child's understanding of number.

We can see the same precedence of the qualitative over the quantitative in the child's conception of time. The first temporal distinctions children learn are those of day and night, of before and after, soon and later. These qualitative "cuts" into the time dimension precede the child's understanding of such unit terms as hour, minute, month, and year which are quantitative in nature. Quantitative notions of time are constructed only gradually as the child struggles to arrive at a concept of uniform motion that is independent of all the relative motions of his environment. Once he arrives at a sense of uniform motion, to which all clock and watch hands conform, regardless of the physical motions to which they are subjected, he is on the way to a true understanding of the measurement of time.

Children's conceptions of age show the same evolution from the qualitative to the quantitative. Young children may judge the age of a person or a tree by its height, as if getting taller were the same as getting older. Taller people are older than shorter people. When a person stops growing taller, he stops growing older. As one young man said to his father on the occasion of his birthday, "You don't need any more birthdays, Daddy, you are already grown up." The understanding of age in unit terms only occurs at about the age of seven or eight.

The child's conception of speed also demonstrates how the qualitative precedes the quantitative. When children observe two toy cars traveling on circular tracks of different circumferences, they make characteristic judgments. When both vehicles are traveling at the same speed, the car on the track with the smaller circumference "overtakes" the car on the longer. Children believe that the car on the smaller track is going faster. On a straight path, the car which has gone farthest is regarded as having gone the fastest even if it was, in fact, going more slowly than the other car which simply did not go as far. The young child first judges speed qualitatively, by "overtaking" and only later by the coordination of measures of time and distance.

In arriving at a true conception of length, children again demonstrate how the qualitative precedes the quantitative. The young child believes that an object that goes beyond another is the "larger" one regardless of how they line up at the other end. Thus, when two rulers of equal length are arranged side by side in a staggered position, the child says that one is longer than the other because one goes beyond the other. Gradually the child is able to deal with the staggered ruler problem as he recognizes that the extent to which one ruler is ahead of the other at one end is exactly the same as at the other end. Eventually the child arrives at a notion of unit length independent of a particular object. It is at this point that the child truly understands what a ruler is.

Perhaps these examples will suffice to demonstrate that in the child's spontaneous or operative learning activities he deals with the qualitative dimensions of the world before he deals with their quantitative dimensions. That is as true for middle and late childhood levels as it is for early childhood. The child needs to observe and classify specimens before he can begin to quantify them in meaningful ways. The adolescent, too, must understand the qualities of the materials he is dealing with before he effectively quantifies them for experimental purposes. A too speedy entrance into quantification is the bane of traditional educational practice and flies in the face of the child's natural modes of learning.

Horizontal elaboration precedes vertical integration. When children, or adults for that matter, are learning a particular skill or subject matter, there is a spontaneous tendency to practice these new acquisitions in as wide an array of situations as possible (cf. Chapter VI). Children who are learning to read, for example, will practice the "left to right" visual swing on a wide range of materials including their examination of pictures. Likewise an adult who is learning a foreign language will practice it on every possible occasion. When we learn, we want to substantiate our new skills and knowledge by applying them to as wide a range of new and different situations as we possibly can. This is horizontal elaboration.

The tendency, indeed necessity, for individuals to elaborate their abilities in the horizontal direction is sometimes forgotten in education. It often appears as if vertical acceleration is regarded as more important than horizontal elaboration. Children are encouraged to move continually to harder and harder problems without ensuring that they have fully elaborated their abilities at a particular level of difficulty. As a consequence they may move ahead too rapidly before they have fully consolidated their cognitive gains.

It is much more natural, however, for children to apply their skills in a wide variety of domains at the same level. At about the age of seven and eight, children have learned to classify and order materials. What they need at this point is the opportunity to classify and order materials of many different kinds. They can begin to distinguish the many different kinds of leaves, fern patterns, geological formations, and fossil forms. They can arrange forms of housing and clothing in rough order from ancient to most modern, and they can order materials according to hardness, softness, durability, and the like. Such orderings need not be, indeed should not be, numerical but rather ordered according to qualitative properties.

Exercises of this sort not only expand the child's realm of experience and re-presentation, they also strengthen his cognitive skills and make further cognitive growth more easy and substantial. Such activities prepare the child for the quantification of experience, which, in the absence of such quantification, might be empty and devoid of real meaning. Once a child has classified and ordered many different kinds of natural elements, quantification of the physical world follows naturally and is a meaningful next step in the way of re-presenting experience. But, as we said earlier, qualitative re-presentation precedes quantitative re-presentation.

As the child elaborates his abilities on many different materials and re-presents his experience in many different modes, he prepares himself for the vertical integration of his knowledge. A child who has learned geometric forms, such as circle and square, can elaborate these skills by looking for circles and squares in all spheres of his experience. He can discover that coins, wheels, and doughnuts all are circles. Through this elaboration of his experience he arrives at a general concept of circles that, combined with general concepts of squares and triangles, will lead naturally to the more general concept of geometrical forms. The horizontal elaboration of experience multiplies the *variety* of the child's encounters with a concept and renders it at once more general and more susceptible to vertical integration within a broader more abstract conceptualization.

The absolute precedes the relative. In the spontaneous learning of children, the understanding of relations is always later than the understanding of absolute properties. The young child first believes that "right" and "left," "up" and "down" are absolute properties of things. Likewise, a five-year-old who knows that he has a brother nonetheless argues that his brother does not have a brother. At this stage "having a brother" is not a reciprocal relation that implies "being a brother." Rather it is like having blue eyes or brown hair, a "property" of the individual. It is only in late childhood that most children understand the relational nature of kinship terms.

It is important to say that these absolute ideas are not "wrong" in the same sense that $4 + 4 = 9$ is wrong. The child's absolute ideas of brother and sister are necessary steps in his construction of relationistic kinship concepts. They are stages along the way to a correct concept in a way that $4 + 4 = 9$ is not. An arithmetic error can be produced by accident, by inattention, or by incorrect understanding, but an absolutist notion is simply a stage in a progression toward a more advanced concept.

Attempts to correct such relational errors merely enlarge the child's fears and inhibit further growth. Relations are hard to learn, and if a child knows that he has a brother, even in an absolute way, then that is an achievement worthy of praise in and for itself.

PRINCIPLES OF CONNOTATIVE LEARNING

Proximal experience precedes distal experience. Recently I visited a school in which six- and seven-year-old children were doing a unit on the San Francisco earthquake of 1906. Most of the compositions were little more than copies of the story as it was told by the teacher. In other schools I have seen children of six or seven doing units on the planets or on maps of the United States. The problem of all these units, from a developmental point of view, is that they are far too distant from the child's experience and level of conceptualization to be comprehended. In order to re-present an experience meaningfully, the experience must be within the child's realm of comprehension. But the San Francisco earthquake, the planets, and the geography of the United States are beyond the realm of the early elementary school child's understanding. Indeed the experience itself must be introduced symbolically, and the child's only alternative is a secondhand re-presentation of what was given him. Not surprisingly, material re-presented in this way is seldom retained for any length of time and rarely becomes a useful component of the child's fund of information.

Connotative learning, particularly in children of preschool and elementary school age, begins with proximal or near experiences. Children attempt to re-present objects, vistas, animals, plants, and buildings that they can see, feel, touch, smell, and manipulate. They will learn more connotatively from a trip to a bakery than from hearing about a trip to the moon. They will learn more from observing a live guinea pig than they will from a story about dinosaurs. And they will learn more from making a map of their room than they will from coloring a map of the United States. The most meaningful experiences children have are those which they can encounter firsthand.*

This is not to say, of course, that the child's experiences must be limited to the proximal, but only that they should *begin* there. If children are to understand a map of the United States, they must first understand a map of their immediate environment. After making maps of the school room, of their homes, of the neighborhood that surrounds school and home, children have a better sense of the nature of maps and what they represent. Maps of larger and more distant regions can be presented after the children have comprehended maps of their immediate environment. The princi-

---

* I still recall the tremendous excitement I felt as a child when the teacher talked about and showed pictures of the Henry Ford museum, which I had visited and seen myself.

ple that proximal precedes distal experience is a procedural and sequential one and does not mean that proximal experience is to be used to the exclusion of distal experience. Rather, it means that children should learn what is near at hand *before* they venture to learn what is far afield.

Interest precedes involvement. By chance I happened to be in England visiting schools at the time of Princess Anne's wedding. The schools were closed for the day and the wedding was at the forefront of newspaper and television discussion. The next day I visited several schools and found the children to be very much involved in writing, drawing, and talking about the wedding. Young children liked the Queen and the carriages, whereas somewhat older children were enthralled by the gowns and uniforms. What was more natural than to capitalize upon this interest to involve children in a variety of activities in which they could re-present their exciting memories of the wedding.

Clearly, children become involved in activities that enable them to pursue and develop their spontaneous interests. Sometimes these interests derive from the development of new abilities. The interest of four- and five-year-old children in quantity comparisons of all sorts ("who has more") reflects the development of concrete operations during this age period (cf. Chapter VI on motivation). It is easy to involve children at this age in quantity-related activities such as counting and size estimation. Sometimes children's interests derive from upcoming holidays such as Thanksgiving, Christmas, or Easter. These can be the occasion for excursions such as visiting a turkey farm, which can then be represented in words, graphically, and in movements (imitation of the turkeys). The child's spontaneous interests are thus guides to experiences that children will attend to and wish to represent in various ways.

In addition to the spontaneous interests that grow out of events common to all children, interests develop out of the experiences of particular children or groups of children. If the children in a particular class visit a railroad yard, doughnut factory, or museum, the experience will generate spontaneous interest. The interest may not always be what the teacher expects. Sometimes children at a museum may be more interested in the snack shop than they are in the museum displays. Sometimes a worm outside the museum may be more interesting than what the children saw inside. The teacher has to be alert to the spontaneous interests of children and allow them to become involved in re-presenting what is important and significant to them.

Occasionally spontaneous interests emerge out of the child's individual life circumstances. Perhaps a new baby has arrived, a trip is to be taken, a new car has been purchased, a new house is to be moved into, or grandparents are to visit. The child has a genuine need to involve herself in these experiences and to re-present and assimilate them. In this process she can expand and elaborate many different skills such as writing and drawing.

Accordingly, whether the spontaneous interests of children come out of their developing mental abilities, out of upcoming events of general interest, from class excursions, or from individual circumstances, they are the prerequisite to the child's active involvement in connotative activities of many different kinds. Children practice and extend their vocabulary, reading, and mathematical skills in the process of re-presenting experiences which elaborate their spontaneous interests.

Fluency precedes accuracy. When I was learning French, I was petrified to speak it for fear of making a fool of myself. Fortunately we were living in Switzerland at the time and I was forced to speak French if I wanted to ask questions and learn anything. I gathered up my courage and began speaking without worrying too much about grammar and pronunciation. To my amazement I was able to communicate—there were, to be sure, grimaces on the part of my French-speaking companions—and this gave me the confidence to continue speaking. I became fluent and gradually cleaned up my grammar, syntax, and pronunciation.

This is not an unusual experience, but is in the very nature of connotative learning. Whether we are talking about motor skills such as swimming or skills of the intellect such as reading, fluency precedes accuracy. In learning to swim, the most important thing for a child to overcome is his fear of the water, of having his head in the water. Once he feels comfortable in the water and overcomes his fear of having his head in the water, he will learn several strokes, such as the dog paddle, and be susceptible to instruction. He needs to overcome his fear of the water, to be fluent in it, before he can develop accuracy in swimming. The same is true for many other skills such as bike riding, skiing, and water skiing.

In academic learning the same holds true. In reading, the child needs to develop a sense of acquiring meaning before he attains complete accuracy in letter recognition and pronunciation. The situation is not really that different from learning to speak a foreign language. The child who is learning to read is afraid he is going to make mistakes and embarrass himself. Once he gets the courage to read, his errors should be overlooked and his courage in reading out loud should be applauded. Later, when he feels comfortable in reading aloud, he can be helped to be more accurate. But initially, while he is gaining the courage to read out loud, it is much more important to reward his fluency than to be concerned with his accuracy.

The same principle holds for a child's writing. In the flush of creating, the child cannot and should not be bothered by spelling and grammar. What is important are getting his thoughts down on paper as they tumble out and experiencing writing as a natural mode of expressing his thoughts. There is plenty of time later to clean up the grammar, spelling, and syntax. This is the way most writers work, anyway. Getting it down on paper is the hard part, while "polishing" the rough spots is the finishing touch.

It should be clear from the foregoing remarks that a too early insistence upon accuracy can inhibit and block connotative learning. Accuracy in any creative endeavor is the luxury of the last or terminal stage of the effort. To insist on accuracy too soon

magnifies the child's fears about his competence and thus undermines the learning process. In helping children construct meaning
our main task is not to correct errors but to encourage fluency in
communication and expression. Once we do this, children will want
to correct their own spelling and grammar to improve the appearance of their work. Eliminating errors should be the fun part of
expressive work.

Please understand, however, that the principle of fluency preceding accuracy holds true for connotative learning but not necessarily
for operative or figurative learning.

PRINCIPLES OF FIGURATIVE LEARNING

Quality of practice is more important than quantity. In traditional
discussions of learning much space was devoted to the advantages
and to the disadvantages of massed versus distributed practice in
learning. Is it better, for example, for the student to study regularly
all semester long or can he or she do equally well by studying for
long hours several days before the exam? The question presupposes
that the kind of knowledge required by the exam is figurative and
that the studying involves memorizing facts, names, and dates. If
this is the case, the question is whether massed or distributed
practice most facilitates memorization. Contemporary opinion,
however, suggests that the issue is more complicated than that
because other variables, such as motivation, enter the equation
regarding the effects of practices.

Indeed, it is now recognized that one of the most crucial variables
in figurative learning is motivation and attention. If someone
engages in distributed practice but is not really concentrating, then
the practice is not going to be worth much. On the other hand,
intense, highly concentrated practice can be quite effective because
it is highly motivated. But there is a danger here as well. A certain
amount of anxiety is healthy to figurative learning, but too much or
too little can interfere with it. In studying regularly for the exam,

there may not be enough anxiety to make studying very profitable. On the other hand, waiting to the last minute may make the anxiety too high for the studying to be of much value. Figurative learning, then, is not necessarily improved by massing or distributing practice. Such learning is enhanced by attaching sufficient motivation to it to make it interesting but not so much as to make it emotionally debilitating. One technique for providing motivation is to provide individual attention. At the Mt. Hope School the children may spend only about an hour and a half a day in reading, less perhaps than is spent in the public school. But if they are reading with a student, they are spending the whole hour and a half on motivated reading, really practicing the task.

In a large classroom, where children cannot be conveniently worked with individually, children can effectively avoid practice even though they are spending two or three hours on "reading." The only way to overcome this inefficient practice is through social motivation and, if possible, individual attention—at least in the beginning. The use of older children, of teacher aids, of small groups among which the teacher can circulate, are all means of improving the quality of practice. The improvement comes about as a result of enhanced social motivation. Once a child acquires attentional skills less individual attention is required.

Present the skill at the child's level of competency. Artistic and musical skills, no less than many academic skills, must often be taught in a figurative way. What is crucial in introducing such tasks is that the skill being taught is within the limits of the child's competence. A nice example is the Suzuki music method. Young children are taught to play the violin and other instruments by ear and in the company of one or both parents, who must take lessons at the same time. (This method makes use of the attachment dynamism to be described in the following chapter.) What the Suzuki method builds upon is the fact that young children can coordinate hand and ear much better than they can coordinate hand and eye. By building upon this coordination ability, the child is able to acquire a skill which brings enjoyment to himself and to others. Reading music, on the other hand, is not taught until much later when children are far along in concrete operations.

Drawing can also be taught in ways that capitalize on the skills which children do have. Too often children begin with material that is much too advanced and they attempt to draw houses, trees, people, and so on. The results are, for the most part, rather stereotyped and quite unsatisfactory. On the other hand, a program that begins where the children are, developmentally, can produce quite lovely work. One art teacher I know starts children out by having them draw straight lines coming up from the bottom of the page in various directions—a kind of fireworks' display. The effect, particularly with the use of a colored pencil or two, is quite pleasant. It is a task well within the child's competence. But one child whom I was observing could not resist putting in the grass and flowers at the bottom and the blue sky at the top!

Printing is one figurative skill on which children do not usually spend enough time and which is well within their competence. By the age of five children can begin printing letters if they demonstrate the necessary motor coordination. Such printing is an excellent prereading exercise and facilitates letter discrimination. Printing also has another function—it helps the child to recognize the symbolic nature of letters and helps to lessen some of the strangeness and mysteriousness young children often experience with respect to printed symbols. When the child discovers that she can make those lines, some of their mystery and frightening quality is lost.

Overcoming the child's fears and apprehensions about a task is, by the way, one of the more important reasons for teaching figurative tasks at the level the child can cope with. When a task is taught which is beyond the child's capabilities, at best the results are innocuous, like drawings of grass and sky. But at the worst, children can experience so much frustration and anger that any possible interest in the skill being taught is destroyed. This often happens when children are given formal instruction in reading before they have attained concrete operations. Many children in this situation cannot understand what it is they are being asked to do and some convince themselves that they, not the task, are stupid. Such children are poor readers because they were taught too early and because as a consequence they convinced themselves they would never be able to learn.

SOCIAL LEARNING

So far we have looked at learning primarily as it pertains to the physical world, to the attainment of tool skills and the culturally imposed school curriculum. But what about the social world? How does the child learn about other people and about social situations? Do the same modes of learning operate or do new ones come into play when the social world has to be dealt with? Although Piaget has not dealt with social learning to any great extent, and did so mostly in his early books, he does suggest that learning about the social world is not different in principle from learning about the physical world.

Although there is not sufficient research and theory to warrant an extensive discussion of social learning from a Piagetian perspective, it might be well to at least give examples of how operative, figurative, and connotative learning serve the child in social situations. Piaget's own examples are primarily concerned with moral development and discipline, and his position on these matters will be summarized in the chapter on the active classroom (Chapter IX). Here we will concentrate on school examples of social learning according to the developmental modes.

In the social domain, as in the physical one, operative learning comes about through the child's active participation and through abstraction from his own activities. Children learn to play with one another by playing with one another. More than anything else such play forces the child to take the other child's point of view when it is different from his own. In some respects, other children serve in the same capacity as the physical world does; they confront the child with contradictions in his own behavior and force him to move to higher-level integrations. Operative learning in the social domain is encouraged when small groups of children are allowed to work cooperatively on joint projects. It is in the context of such joint efforts that children learn the concepts of cooperation, sympathy, and mutual respect.

Operative learning is also involved in constructing concepts of other people. As a result of his active encounters with his parents, the child constructs a conception of them. He does the same with his teacher and with his playmates. His constructions will always reflect what he has actually experienced, filtered by his own pre-existing conceptions. It has to be emphasized that these conceptions of others are often unconscious, like much practical intelligence, and guide the child's behavior without his being completely aware of why he is acting as he is. Children may describe a teacher as "nice" and relate positively to her without being able to verbalize the many and varied things which she does that have led to this conception.

Figurative learning in the social domain is also quite common in the classroom. Often it involves matters of dress and appearance. Judging people by appearance is a kind of figurative learning. Unfortunately, children do this all of the time. They will laugh at a child who is dressed differently from them or at an adult who is disfigured in some way. Such judgments reflect simple associative learning wherein certain perceptual features are associated with certain types of persons. In some respects judging a person by appearances is like judging quantity on the same basis—it is misleading.

Children also engage in social learning by connotative means. As a matter of fact, this is perhaps the most frequent mode of learning in the child's social experience. Again and again the child has to make sense out of words, behaviors, and gestures of both adults and children. What does it mean if the teacher doesn't notice it when your hand is up? What did the teacher think when you gave that wrong answer? Why did the other children no longer want to play the game when you joined them? In trying to make sense out of these experiences the child relates them to pre-existing concepts about himself and others. The resulting re-presentations can be used to reinforce negative or positive self-conceptions as well as negative and positive conceptions about others.

This has been a very brief description of social learning from a developmental and cognitive perspective. Clearly, this is a very important field of learning and warrants much more lengthy treatment. All I have tried to do is to suggest how the modes of learning described earlier might operate in learning about social situations and about people. Much more research and theory are necessary before a comprehensive treatment of social learning from a cognitive developmental perspective can be given.

VI
MOTIVATION AND DEVELOPMENT

"Whether we study children in Geneva, Paris, New York or Moscow, in the Iranian mountains, in the heart of Africa, or on a Pacific Island, everywhere we observe certain social conduct of exchange between children, or between children and adults, which takes effect by their very functioning, independent of the content of educative transmissions."

J. PIAGET

In the preceding chapter we dealt with some aspects of *how* children learn, with the processes and principles of learning. The present chapter deals with some of the *whys* of learning—the forces that energize the child's learning activities. Traditional discussions of motivation usually deal with primary drives such as hunger and thirst and with secondary drives such as the need for approval. But motivation can also be looked at from the developmental point of view, from the standpoint of the forces that prompt the growth of mental structures and which ensure their utilization. These developmental and social forces will be the concern of the present chapter.

Before proceeding to a discussion of these developmental and social motivations, it is important to point out some of the similarities of and differences between growth forces and drives. Growth forces and drives are both essentially cyclical in nature. But drives are essentially short-term cycles (minutes and hours) whereas growth forces manifest cycles that last months and years. Secondly, drives follow a cycle which involves gradually increasing tension (hunger, thirst, or bladder or bowel distension) and a more or less sudden diminution of the tension. As we shall see in more detail below, growth forces follow a different pattern and begin with a period of stimulus-seeking and end with a pattern of play. After describing the cycles of growth forces we shall look at the social motivations that succeed them, namely, the attachment, age, and imitation-avoidance dynamisms.

COGNITIVE GROWTH CYCLES

A cognitive ability in the process of development shows characteristic phases. In the first phase there is a period of *stimulus-seeking* in which the sought after stimuli become the *nutriments* of further cognitive growth. This stimulus-seeking activity must be distinguished from "novelty," "exploratory," and "curiosity" drives as a dynamic of action. In all of the latter cases it appears to be the stimulus which in part or in whole, is the goad to action and without the appropriate stimuli there is no novelty, exploratory, or curiosity behavior (cf. Berlyne, 1960).

In the case of stimulus-nutriment-seeking, however, the nature of the stimulus plays a more or less insignificant role, at least initially. As far as the developing mental process is concerned, there is considerable flexibility as to environmental stimuli so long as the basic nutritional ingredients are there. A close analogy is the child's ability to use a wide variety of different foods to foster physical growth. Children all over the world grow in roughly the same way despite extremely different diets. Apparently they are able to get the essential nutriments out of many different forms of food. Mental growth via stimulus-nutriment seeking seems to occur in the same way. It should be said, however, that once a child gets adapted to particular foods, long-range preferences are established. The same probably holds true for the stimuli upon which children nourish their mental abilities.

Stimulus-nutriment-seeking in the course of mental growth is often observed in *repetitive behavior*. The circular reactions of infancy, wherein the child pulls his mobile, sees it move, then pulls it again, provide stimulus nutriment for his developing abilities to coordinate perceptual and motor schemata. At a somewhat later age, the proverbial "why" questions of the three-year-old are probably aimed, in part at least, at providing verbal stimulus-nutriment for the child's developing linguistic structures. Again at the elementary school level, the involvement in doing, making, and collecting provides stimulus nutriment for the maturing structures of practical intelligence.

Another characteristic of mental growth cycles is what might be called stimulus-*gating* and *storage*. In order to pursue stimulus nutriment the child must frequently ignore or tune out distracting stimuli. That is what I mean by stimulus-gating. Whenever the child has found nutriment for his mental growth and is utilizing it, he tends to be impervious to other intruding stimuli.

In some cases the stimuli gated by the child may not be registered at all. But this is not always the case, and occasionally the stimuli may be gated from conscious elaboration but stored unconsciously for later elaboration. This is particularly true when the stimuli may have nutritional value for the child but come in too big amounts to be digested all at once. One sees this, for example, when young children are taken to the zoo or to the circus. Although the stimuli are valuable to the child, they are too much to be utilized all at once, and the child may not begin to talk about or to draw the zoo or circus animals until weeks after the fact of his visit. Obviously, stimulus-gating and storage occur after a cognitive ability is established but during the formation of an ability they ensure the effective utilization of stimulus nutriment for that ability.

A final phase in the cycle of cognitive structure formation is the appearance of intellectual *play*. Play has been described as a preparation for life (Groos, 1914), as the discharge of surplus energy (Spencer, 1896), and as a mechanism for attaining catharsis and mastery (Waelder, 1933; Erikson, 1950). In the case of mental growth, however, play appears to serve a complex of these functions. It is first and foremost an expression of *having attained** mastery, and portrays in action the joy of being in control. When an infant has attained a sense of permanent objects that exist when no longer present to the senses, then he plays at such games as "peek a boo." Part of the joy of the game derives from the sense of knowing what to expect, of having mastered the situation. Likewise, children who have mastered the distinction between words and things can then engage in word play and in "name calling."

Play has another function in mental growth as well, and this lies in its preparation for further growth. The infant playing at "peek a boo" is not only enjoying his new-found sense of permanent objects but is also becoming aware of spatial relations that will later suggest new intellectual problems. Likewise, the child who engages in "name calling" is preparing for an understanding of the metaphorical use and meaning of words. In the context of cognitive growth cycles, therefore, play points backwards to past achievements and forward to new intellectual challenges.

Stimulus-nutriment-seeking, repetitious practice, stimulus-gating and storage, and play are thus the major components of cognitive growth cycles. We need now to look at these cycles in more detail as they apply to the development of mental abilities from the simple to the complex, namely, from rote memory to perception, language, and reasoning.

ROTE MEMORY

In general, rote memory refers to the ability to recall material that was presented more or less outside a context of significant issues and events as regards the individual involved. The digit span test, in which the subject is required to repeat after the examiner a string of

---

* Play as an expression of having attained mastery suggests that some play is a reaction *to* the relief of tension and is not always, as dynamic theories posit, a mechanism *for* the relief of tension.

digits is the most popular test of this mental ability. From a structural point of view, rote memory ability seems to appear relatively early in life, and the structures that mediate it do not seem to change much with age (Miller, 1956). In recalling digits adults are forced to use the same mechanisms as children (although adults may group more effectively).

Evidence for cognitive growth cycles in the attainment of rote memory ability is anecdotal but so common that its existence is easy to document. Young children memorize materials of all kinds without being told to do so and apparently without any conscious intention of so doing. Most parents have had the experience of reading a book to a preschooler for the third or fourth time, and of then discovering that the child knows the story by heart. Indeed the child will quickly correct the adult who misreads a word or who skips a page. But the adult, who has heard the story equally often, does not have it memorized. One explanation of this phenomenon is that young children are just in the process of attaining rote memory ability and are, therefore, using any stimulus available upon which to practice their emerging memory skill.

Gating and storage with respect to rote memory is evident in what Piaget (1951c) has called "deferred imitation." Piaget gives many illustrations of children who observe a phenomenon early in the day and imitate it later in the day or on following days. A girl may observe a woman painting a picture and will later make believe she is painting one herself. Likewise, frequently young children will listen to songs which they will not repeat at the time but will sing at some later point. In addition, children who scold their siblings and peers in just the words and tone of voice of their parents—"What am I going to do with you!"—are demonstrating deferred imitation which consists of gating the stimulus before it can precipitate immediate action yet storing it for later utilization.

Psychometric data as well as research studies suggest that rote memory matures relatively early in life and remains relatively constant thereafter until senescence. With advancing age, immediate memory is among the abilities most subject to deteriorization. As it pertains to cognitive growth cycles, the early maturity of rote memory would lead us to expect evidence of rote memory "play" during the elementary school years. Such evidence can be found. A well-known formalized game of rote memory is the "spelling bee." While the spelling bee originated out of the spontaneous play of children seeing how many words they could spell, it became a highly competitive activity which lost most of its "playful" or freedom-from-tension aspect.

Other rote memory games that children used to play have become obsolete through the growth of technology. At one time many young children took delight in identifying and naming every make and model of car they saw go down the street. Today, however, the variety of models is so great that this game is no longer possible. Likewise, the collections of baseball and football player cards that were once so popular are a little less so today because of the large number of teams and players. Many young children, however, still delight in knowing the names of all the members on their favorite teams, and this is a playful use of their rote memory skills.

From the point of view of cognitive growth cycles, the early termination of the cycle for rote memory raises an important question. What becomes of the intrinsic growth forces that motivated its development and what determines its later utilization? If we look at the fate of rote memory, some answers are suggested. In contrast to the preschool child, who spontaneously uses rote memory, the school-age child resists memorization and educators are up in arms against it. Apparently, therefore, the growth forces that led to the structurization of rote memory are dissipated once the structures are formed. Thereafter, as we shall discuss later, memorization is put in the service of various social motives which take up where the growth forces left off.

PERCEPTION

In the most general sense, perception can be said to involve the processes by which we read the information which comes to us through our senses. Although perception has to do with all of the senses, I will limit my remarks here to the development of visual perception. The discussion will lean heavily upon Piaget's (1969) developmental theory and some of my own research regarding age changes in this domain.

Perception presents us with an evolution which is much more complex and intricate than the development of rote memory but which nonetheless manifests the characteristics of the cognitive growth cycle described earlier. Unlike rote memory, which does not appear until the emergence of the symbolic function, perceptual processes are already well established at birth or soon after. During the first weeks of life, infants respond selectively to different visual patterns and forms. Moreover, infants appear to prefer more complex forms as evidenced in their tendency to observe such patterns for longer periods than less complex forms (Fantz, 1965).

These earlier perceptual activities and processes are, however, not truly developmental in the sense in which that term is used here, because they do not show the sequential, age-related changes in performance. They are, in Piaget's terms, "field effects," Gestalt-like organizational structures which are part of the infant's initial equipment. Field effects organize experience according to Gestalt-like principles of good form, closure, and so on, and continue to do so in more or less the same way across the entire life span. Indeed, field effects appear to be basic organizing forms somewhat analogous to those of space, time, and causality in cognition.

In contrast to the appearance of field effects soon after birth, perceptual development proper begins only in the preschool years. Starting at about the age of three one comes to see the gradual appearance of what Piaget calls *perceptual regulations*, perceptual structures which, in their manner of operation resemble the structures of intelligence. As these structures begin to develop, children start to manifest the phases of the cognitive growth cycle we have already described with respect to rote memory. That is to say, perception begins to show the stimulus-nutriment-seeking, the repetition, the gating and storage, and the spontaneous play which are evidenced in the realization of other cognitive abilities.

With regard to stimulus-nutriment-seeking activities, we can first refer to anecdotal descriptive data and then to research findings. Elsewhere (Elkind, 1975) I have suggested that perceptual regulations play an essential role in reading and made the point that printed material can therefore provide the stimulus nutriment for developing perceptual regulations. Montessori (1964) provides the corollary anecdotal evidence describing in vivid terms children who, literally, burst into reading, how they dance about reading everything in sight including signs, labels, and book jackets. During this period children read any and all printed material available, much as younger children at the same stage in acquiring rote memory memorize any material with which they come into contact.

Turning to some research evidence, we found a similar phenomenon in a study of perceptual exploration (Elkind and Weiss, 1967). One part of the study involved presenting children at different age levels with a card on which eighteen pictures of familiar objects were pasted in a triangular array. The child's task was to name every picture on the card. Results showed a striking similarity between kindergarten and third-grade children, all of whom did the same thing, namely, they read the pictures starting at the apex and along the sides of the triangle. This would have been predicted by a Gestalt psychologist since the triangle constitutes a "good form."

What the Gestalt psychologist might have had trouble predicting were the results from the first- and second-grade youngsters. These children surprised us because about half of them read the array from left to right and from top to bottom! That is they named the picture on one side of the triangle and then its paired opposite on the other side and so on to the bottom of the array. Kugelmass and

Lieblich (1970) have replicated this finding with Israeli children. The only exception they found was that the Israeli children, schooled in Hebrew, read the pictures on the triangle from right to left and from top to bottom.

Clearly the tendency to read the figures in this way in the case of first- and second-graders was in part attributable to the fact that they were learning to read. I have already suggested that reading requires regulations, and these children were also at the age when the development of perceptual regulations is in the ascendance, as we have shown in other investigations (Elkind, 1975). Learning to read from left to right can thus be interpreted as an exercise for perceptual regulations and stimuli which permit this activity to be used as stimulus nutriment for the attainment of these abilities. Once the regulations are fully formed, stimulus-nutriment-seeking disappears and children revert to the path of least effort and Gestalt principles of organization. Perceptual regulations have, at that point, lost their growth impetus and hence their spontaneous utilization in appropriate situations.

It should be said that these studies also revealed evidence of the final or play stage in the cognitive realization cycle. Youngsters who participated in both our study and that of Kugelmass and Lieblich (1970) were also shown a card on which familiar pictures were pasted in a disordered array. First- and second-grade children read the pictures from top to bottom and from left to right, that is to say, they imposed an organization upon the disordered array. Third grade children, however, did not limit themselves with respect to top to bottom and right to left. They explored the array in new and unexpected ways, up, down, and across. It was as if, now being in full command of their perceptual regulations, they could afford to play with different organizations of the stimulus materials.

With regard to stimulus-gating and storage we found other results of interest. In an unpublished study we used strips of black tape to unite the pictures on the disordered array card into distinct rows. The subjects were kindergarten children who were tested on cards with and without lines. On the first testing the lines had a negative effect, the children made many more errors of commission (naming the same figure twice) and of omission (failing to name the figure at all) on the card with the lines than on the card without the lines. Several weeks later when the testing was repeated the reverse held true. On the second testing the children were effectively able to gate the distracting component of the lines and yet to use the lines to facilitate their exploration of the array. Performance on the unlined cards improved also, but to a lesser degree. Effective gating, it appears, can be improved with practice.*

It might be well here to say something about the nature of stimulus nutriment in the growth of perceptual abilities. By and large it appears that children can generally find nourishment for developing perceptual structures in almost any environment. I once tested large numbers of Sioux Indian children on the Pine Ridge reservation in South Dakota. These children had grown up in Wickiups in barren fields and valleys with few if any toys, books, or other structured play or educational materials. On the perceptual tests, these youngsters did at least as well as children in the suburbs of cities in the Northeast and Southwest. Indeed, many of the Sioux children were artistically gifted. Even on the borders of the barren badlands they were able to find nourishment for their developing perceptual abilities.

Once perceptual regulations become established, which usually occurs in late childhood, their spontaneous utilization comes to an end. Interestingly, this lack of spontaneous use of perceptual regulations for reorganizing and exploring the perceptual world appears to diminish at about the same time as the child's spontaneous interest in drawing. The urge to draw like the urge to perceive creatively seems to dissipate once the basic abilities (understanding of perspective, etc.) have been acquired. Thereafter,

---

* This may be what happens to children in some of the new "open" school with few walls. At first the children find the noise and bustle distracting, but after a while many children adapt to it and are able to gate out the distracting stimuli.

other motivations are needed to bring them into operation. In perception, as in rote memory, the control of the attained structures shifts from the growth forces inherent in their formation to social motivations, which then determine the nature and direction of creative perceptual activity.

The past decade has in many ways constituted a new era in the study of language growth and development. Mightily stimulated by the work of Chomsky (1957), investigators have begun to look at the child's acquisition of grammar and his skill in language production. This new trend complements much of the earlier work on language, which involved developmental descriptive studies of vocabulary, sentence structure, and parts of speech. Just as earlier works found a sequential development in "parts of speech" such that nouns appeared before prepositions, there appears to be a comparable sequence in the evolution of children's linguistic constructions (Brown, 1973), which suggests that they are also developmental in nature and should, therefore, manifest the same structural growth cycle evident in the formation of other cognitive abilities. Language ability is, however, even more complex than perception and it is not possible to deal with it in any complete or comprehensive way here. Accordingly, I will limit myself here to examples from the research on the growth of two-word utterances and of semantic structures to illustrate the stages of the structural growth cycle.

In considering the growth of two-word utterances and of language generally, one point requires special attention, namely, the fact that the child can use his own activity as nutriment to further his own linguistic growth. We will encounter the same phenomenon again when we discuss the development of reasoning. What this means is that evidence for stimulus-nutriment-seeking in language development can be observed on the child's increasing tendency to produce language. In this connection Braine (1963) found, for a single child who had just begun to use a two-word utterance (Bobby up, Bobby go, Bobby eat, and so on), the following numbers of *new distinct* utterances in successive months: 14, 10, 30, 35, 261, 1050, 1100. This is a dramatic example of stimulus-nutriment production, as well as seeking.

Children's learning of language also gives many evidences of gating and storage. There is, first of all, the phenomenon of over-regularization, the fact that the child knows the rules but not the exceptions. Children learning English say "feets, comed, broked" because they know the rules and gate out the exceptions. It is really not unlike what children do when they draw, namely, portray what they know rather than what they perceive. Accordingly, they draw a profile with two eyes because they know a person has two eyes but ignore that fact that from the profile perspective both eyes cannot be seen. In language learning, the child too may *hear what he knows* rather than what he listens to.

There is considerable evidence that children play with language forms once they are well established. This evidence is particularly prominent in the cultural lore of school children. While the songs and chants of children have many functions, such as providing an introduction to the peer group, they also provide a vehicle for playing with language and expressing mastery of language forms. When a child recites:

> Rain rain, go away
> Come again
> another day

he is playing with conventional subject-verb-object linguistic forms as well as demonstrating a knowledge of childhood lore.

Such play with verbal forms is also observed when children tease one another by resorting to "baby talk." An eight-year-old, for example, was heard to say this to his younger sibling:

> Davy want a candy?
> Me want a candy too.

Here mastery is expressed by shifting to verbal forms which the child no longer uses in everyday speech but which can be employed to tease and make fun of other children.

This is but one example of the many ways in which children play with language forms once they are mastered. One reason older children enjoy "Sesame Street" and "Electric Company" is because of the amount of verbal play that goes on. For the young child who is just learning language, seeing words and pictures together may be instructive, but for older children it is sheer fun, particularly when the pictures or skits used to identify the words are a little offbeat. On these programs what is the young child's work is the older child's play.

Similar evidence for cognitive growth cycles can be observed in the semantic aspects of language growth. In the realm of semantics, the repetitious questions of young children are proverbial and reflect the stimulus-nutriment-seeking phase. Here are some examples:

> Do I look like a little baby?
> Can't you get it?
> Can't it be a bigger truck?
> Am I silly?
> Does turtles crawl?
> Did you broke that part?
> Does the kitty stands up?

In talking to a child at this phase each answer merely elicits another question. It becomes clear then that the adult has become part of a circular reaction in which he or she provides verbal-stimulus nutriment for the child's growing semantic and grammatical comprehension.

Gating and storage are likewise present at the semantic level. With regard to gating, Piaget (1952a) long ago described what he called "parallel play." In such play two children talk *at* rather than *to* one another. One child talks about his new jacket while the other talks about a trip to the store, and neither child acknowledges the other's utterance. In such parallel play, the child effectively gates out the semantic input of his companion. It is important to point out that the child could understand the utterances—he certainly does so when he is talking to an adult—but when engaged in play his language accompanies and reinforces his actions—distracting stimuli are effectively gated from consciousness.

Anecdotal examples of semantic storage are easy to come by. Most parents are surprised when a child recalls the name of a person or place he may have seen six months or a year before. We do not expect children to store for such long periods. More experimental evidence comes from the studies of Burtt (1932, 1941), who read his young child passages in Greek and found that this facilitated the learning of these passages at a much later point in life. Children exposed to a foreign language early in life, even if this experience is not prolonged, seem to learn the language later more readily than young people who have not been so exposed.

Finally, the mastery of elementary semantics involving the distinction between words and things gives rise to a great deal of verbal play. Such play is particularly evident in "name calling." Young children are upset when called names by older children because they have trouble distinguishing between the word and the reality. Older children delight in calling others "stupid," "dum dum," "fatso," and so on. While such verbal play has emotional overtones, it also expresses the child's mastery of the distinction between words and reality and the recognition that the two do not always need to coincide. In other words, they appreciate that being called dumb is not the same as being dumb. This distinction is marked most dramatically in the familiar jingle: "Sticks and stones will break my bones but names will never hurt me."

By and large the language system, like the perceptual system, seems to be more or less structurally complete by middle childhood (7 to 11). Thereafter, growth in language is a matter of vocabulary growth and increased comprehension associated with the development of reasoning and thought. Again, once the basic structures of

language are formed, their inherent dynamic seems to be dissipated, and language utilization and efficiency come under the
domination of social forms of motivation. This helps to account for
the fact that while all individuals share the same grammatical
structures, there are extraordinary individual differences in volubil-
ity and articulateness. These individual differences in linguistic
prowess become especially evident in adolescence when language
begins to express the differentiation of individual emotions, motives, and identities characteristic of this period.

REASONING

As the term is most generally used, reasoning has to do with the
processes by which we arrive at knowledge that is implicit in what
we already know. As Piaget (1950) has shown, reasoning is the most
complex of human mental abilities. With regard to cognitive
growth cycles, for example, we have to allow for a major cycle from
birth to the middle of adolescence (14 or 15), the period during
which the reasoning structures as a whole attain their final form. In
addition there are minor cycles corresponding to Piaget's sensorimotor, preoperational, concrete operational, and formal operational
stages. Finally there are subcycles for the attainment of particular
concepts such as the conservation of number, of mass and weight,
and of volume.

While it is unnecessary to repeat all the Piagetean stages here (cf.
pp. 84–102), I do believe that, at whatever level we look at the
development of reasoning, the behavioral manifestations of the
three phases of cognitive growth cycles will be in evidence. To
illustrate these phases in the growth of reasoning ability we can
look again at the attainment of concrete operations in young
children. Beginning at about the age of four or five, most children
start to develop the mental structures that will make possible
elementary reasoning and mathematical thinking as well as classification and seriation (Piaget, 1952a). As these operations come into

being we again see evidences of stimulus-nutriment-seeking, repetition, gating and storage, and eventually play, as the attainment of structures is completed and consolidated.

Evidence for stimulus-nutriment-seeking in the attainment of elementary reasoning ability is both indirect and direct. First, with respect to the indirect evidence, children all over the world appear to attain concrete operations at about the same age level (e.g., Goodnow, 1969). Indeed, we have more replication studies, and hence more comparable data, on Piaget's conservation tasks than on any other experiment in psychology today. The uniformity of the results across wide variations in cultural background, environmental stimulation, and child-rearing practices suggests that the attainment of operations is not a function of the variations in these general factors. What it does suggest is that children all over the world are able to use whatever stimuli are available to nourish their mental growth.

More direct, if more anecdotal, evidence comes from behavioral observations of children who are moving out of the pre-operational stage to the concrete operational stage. Children at this level are inordinately concerned with quantitative gradations and the preoccupation with "who has more" is very evident. This concern with "who has more" could certainly be interpreted from a psychoanalytic point of view (as greed, sibling rivalry, etc.). While such an interpretation would probably be justified in part, it does not exclude the stimulus-nutriment interpretation. Behavior has multiple determinants, and child behavior directed at obtaining stimulus nutriment could at the same time symbolically represent more deep-seated concerns.

Other stimulus-nutriment-seeking behaviors evident during this period are subject to the same dual interpretation. Many young children who have learned to count will count to a hundred, or a thousand over and over again in a manner reminiscent of the circular reactions evident in infancy. The clinician might interpret this behavior as a compulsive action that seeks to undo some feeling of guilt. While this may be true, it is probably again true only in part. The child who counts over and over again is also nourishing his growing quantitative skills. As in the case of language, the child's own activity creates the nourishment for further mental growth.

We see the same duality of interpretation in the case of children's fairy tales. Such tales abound in quantitative terms and gradations. "Goldilocks and the Three Bears" illustrates the point. The three bowls of porridge are of different sizes, the porridge itself is at different temperatures, the beds are of different size and degrees of hardness. The elements of the stories could be given a psychodynamic interpretation that would make sense. The stimulus-nutriment argument also makes sense, however, and children like to hear fairy tales again and again, in part at least, because they provide nourishment for the child's growing quantitative abilities.

With regard to stimulus-gating and storage, Piaget and Inhelder's work on memory (1973), which was mentioned briefly in Chapter III, is apropos. In one study children aged three to eight were presented with a step-wise arrangement of sticks which were from nine to fifteen centimeters in length. The children were instructed to look at the arrangement and told to remember it. The children were allowed to look at the arrangement for as long as they liked. After a week they were asked to recall what they had seen and to demonstrate this with gestures and with a drawing. Six to eight months later they were again asked to draw from memory the series arrangement which they had not actually seen since the first presentation. After each recall test, the children were given the sticks and asked to make a seriation themselves.

Results of this study were quite remarkable. Initially the stages that Piaget had reported earlier were clearly present in the children's drawings and in their constructions. At the first stage (usually three to four years of age) children drew a number of lines in a row but the lines were roughly equal in length. Then at the next stages (usually four to five years of age) children either drew the sticks in pairs, one big and one small, or in groups of big and small lines or in smaller groups of big, little, and middle sized lines. At the third stage (usually ages five and six) the children drew actual series but with only a few lines in the series. Then, at the fourth stage, (usually ages six to seven) children were usually able to draw a correct seriation.

After an interval of six to eight months, and without their having been presented with the original seriation again, 90 percent of the five- to eight-year-old children had advanced at least one stage in their drawing of the series! One interpretation of this finding is that the memory of the series was not a simple copy of the perceived arrangement but rather a construction resulting from an active assimilation of the stimulus material. In the course of mental development the resulting schemata change as the operations from which they are constructed differentiate and become more hierarchically integrated. These data give evidence that storage during the period of structural growth involves mental activity and reconstruction and is not a passive warehousing of impressions.

With the attainment of concrete operational structures at about the age of seven and eight, children begin to play with these elementary reasoning structures. The evidence is again anecdotal but familiar. Children of six and seven often tease their younger brothers or sisters by surreptitiously adding liquid to their drinks or by putting the drink to their mouths without drinking so they continue to "have more" even though they are drinking! This behavior implies a sophisticated understanding of continuous quantity and a tendency to play with these ideas. Another trick that older children like to play on younger children is to offer them a dime and a nickel to see which one they will choose. The young child often chooses the nickel, which is larger, and this amuses the older child who knows the differences between size and value.

As in the case of the interest in fairy tales of younger children, the interest in quantity play and games of older children can be given a dynamic as well as a cognitive interpretation. The enjoyment that six- to seven-year-old children get out of quantity play of all sorts, including cards and spinner games, is probably determined in multiple ways. It certainly seems, however, that some of the pleasure children take from quantity games arises from the joy of having mastered the abilities required to play them.

It would be possible to give other illustrations of cognitive growth cycles, but the few described here should suffice to describe their major characteristics. What these cycles suggest from an educational point of view is that we cannot always rely upon intrinsic growth forces, the child's "eagerness to learn," as if it were a general and unlimited thirst for knowledge. In fact, as I have tried to demonstrate here, growth cycles are rather specific both in terms of the age period during which they run their course and the abilities with which they are concerned. Young children of four and five are spontaneously interested in quantity, but this interest is no longer universally in evidence by the time they reach the age of eight or nine.

In my opinion, it is important for teachers (and parents) to be aware of the behavioral signs of cognitive growth cycles. When children are in the stimulus-nutriment-seeking stage, they need to be provided with appropriate materials for practicing their emerging abilities. And when young people are at the end of a cycle, they need to be permitted the freedom to explore and to experiment with their newly achieved abilities. In addition, when children are in a play phase of a cognitive growth cycle, this should be a clue to the teacher that the child or children are ready to go on to new and more challenging intellectual skills and materials.

But what happens when the growth cycle is dissipated? What new motivations underlie the child's continuing utilization of his mental abilities? Once the cycle is at an end is it necessary to fall back on biological drives and their derivatives, or are there social processes which take over and energize the utilization of mental structures once they are fully formed? It is to this issue that the next section of this chapter is addressed. My aim is to demonstrate that, in addition to drives, there are growth forces (just described) and social forces (to be described below) which are also operative in learning and which are neither derived from nor reducible to biological drives.

SOCIAL–EXPERIENCE DYNAMISMS

Social experience, the sum of the child's interpersonal relationships, bears a complementary relationship to cognitive growth. This is true because the child's level of mental development structures the level of his social experiences and because his social experiences serve as a motivation for the utilization and further elaboration of his cognitive abilities. In Chapter IV, I described some of the ways in which the child's mental abilities serve to organize his interpersonal relationships. As we have seen, the egocentrism of the preschool child makes him impervious to the needs and feelings of others when these are different from his own. In the same way, the egocentrism of the adolescent make him assume that everyone about him is as concerned as he about his long nose or acne. The child's mental abilities determine the way he interprets and reacts to social interchanges.

In stressing the role of cognitive structure in social experience in the chapter on understanding children, I did not mean to gainsay the importance of social experience in determining cognitive functioning. Indeed, the present section is concerned with some of the ways in which the child's interpersonal experiences encourage the utilization and further elaboration of the child's mental powers. After a discussion of the role of these social motives in normative cognitive development and education, the part they play in learning disabilities will be briefly reviewed.

With these preliminaries out of the way, I want to talk about several different types of social motivations which seem, to me at any rate, to be of critical importance for the continued utilization of fully formed cognitive structures. In this discussion, as in others in this book, it is necessary to draw upon clinical and anecdotal material as well as upon research data. We are, however, still at a very early point in our experimental understanding of the nature of social relations and may still have to rely upon the consensual validation of our observations rather than upon statistics as a basis for agreement if not for belief. There are three types of social interactions that seem to be of particular motivational significance, and I have called them, respectively, the attachment dynamism, the age dynamism, and the imitation-avoidance dynamism.

THE ATTACHMENT DYNAMISM

There is now a good deal of evidence (Bowlby, 1973; Ainsworth, 1969) that the attachment of the infant to particular adults comes about during the last trimester of the first year of life and that this attachment is increased during the second year of life, when fear of strangers and strange places is inordinate. By and large the infant remains attached to only a very small coterie of adults, usually his mother, father, and perhaps a caretaker. The adults to whom the child is attached are his primary source of self-esteem, and hence wield considerable power over the youngster without his always being aware of this fact. This attachment of the child to significant adults is perhaps the most powerful motivation for the elaboration and utilization of mental abilities. Although the phenomenon of attachment that I have just described is quite familiar, it seems to me that its implications for mental development have not always been emphasized, particularly in special education.

The importance of attachment in mental growth can be demonstrated in many different domains, but I would like to illustrate its importance in two practical situations. These situations are the teaching of reading to normal children and the teaching of tool subjects to youngsters with learning disabilities. In both of these contexts the role of attachment is often overlooked, and those concerned with instructing children in these situations may be primarily concerned with curriculum materials and instructional techniques rather than with interpersonal relationships. It is often assumed that the selection of the right curriculum materials and instructional techniques will release the child's "innate" curiosity and eagerness to learn. But as I have already suggested, I do not think one can hope to build upon intrinsic motivation in each and every learning situation. Indeed, I am very much afraid that what appears to be intrinsic motivation is, in a good many cases, social motivation derived from the adults to whom the child is attached.*

Learning to read is a case in point. Unlike walking and talking, reading is not something a child acquires spontaneously as a part of his normal, expectable, adaptive apparatus. Learning to read is a difficult task and, in addition to having the requisite mental abilities and experiences, children need powerful motivation. In the majority of cases this motivation comes from attachment to adults who encourage and reward the child's efforts. In our study of early readers (children who read before coming to school) (Briggs and Elkind, 1973), we found that many had a close friend (either an older child or adult) who spent a great deal of time helping the child to read. And in the biographies of blacks who have gotten out of the ghetto (Brown, 1965) one often reads of particular adults or teachers who recognized and encouraged abilities and talents. Attachment to adults who encourage and reward reading behavior is probably of major significance in all academic achievement.

One other example of the role of attachment in academic achievement might help to strengthen the argument for its importance. For the past six years I have been supervising, at the University of Rochester, an undergraduate practicum wherein the college students tutor children with learning handicaps for an entire year. Among the many things we learned in the course of running this program was that remedial work could not be introduced or

* For a recent comprehensive discussion of many positions on motivation see Deci (1975).

used effectively until an emotional relationship, an attachment, occurred between the tutor and the child. Once this occurred, the child's behavior began to change at home and at school. Once a child began to feel that he was worthy of a young adult's liking and respect, there was a kind of *spread of affect* which made him feel good about himself and his abilities to learn in a variety of situations.

It seems to me that this spread of affect phenomenon is of crucial importance in working with learning-disabled children. Whatever the child's physical, neurological, or physiological handicaps, his impaired sense of self-esteem always plays a part in his difficulties with learning. When such a youngster is made to feel better about himself, from the attention, concern, and liking of another person, he feels better about himself in general and about his capacity to cope with new learning situations. We have often observed how children in our program begin to do better work at school and begin to be more tractable at home as a result of the nonacademic, but self-esteem-bolstering experience of our program.

Actually, the importance of emotional attachment in academic achievement is already implicit in Freud's conception of transference. In Freud's (1953a) view, a patient could not really begin to change his ideas about himself and his world until he established an emotional attachment to the therapist. This attachment was conceptualized as a failure to differentiate between the patient's parents and the therapist and hence involved "transferring" their feelings for the parents to the therapist. It is this "transferred" emotional attachment which, in therapy, motivates cognitive as well as emotional change in the patient. The importance of such attachments in educational settings has been made explicit by Redl and Wattenberg (1959).

It is important to say, however, that not all attachments between children and nonparental adults are of the transference variety. Transference is a specific form of attachment which derives from the peculiarities of the therapeutic situation. In a less intense context, children, like adults, can become attached to other people on the basis of shared experiences and mutual positive regard. In such forms of attachment, although the patterns of attachment may be modeled after familial patterns (of attachment to parents and siblings), the feelings are less intense and involve a clear differentiation between the adult and familial figures. In short, there are many degrees of attachment of which the transference in psychotherapy is perhaps a more extreme form. Even less intense modes of attachment can, however, have positive motivational effects.

Although attachment to adults is a primary social motive for learning in young elementary school children, this effect diminishes with age. Between the third and fourth grades—when children are between eight and nine years of age—the peer group becomes more important and parents and teachers become less important. How the peer group feels about academic achievement then becomes a powerful motive for doing or not doing school work. In adolescence, the attachment to friends and peer group almost completely eclipses the parents and teachers as the source of the attachment dynamism and as the motivation for succeeding in school.

The relation between attachment and cognitive functioning does not cease in childhood. But in adulthood the causal directions can be reversed. An adult who is intellectually stimulated by a particular author or theorist not infrequently experiences an emotional attachment as well. One example of the relation between intellectual stimulation and attachment is provided by some of Freud's followers. Among some of these disciples, the commitment to Freud as a person was every bit as great as their commitment to him as a theorist. When Freud's words are taken as a gospel from which deviation is unthinkable, we have the end result of an attachment dynamism. In this case, the attachment to Freud as a person made it impossible to challenge him as a theorist. This melding of intellectual stimulation and attachment is to be found among at least some of the followers of Hull, Skinner, Chomsky, and Piaget. Although the end result is seldom as glaring as it was in the case of some of Freud's followers, emotional attachment to the master sometimes blurs critical judgment.

As the foregoing discussion suggests, the relationship between emotional attachment and intellectual stimulation among adults is fraught with dangers. Such attachment can make the followers of an intellectual innovator become protective of the master's work and thus violate the spirit of openness which the innovator espoused. The history of science is replete with stories of men who made dogmas of new scientific theories and gods of the men who created them. The urge to deification is apparently a deep-seated archetype in man and it is easily released by the intellectual genius. In adults, therefore, the relation between attachment and intelligence can be just the opposite from what it was in childhood. Among children, emotional attachment can be the motivation for further intellectual growth, whereas in adults such attachment can lead to mental stultification and rigidity.

THE AGE DYNAMISM

In a rigidly age-graded society such as our own, age-related and age-appropriate behaviors are often clearly marked. Smoking and drinking are allowed after age eighteen and not before. Likewise, driving and voting are permitted only at a certain age as prescribed by law. There are many informal age rules as well. After about the age of eleven or twelve, it is no longer appropriate for young people to go out "tricking and treating" on Halloween. Adolescent girls may wear pantyhose and makeup but preadolescent girls, except on special occasions, may not. Many more examples could be given, but these may suffice to illustrate the many age-related behaviors operative in our society. The age dynamism is essentially an awareness of these age-graded behaviors that serves to motivate cognitive growth. The age dynamism, like the attachment dynamism, operates at all levels of development and takes different forms at different phases of the life cycle.

The following incident illustrates how the age dynamism works. Last spring I visited a school at the time the children were preparing decorations for an Easter program. I had the opportunity to talk about the activities with the children. In the course of our discussion, one third-grade youngster remarked that he "used to" believe in the Easter Bunny, but that he did not believe in it any longer. There was a certain quiet pride and a sense of new maturity in his recitation of this fact and, for him, it was clearly a step forward in personal intellectual growth. Children demonstrate the same sense of pride and maturity when they announce that they no longer believe in Santa Claus or in fairy tales. In all of these instances we see the age dynamism at work. In essence there is pleasure in giving up ideas held at an earlier age and in mastering ideas common to a later age. Once a child has passed a certain stage, awareness of this circumstance motivates him to consolidate his gains and to move toward further differentiation from "childish" ways of thinking and behaving.

The age dynamism involves more than the giving up of "childish" ideas; it also involves the tendency on the part of children to imitate and copy the behaviors of young people who are slightly older than themselves. This aspect of the age dynamism helps to account for the perpetuation of the vast language and lore of children from generation to generation (Opie and Opie, 1960). The language and lore include everything from incantations about ladybugs and cracks in the sidewalk to parodies of adult manners and morals. Much of this language and lore originated hundreds of years ago and has been passed down by oral tradition from older to younger children in the course of their spontaneous play. The existence of this extensive language and lore is ample witness to the proclivity of younger children to ape the behavior of their elders.

Evidence of this aspect of the age dynamism can be seen in

children's choice of fictional heroes. Most authors who write for children know that the hero or heroine of the story has to be several years older than the children for whom the story is written. Peter Pan, who is about age ten, appeals to children of six, seven, and eight as does Christopher Robin who is about the same age. Tom Sawyer and Huckleberry Finn, however, who are young adolescents, appeal to the nine- and ten-year-old children. The same holds true for the heroines in fiction for girls. Young adolescent girls eagerly read about Nancy Drew, a late adolescent girl. At least some of the appeal of these stories is the opportunity they provide for younger children to identify with leading characters who are older than themselves.

An example of the age dynamism which reflects both the pleasure of overcoming childish ideas and the satisfaction inherent in acquiring more mature ones comes from the recent work on peer teaching. The effectiveness of having older children tutor younger children rests, in part, on the operation of the age dynamism. In such tutoring situations the younger child is pleased to be the object of attention of an older one. In his turn, the older child takes a certain satisfaction in recognizing how much more he knows and how much more mature he is than his younger counterpart. Of course the peer situation may not always operate this harmoniously. In the family situation the aspirations of the younger child to ape the older one, in manner of dress and speech, may be a cause of friction and conflict.

If we look at the age dynamism in childhood more closely, we see that it involves a number of different elements. There is, on the one hand, a sense of having passed a particular stage and being superior to it. There is also the sense that there are still further secrets, freedoms, and pleasures that await one at the next stage of development. The age dynamism in younger children is a kind of hunger for the special privileges and freedoms of those who are older and more mature. It is perhaps the prime motivation for younger children to model the behavior and attitudes of older children. As in the case of the attachment dynamism, doing what the older children do enhances self-esteem.

The age dynamism, which appears in childhood, does not really disappear but rather undergoes a sort of metamorphosis in adolescence. At a certain point in development, within our society at any rate, the behavior of adults no longer seems worthy of emulation. To be sure, adolescents still smoke, drink, and have sex in part at least as a continuation of the attempt to give up childish things and adopt older "more mature" behaviors. But adopting adult manners, morals, and values begins to take on an aversive quality, hence the metamorphosis of the age dynamism.

What happens after adolescence, I believe, is that the age dynamism gets separated from age and becomes a "newness" or "novelty" dynamism. Rather than enhancing self-esteem through emulating their elders, adolescents seek new language, modes of dress, and music as a means of enhancing self-esteem through giving up what is old and acquiring what is new. The creativity of adolescence is, in part at least, stimulated by this need to get rid of the old and to latch on to the new, which in childhood was the age dynamism.

In adulthood, the age dynamism can take on several different forms. Among many adults the original impetus to give up the immature ideas of an earlier age and adopt more mature notions becomes a desire to "keep up with the times," to keep abreast of local and national political and social events. In substituting a kind of "keeping up with the times" for a "catching up with the next age group," there is a shift from self-esteem enhancement to self-esteem maintenance. Among adults who take this path, keeping up with contemporary events is a means of sustaining and nourishing an established and solidly positive self-concept. Such individuals continue to grow by *integrating* the new with the old, which expands their knowledge and leads to a progressive enhancement and enrichment of the self.

Other adults handle the age dynamism differently. For these

individuals the passing of adolescence was seen as a great loss, and they try to perpetuate or maintain adolescence by an *inversion* of the age dynamism. Instead of emulating those who are older, or trying to keep up with the times, these adults adopt the manners, dress, and morals of adolescents. Just as among children the behavior of younger children is regarded as negative and something to be avoided, so these adults are aversive to the behavior and appearance of more mature people and they strive to emulate those who are younger. In effect these people invert the age dynamism by imitating the behavior of younger age groups and avoiding behavior, dress, and manners characteristic of an older generation.

To be sure, in our society, the inversion of the age dynamism occurs to a certain extent in all individuals. In a society wherein youth and beauty are ultimate goods, no one wants to grow older, gracefully or otherwise. Most people eventually accept the inevitable but extreme cases of age-dynamism inversion are common, and quite easily recognizable. It should be said, too, that in our society this inversion is likely to occur earlier among women than among men. This is true because, as matters stand now, men continue to advance in their careers in early adulthood and still seek to model their behavior after older, more mature, sophisticated, successful men. The inversion of the age dynamism in men is more likely to occur in middle age when the next older generation of men is seen to be on the decline and the middle-aged man recognizes that a similar fate is in store for him. The crises of middle age in the male would be much alleviated if there were more available models of men who continue to function successfully in more mature years. While this is true for statesmen and intellectuals, it is not true for many white-collar, and blue-collar workers who provide the models for the majority of men in our society.

Among women the inversion of the age dynamism comes earlier and is more gradual. A recent study (Jourard and Lasakew, 1973) supports the clinical observation that in women the inversion of the age dynamism occurs in young adulthood. The study in question dealt with self-disclosure between college women and young married women recently out of college. Results showed that the married women inevitably followed the college women's lead as to self-disclosure, but that the reverse was not true. If the college student was open, the young married woman was likely to follow suit and if the college woman was closed, the young married woman was also reluctant to reveal herself. College students, in contrast, disclosed or did not disclose depending upon their own predilections and were not guided in their behavior by the model set by the young married women. My guess is that just the opposite results would be obtained with college student and young married males.

The tendency of women to emulate younger women would seem to begin in young adulthood and is then gradually given up with increased maturity, family responsibilities, or career involvement. As more older women join the work force and occupy more visible and responsible jobs, the inversion of the age dynamism in women is likely to parallel more closely the pattern of age dynamism inversion that one observes in males. (It might be said—parenthetically because this is not the place to deal with the issue—that the discrepancy between the age at which the age dynamism undergoes inversion in men and in women can be, and frequently is, a cause of marital disharmony.)

In adults, therefore, the age dynamism can be transferred into a keeping up with the times which results in continued self-esteem maintenance and self-realization or it can be inverted, in which case there can be intellectual and personality stagnation. In the majority of individuals the age dynamism probably takes both forms to a certain extent and at different times in their lives.

THE IMITATION–AVOIDANCE DYNAMISM

Within the social-psychological literature, imitation is usually regarded as a process whereby children learn a variety of social behaviors. But imitation has another indirect interpersonal function which is often overlooked, and which plays an important role in cognitive development. Moreover, in contrast to the other dynamisms described so far, the imitation-avoidance dynamism pushes individuals toward uniqueness and difference rather than toward uniformity. Put more directly, when one person imitates another, the imitated person is often motivated to change and to be different. Contrariwise, many individuals strive not to imitate themselves or others. Both are instances of the imitation-avoidance dynamism.

Again, I will begin with an anecdotal observation. For many years I served as a consultant to various family courts and worked with many different delinquent youths. One young man was brought to court because he had stolen a thousand dollars from the prize money at a golf tournament at a course where he was a caddy. He had a history of petty thefts and nuisance behaviors and always managed to get caught. It turned out that he was the youngest of three sons. The oldest boy was an athlete and a scholar who had won a National Merit Award. The middle son was a good athlete but also a musician, and a social leader. In some ways the identity options for the younger boy had been, or so he imagined, pre-empted. He sought to find his own identity by becoming a thief and a trouble-maker. He was trying hard to avoid imitating the identities carved out by his brothers with whom he was constantly being compared by his parents and teachers.

In talking about the age dynamism, I suggested that younger children wanted to behave like the next older age group. And, in fact, younger children are constantly emulating their older siblings. But the older children do not like to be copied, as it detracts from their aspirations to being older and more mature. When young children begin to wear their hair as long as their adolescent brothers, there is an impetus for the older brothers to begin wearing their hair in a different style. The use of drugs by high school students is a reflection of the age dynamism, but now that it has become a "high school" thing, fewer college students are getting involved with drugs. This moving away from behaviors in which they once engaged is an example of the imitation-avoidance dynamism.

It is this combination of the age and imitation-avoidance dynamism which, it seems to me, plays a large part in the creative and transient nature of adolescent society. The age dynamism is the motivation for change and innovation, and this motivation is heightened by the imitation of the adolescent by the younger generation on the one hand, and by the older generation (because of the age-dynamism inversion) on the other. As soon as a given adolescent society creates its own language, dress, and music, this is taken over by the next younger and next older generations. The young people who copied their adolescent elders find, when they are adolescent, that they must create new cultural mores to express their group identity. As a consequence, each adolescent generation does have, to a greater or lesser extent, its own social identity, its own heroes, music, and special mode of dress.

At the individual level, the imitation-avoidance dynamism operates intrapersonally as well as interpersonally. Intrapersonally, the imitation-avoidance dynamism is the impetus not to imitate oneself, to go beyond what one knows she can do well to those tasks which have not been tried and where there is always threat of failure as well as of success. The child who competes with herself to do better than she did before manifests a kind of imitation-avoidance dynamism. Such a child does not want merely to repeat what she has done before but to go further to test herself in new ways and to reassess her limits.

Among creative adults in all walks of life one can observe the imitation-avoidance dynamism at work, both in its interpersonal and intrapersonal forms. The artist who created a new style moves away from it once she begins to be imitated by others, both to test herself and to avoid being copied. Likewise the scientist who initiated a new field of study may leave it once that field becomes crowded with other investigators. Writers, too, may move away from familiar themes and forms to avoid repeating themselves and to challenge their creative powers. The imitation-avoidance dynamism, like the attachment and age dynamism relates to self-esteem. The motivation is to protect and defend one's own uniqueness as a person.

SOCIAL DYNAMICS IN LEARNING DISABILITIES

The foregoing description of the role of social dynamisms in mental development has numerous educational implications. When the attachment, age, or imitation-avoidance dynamisms fail to operate in the "normative" manner there can be hindrances and impairments in cognitive functioning which reverberate through the whole pattern of the individual's interpersonal relationships. In the following discussion I would like to suggest some of the ways in which disruption of the social dynamisms can contribute to the familiar problem of learning disability.

Learning disabilities. It has already been suggested that academic success is, at least in part, a function of attachment to significant people who reward and support the child's intellectual efforts. When such attachments are not a part of a child's life-experience there are dislocations in the other social dynamisms as well. A child who is doing poorly in school and who has a negative and inferior self-concept has difficulties with the age dynamism and with the imitation-avoidance dynamism as well, which further complicates and compounds his problems.

A child who feels inadequate and inferior is not as likely to ape older children and to avoid behaving like younger children. Indeed, many children with learning problems tend to play with younger children and to display behaviors such as interest in toys which their age peers have more or less outgrown. The child who feels inadequate is afraid to model his behavior after older children for fear of failure and ridicule. Behaving like a younger child is much safer and much less threatening, but the price is enormous. What the child loses is the force of the age dynamism for further development and elaboration of his abilities. One reason that untreated learning problems become more extensive and pervasive with increasing age is the damage which has been done to the motivating power of the age dynamism.

In such children the imitation-avoidance dynamism is also interfered with. Learning-disabled children welcome imitation of any kind because to them it means that someone else is interested and concerned with them. Even derogatory, teasing imitation is welcomed, not as motivation for change but as some recognition of the child's existence if not of his personal worth. The learning-disabled child who is falling farther and farther behind is hardly challenged to compete with himself and do better. He has enough trouble holding his own and maintaining his minimal academic gains.

Children who have difficulties learning can thus be described as children whose social dynamisms are disrupted and who lack the self-esteem to utilize the social dynamisms effectively. These dynamisms are, in turn, the major dynamic in the utilization and elaboration of mental abilities once the intrinsic motivation which determines the formation of these abilities has been dissipated. Every child with a learning disability has, as well, a social disability, an impairment of his social dynamisms. In helping children with learning disabilities, therefore, as much attention must be paid to revitalizing the motivational dynamisms as to re-enhancement of academic skills.

In closing this section on motivation, it might be helpful to tie it, even if in a cursory way, to the material on learning which was presented in the previous chapter. This can be done by relating the different kinds of motivation described here to the three different modes of learning. Growth-cycle motivation is clearly related to the development of operative learning, which is usually spontaneous and self-directed. Primary and secondary biological drives, which were not discussed in detail, are involved in figurative learning, which is usually externally motivated. Finally, connotative learning, the search for meaning, is related to the social dynamisms. The search for meanings is the most conscious mode of learning and is most closely related to the need for self-esteem, maintenance, enhancement, and defense. Each time a child discovers something about the world he also discovers something about himself.

APPLICATIONS

VII
DEVELOPMENTAL ASSESSMENT

"The test method has its uses, but for the present problem (studying the child's conception of the world) it tends to falsify the perspective by diverting the child from his natural inclinations."　　　J. PIAGET

Much of the value of Piaget's work for education lies in his description of the stages of mental development. In the next chapter, the ways in which knowledge about the stages of development can be used in curriculum analysis and planning will be described. In the present chapter some different methods for assessing a child's level of conceptual development will be presented. Some of the methods are observational, others involve presenting children with brief tasks. All of the methods are individual but, once they are mastered, take little time and can be utilized during any educational activity. We will begin with observational methods and then describe material-based assessment techniques. A final section will speak briefly to the matter of achievement testing and grading.

Before proceeding to the discussion of assessment methods, some comments about observation in general are in order. Observational skills are among the most important tools a teacher can acquire. Most teachers acquire them on their own as a consequence of classroom experience. While such self-taught skills are quite often efficacious, they sometimes have gaps or inadequacies. An analogy would be learning a motor skill such as tennis, swimming, or skating. Some people pick up these skills naturally and without instruction, but in so doing they may have also acquired habits and reactions that prevent them from ever being as good as they might have been with instruction and guidance.

The same is true for observational skills. Most teachers become pretty good observers on their own. But in many cases their observational skills might be improved with some guidance and instruction. In the course of teaching observational skills to students over the years, I have found some exercises useful both for the teacher in training and the teacher with extensive classroom experience. Since careful observation is essential to the assessment methods described later in the chapter, some of the exercises for developing observational abilities are described below.

Perhaps the most helpful exercise in the attainment of observational skills is the verbatim transcription of children's conversations. The conversations can be those which are simply overheard or which are teacher-initiated. If possible, the transcript should be compared with a tape-recorded version. Below is a beginning teacher's transcript of a young boy's monologue followed by a transcript of the tape.

Teacher's transcript: "Hey, where are the papers, they were supposed to be here. How am I going to make a tree without any more papers? Man that makes me mad, never have the stuff you are supposed to have."

Transcript from the tape: "Hey, where da papers, where da dumb papers? They was supposed to be here. How ma gonna make a tree widout them dumb papers. Man that makes me mad, never have da stuff you supposed to have."

It is clear from the example that when adults transcribe child language they in effect "clean it up" in terms of pronunciation, grammar, and even vocabulary. In so doing they may miss the peculiar terms of phrase, the grammatical lapses, and the vocabulary gaps that could have significance for cognitive assessment. Learning to listen, really listen to children, and to record accurately what it is they say, is a very important attainment. Teachers who hope to be good observers should practice this skill until they are truly proficient. Efforts in this regard will be more than repaid because they will help the teacher detect misunderstandings and cognitive deficiences that might otherwise go unnoticed but could be the cause of academic failure and classroom disruption.

Another observational skill is the ability to describe as accurately and in as detailed a fashion as possible particular behavioral events and episodes. The following descriptions were written by two student observers of the same classroom episode.

> A: "John and Bill got into a fight and the teacher stopped it."
> B: "John was sitting at his desk printing a sign for the teacher when Bill walked by, brushed John's arm, and made him mess up the P he was making. John got angry and said that Bill had done it on purpose. He got up and started to push Bill who started to push him back. That is when Mrs. L. came up and asked what had happened."

The difference between the two observational records is obvious —one is quite general, the other detailed and factual. The trick in observing, as in listening, is not to interpret, not to generalize, but merely to record as simply, as directly, and as completely as one can. In this regard useful exercises include not only describing episodes but also describing children. How big is the child, is he or she thin, fat, or medium? What color is the hair, the eyes; how does he or she dress (in well- or ill-fitting clothes, in jeans like the other children or in regular slacks or dresses)? What is the voice like, is it high and whiney, or deep and husky? Writing exact and detailed descriptions of this sort will often suggest or reveal why a child is popular or unpopular, and what sort of self-concept he has. A child who does not care for his or her appearance usually has a negative self-concept.

These exercises can help one become a better observer of children. It is useful to keep a little notebook about each child in the class and to record his or her academic progress during the year.

If notes about the child's appearance, voice, and manner of relating to adults and other children are kept as well, the teacher will have a good record of the pupil's progress that is far richer and more meaningful than a record of achievement scores.

OBSERVATIONAL ASSESSMENT

In the chapter on motivation (Chapter VI) it was suggested that when an ability is in the process of formation, a child prefers materials that nourish the growth of that ability. Likewise it was suggested that once a child masters an ability he begins to play with it and to exploit its potentialities. Accordingly, children's preferences for materials and the kinds of intellectual play that they engage in provide clues to their level of conceptual development. So does their language. But not all of it, and it is particularly in the area of quantity and in logical propositions that children reveal their level of cognitive growth in language.

PREFERENCES

Sometimes children's preferences for material which is nourishing to their cognitive development is revealed in repetitive activity. Montessori (1964) gives a description of a child engaged in repetitive activity that is nourishing cognitive growth and is also an index of new abilities in the making. Here is Montessori's (1964) observation of a child using the cylinder block, a wooden block with holes of different sizes that take cylinders of corresponding sizes.

> I watched the child intently without disturbing her at first, and began to count how many times she repeated the exercise; then, seeing that she was continuing for a long time, I picked up the little arm chair in which she was seated and placed chair and child upon the table, the little creature hastily caught up her case of insets, laid it across the arms of the chair and

> gathering the cylinders into her lap, set to work again. Then I
> called upon the children to sing; they sang, but the little girl
> continued, undisturbed, repeating her exercise even after the
> short song had come to an end. I counted forty-four repeti-
> tions; when at last she ceased, it was quite independently of
> any surrounding stimuli which might have distracted her, and
> she looked around with a satisfied air, as if awakening from a
> refreshing nap [pp. 67–68].

One must be careful, however, because repetitive behavior in
some children may be an indication of an unwillingness, usually
based on fear, to move on to new and more challenging tasks. Such
defensive repetitiveness need not necessarily be a sign of mental
slowness either. I once encountered a bright young girl who early in
her school career had learned to draw horses and to draw them
well. Her horses won a great deal of admiration from the other
children, the teacher, and her parents. But thereafter she would
only draw horses of the kind she had drawn before. She was afraid
that if she drew anything else it would not be as good and that she
would lose the special prestige that her excellent horses had won
her. In this instance repetition was not a sign of mental growth, but
rather of intellectual stagnation.

The stories children choose to read and listen to are another
index of their emerging cognitive abilities. Stories are quite useful
in this regard since their structure, if they are well written, often
mirrors the stages of cognitive growth. Simple "repetition" stories,
for example, are consonant with preoperational thinking. The
characters are one-dimensional (either bad or good); there is only a
single plot line with no subplots, and the time and place of the story
are not made very precise. Continuity of plot is by way of
repetition. These characteristics are in accord with preoperational
thought, when the child cannot deal with one person having
contradictory traits (bad and good ones), cannot depart from one
major course of action, and has little if any quantitive sense of time
or space.

The following excerpts make these aspects of literature for the preoperational child more tangible.

Whose mouse are you?

Whose mouse are you?
Nobody's mouse
Where is your mother?
Inside the cat.
Where is your father?
Caught in a trap.
Where is your sister?
Far from home
Where is your brother?
I have none.
(ROBERT KRAUS, 1970)

The Surprise Party

"I'm having a party tomorrow," whispered
        Rabbit. "It's a surprise."
"Rabbit is hoeing parsley tomorrow,"
        whispered Owl. "It's a surprise."
"Rabbit is going to sea tomorrow," whispered
        Squirrel. "It's a surprise."
"Rabbit is climbing a tree tomorrow," whispered
        Duck. "It's a surprise."
(P. HUTCHINS, 1969)

For contrast, compare this passage from *Winnie-the-Pooh* and note the complexity of plot, character, and setting that is involved.

"And how are you?" said Winnie-the-Pooh.
Eeyore shook his head from side to side. "Not very how," he said. "I don't seem to have felt at all how for a long time."
"Dear, dear," said Pooh, "I'm sorry about that. Let's have a look at you."
So Eeyore stood there, gazing sadly at the ground, and Winnie-the-Pooh walked around him once. "Why what happened to your tail?" he said in surprise.
"What happened to it?" said Eeyore.

> "It isn't there!"
> "Are you sure?"
> "Well, either a tail is there or it isn't there, you can't make a mistake about it. And yours isn't there."

Children who prefer such stories have clearly reached the concrete operational level of cognitive development.

And if an elementary school child begins to read and enjoy Tolkien's *The Hobbit* (1966; first publ. 1937), one can be pretty sure that he has reached the formal-operational level of thinking. Compare the following passage in terms of complexity of character setting and plot with the other two:

> As he listened to the talk of the raftmen and pieced together the scraps of information they let fall, he soon realized that he was very fortunate ever to have seen it all even from this distance. Dreary as had been his imprisonment and unpleasant as was his position (to say nothing of the poor dwarfs underneath him) still he had been more lucky than he had guessed. The talk was all of the trade that came and went in the waterways and the growth of traffic on the river, as the roads out of the East towards Mirkwood vanished or fell into disuse; and of the bickerings of the Lake-men and the Wood-elves about the upkeep of the Forest River and the care of the banks. Those lands had changed much since the days when dwarfs dwelt in the mountain, days which most people now remembered only as a very shadowy tradition [pp. 183–84].

In such stories the multidimensional characters and the references to different historical epochs, varied geographical features, and different peoples are too complex for the concrete operational child.

In addition to story preferences, game preferences are also useful cues to a child's cognitive level. At the kindergarten and first-grade level, children who enjoy playing games with rules, such as tic-tac-toe, give evidence of the attainment of concrete operations. Checkers is another game that children just developing concrete operations appreciate. It is useful to have several such games available in the classroom. Interest in games like chess and Monopoly appears a little later, usually eight or nine, and reflect better developed and fully established concrete operations. Interest in collections of all sorts is still another index of firmly established concrete operations.

CHILDREN'S HUMOR

What makes people laugh is generally an unthreatening failure of expectancy. Jokes, for example, are funny because of the unexpected and nonthreatening punch line: "Do you know what a henweigh is?" "No, what's a henweigh?" "About three pounds." The appreciation of humor then, reflects, in part at least, the child's level of cognitive development because expectancies are cognitive constructions. Accordingly, the kind of humor children appreciate suggests the sort of expectancies they can construct and laugh at when the expectancy is not fulfilled.

At the preschool level, children have mastered a good many sensory-motor skills and have a reasonably good sense of practical intelligence. Accordingly, when they see someone walking along and trip suddenly, or if they see someone drop something, they are likely to laugh. Because they expect the motions to be carried out without difficulty, the unexpected clumsiness appears humorous. Clowns are particularly adept at preoperational humor. Recall the fellow who fires a gun that shoots out a flag, and the minicar from which innumerable clowns pile out. In all these instances, there is a failure of expectancy at the level of basic coordinations or at the level of simple causal or spatial relations.

In practice, laughter at "preoperational" humor is not always diagnostic because concrete-operational children enjoy it too—but often less than the preoperational child. Indeed many concrete-operational children will not laugh at clowns because they regard this as too juvenile (see the section The Age Dynamism in Chapter VI). But they will enjoy the slapstick of Laurel and Hardy, which is a bit more sophisticated. When Laurel and Hardy dress in strange clothes—for example, when one plays a maid and the other an English lord—the fun is in their altered appearance and language. Knowing they are the same but different requires concrete operations, and children who appreciate Laurel and Hardy are likely to be concrete-operational.

Verbal jokes of all sorts also are popular at the concrete-operational level but are usually not understood at the preoperational level. Rhymes are also very popular as are stories which put down adults or which deal with taboo topics such as sex or toilet functions.

> Harry Brown went to town
> to buy a pair of britches
> Everytime he tumbled down
> He bursted all his stitches.

> I'm dirty Bill from Vinegar Hill
> Never had a bath and never will.

> Inky, pinky, pen and inky
> I smell a dirty stinky.

Riddles too are conspicuous in the humor of the concrete-operational child:

> "Why did the lobster blush?"
> "Because it saw the salad dressing."

> "What did the monkey say when he was cutting off his tail?"
> "It won't be long now!"

And a riddle which is currently making the rounds among American school children is the following:

> "How do you get a Burger King?"
> "Marry him to a Dairy Queen."

The humor of adolescents is of quite a different sort than that of children. For one thing, new forms of humor emerge including that scourge of us all, puns and punning.

When two Vampires fight there's generally bad blood between them.

A woman who buys a cheap pair of nylons is sure to get a run for her money.

Banter is another form of humor that makes its appearance in adolescence. The magazine *Mad* provides many examples. Children who read and appreciate *Mad* are most probably formal-operational. Here are some examples from that venerable journal.

Father: "Haven't I always been a fair father to you?"
Son: "Well let's say fair to poor. Now how about trying fair to good?"

Mother: "I have to bend down and pick up after you all day long."
Son: "Well, it's cheaper than going to Jack LaLanne."

Mother: (*to son and daughter*) "I don't play favorites, I love you both the same."
Son: "Gee sis, I didn't know you had a lousy deal too."

In short, there is a regular developmental progression in the appreciation of humor from the "sight gags" of the preoperational child to the riddles and jokes of the concrete-operational child to the puns and banter of the formal-operational young person. What sort of humor young people appreciate thus provides a rough gauge of their level of cognitive development.

Children's language is usually a good index of cognitive development. Of particular value in this regard is children's use of quantifiers. For example a child who describes a big block as the "daddy" and the little block as the "baby" or the "little one" is not likely to have concrete operations. The child who describes a block as "wide and fat" or as "tall and thin" shows that he or she is able to coordinate relations and deal with two relations at a time—an index of concrete operations.

Indices of more advanced concrete operations are the use of compound and complex sentences. "Mary ate the pie, but she didn't like it." One way to get samples of children's language is to have them tell a story, or the plot of a recent movie or television program in their own words. This is useful as an indication of the child's understanding of the plot line and characters, which can be another reflection of the stage of development of their concrete operations. Samples of children's writing can also be used in the assessment of cognitive level. It is not difficult, for example, to rank the following "dreams" in terms of the level of cognitive functioning that they represent.

Del: "I dreamed about a big ice cream cone."

Pat: "I dreamed about a bear; it was scary."

Cir: "I dreamed that I was a king and I had lots of money. My wife was a princess. Her name was Tracey. My kid's names were James, Glenn, and Conk. We had a wagon. It was red, white, and blue."

Ann: "I dream that I live in a candy world, with a candy policeman and a big $100,000 candy bar for breakfast, lunch, and dinner. Whenever I'm in bed, I don't have to get up to eat because my bed is a hot ball. I work in an ice cream shop. I get to take breaks and eat ice cream cones as big as a 44-inch table. I always eat chocolate. My bathroom is a banana split. My walls are made out of candy canes and my roof is made up of chewing gum."

"ERRORS" AND "LEARNING BLOCKS"

Some of the most revealing cues to a child's level of cognitive development are his or her "errors" and learning difficulties. Piaget assumed that children's "errors" were not chance or accidental, but rather that they were determined by modes of thought different from those usually engaged in by adults. For example, when a child asks, "If I eat spaghetti, will I become Italian?" this might be taken as an amusing, accidental, and erroneous remark. Taken seriously, however, it would suggest that the child may not distinguish clearly between what comes from nature and what comes from nurture. Such a question reflects a child's concern with origins, with where babies come from, with how some people become men, others women, some Jewish, some Italian. In effect, the child was voicing a theory about origins, about how we get to be and how we get to be in certain categories.

Children's spontaneous remarks can, therefore, often be quite revealing of their modes of thinking. Sometimes these remarks have to be followed up in order to help the child fully elaborate his thought. For example, my (then) six-year-old son asked me why we bury people in the ground. Taken aback, I asked, "Rick, where do you think we should bury them?" To this he replied, "In the garbage can, like we did with the dead bird." "But why," I persisted, "is burying someone in the garbage can better than burying them in the ground?" To which Rick replied, "The garbage can is cleaner and easier to get out of!" For Ricky there was a connection between death and burial but he did not really grasp the concept of death as the termination of life. Hence he believed that death was a temporary condition in which staying in a garbage can would be preferable to staying in the ground.

This conversation reveals much about the child's concept of death and how difficult it is for children to grasp intricate biological concepts. Such conversations are useful to remind us again and again how concrete and limited the child's thought is and how necessary it is to gear instructions, tasks, and materials to somewhere near the child's level.

Sometimes, of course, it is not possible to follow up a child's "error" on the spot. In such cases it is useful to record it and hold it for a more appropriate time. Occasionally the statement or question can be used to stimulate group discussion. When the children are sitting together one might ask, "Why do you think we bury dead people in the ground?" When the statements or questions come from children themselves, they often tap a rather deep-seated interest and are likely to stimulate a lively discussion. Such discussions are fruitful sources of information about levels of cognitive development. The varying answers will suggest the range of cognitive abilities in the group as well as the relative positions of individual children within it.

In addition to statements and questions that seem erroneous, learning difficulties are often indicative of cognitive level. For example, one of the teachers at the Mt. Hope School observed that some children just couldn't do number lines. Such inability to learn has sometimes been called a "learning block." From her observations of their remarks, preferences, and so on she suspected that they were preoperational and that their failure with the number lines meant that they lacked the cognitive ability required to grasp number lines. Essentially number lines require a sense of reversibility, an understanding that you can get back to the starting point of an arithmetic operation by employing the same or other operations. This observation suggested that these children needed to work on preliminary material such as classifying and ordering size-graded sticks, blocks, and other materials. In other words, they needed horizontal elaboration of their preoperational skills.

Another sort of learning difficulty that can reveal cognitive level is what has sometimes been called a "retention block." In such instances the child appears to learn the material but appears unable to retain it. We encountered one such child at the Mt. Hope School. She would learn the names of geometric forms—square, triangle, rectangle—one day but not remember them the next. When I heard about it, the thought occurred that perhaps she had her own names for geometric forms and that it was her own labels that interfered with her learning the prescribed names.

To test out this idea the teacher asked the child whether indeed she had her own names for the geometric forms. It turned out that she did and that she called a square a "box," a circle a "round," and a triangle a "point." These terms were concrete, in that they focused upon a particular rather than a general feature of the forms, and suggested that the girl was still preoperational. We therefore, allowed her to use her own names for the forms, while we continued to use the conventional names. Gradually, as she progressed intellectually, she switched to the more conventional terms.

A child's specific learning difficulties can, then, provide important insights into a child's level of cognitive development. It is important not to dismiss these difficulties either as reflecting the child's lack of motivation or concentration or as reflecting some deficiency in the instruction. In fact, such difficulties reflect not so much on the child or on the teacher as on the curriculum, which may be too difficult or too poorly presented for the child to handle effectively. "Errors" can be cues both to the child's level of cognitive ability and to the necessity for curriculum analysis and revision.

PIAGET'S CONSERVATION TASKS

One of the more direct ways of assessing the child's level of cognitive development is with the aid of Piaget's conservation tasks. Although such tasks are commercially available, there is really no need to go to the expense of purchasing such equipment. The tasks can be presented to children with a wide variety of materials that are readily available at home and at shcool. Indeed, once the teacher appreciates the principles of the conservation tasks, it is a challenge to find and use new materials to demonstrate them.

Basically a conservation task presents the child with a conflict between a conclusion based on reason and one based on perception. For example, if a child is asked to judge whether eight pennies in a pile are the same number as eight in a row, he is confronted with a conflict between reason and perception. A row of pennies looks like it has more elements than a pile, it is a kind of visual illusion. But if the child counts the pennies he can discover whether or not they are equal in fact. If he judges the two amounts by how they look, he is judging on the basis of perception. But if he counts first, an act of intelligence, he is judging with the aid of reason.

In general, if children are presented with a task in which conclusions based on appearance and on reason are both possible, their answers will reflect their level of cognitive development. Children who respond on the basis of perceptual appearance can be regarded as at a lower level of cognitive development than children whose reactions are dictated by reason. The conservation tasks are useful for distinguishing between preoperational and concrete-operational children and between concrete operational children at different levels of mastery of logical processes. They can also be used to distinguish between young people at the concrete and formal operational levels of intelligence. A few tasks that can help the teacher make these discriminations will now be described.

VERBAL CONSERVATION TASKS

Some conservation tasks can be conducted verbally and without the use of actual materials. Several of these tasks can be used to discriminate between preoperational and concrete-operational children and others to discriminate between concrete- and formal-operational young people. It should be said, however, that these methods are suggestive rather than definitive and the indications should be confirmed or discarded on the basis of the child's actual performance in the classroom.

Nesting Classes. At the kindergarten or first-grade level a simple class-inclusion task can be built upon class attendance. A child can be asked:

How many boys are there in the room?
How many girls are there in the room?
Are there more boys or more girls?
Are there more boys (*or girls*) than children?

A preoperational child's answer to the last question will reflect the fact that he or she cannot yet deal with the understanding that one and the same person can belong to two classes at the same time. Such a child will insist that there are "more boys than girls" (or vice versa) but will not contrast boys and girls with children.

Similar tasks can be constructed with a variety of materials. For example, one might use red and white poker chips, or blocks, or pennies, or different kinds of nuts. Objects of this sort can also be brought for preoperational children to work with. Grouping these objects according to different criteria (color, size, etc.) is good preparation for the establishment of concrete operations.

Mastering Relations. A verbal task that measures concrete operations at a slightly more advanced level has to do with kinship relations. Children who may have reversibility (get back to the starting point with compensatory operations in the way that addition can reverse subtraction) may yet have trouble with kinship relations that are more abstract. To get at this more advanced level, ask:

Do you have any brothers or sisters?
How many?
What is your brother's (*sister's*) name?
Does (*brother or sister's name*) have a brother (*or sister*)?

Children who are not well advanced in concrete operations will say that their brothers and sisters do not have brothers and sisters. They do not yet appreciate that *having* a brother implies *being* a brother.

As in the case of nesting classes, the difficulty here lies in seeing that one and the same person can be in two relations at once, that of being and that of having a brother. Other kinship terms are easier for this reason. For example, "Do you have a mother?" "Yes." "Does your mother have a mother?" Mother is not a reversible relationship and hence it is easier to grasp. Children who are doing poorly on relationships need to work on concrete materials with different gradations. "This is longer than this, this is shorter than this." "This is heavier," or "darker" or "more full" than this. Quantitative comparisons of all sorts offer good practice experience for solidifying concrete operations.

Verbal Seriation. A more advanced task, which reveals children who are moving into formal operations, is a verbal variation of a seriation task (arranging a set of objects according to size). Even though a concrete-operational child can solve this problem when it is posed with respect to real objects, he or she has difficulty when it is posed purely at the verbal level.

> Mays is a better player than Mantle and Mantle is a better player than Moskovitz, who is the best player of the three?

Children who are moving into formal operations can begin to solve such problems which require reasoning at the purely verbal or formal level. Arithmetic problems that are posed verbally, and indeed verbal puzzles of all sorts, are good training materials, preparatory to moving into formal operations. Contrariwise, children who have trouble with the purely verbal tasks need more work with concrete materials where the verbal labels can be tied, at every point, to observable qualities and dimensions.

Proverbs. A very revealing technique with respect to differentiating concrete- from formal-operational children is the use of proverbs. The beauty of proverbs is that they are interesting and that children's responses are qualitatively rich at almost all levels of development. For example, "The squeaking wheel gets the grease." What does that mean? The child who says, "When a wheel squeaks you put grease on it," is concrete-operational, whereas the child who says, "The one who makes the noise gets the attention," is clearly at the formal-operational stage. In effect, proverbs involve simile and metaphor, which are usually not fully understood until children attain formal operations.

The proverb above is only one of many that might be used. Proverbs sometimes are good for group discussion and the teacher can get some idea of where different children are when they are all working on the same proverb. A few other proverbs that might be used are:

A bird in the hand is worth two in the bush.
A rolling stone gathers no moss.
All that glitters is not gold.
You cannot serve one sparrow on twelve plates.
If you fear the wolf, keep out of the forest.

Children who interpret these proverbs in a very literal, concrete way need more work in reasoning about actual things.

It should be said that all of these verbal tasks involve one or another form of conservation. That is to say, they require that the child appreciate that something remains the same across a transformation. In the brother-sister task, for example, the child has to understand that the relation remains the same no matter which sibling is involved. And the proverbs deal with the conservation of a rule which can appear in many different concrete guises. The grasp of sameness across apparent change (the victory of reason over perception), first at the concrete and then at the verbal, or symbolic level, is at the heart of intellectual development.

TASKS WITH MATERIALS

As in the purely verbal tasks, the tasks using materials can be varied in many ways. The important point is to make sure that the child is attending to the task and that he or she fully understands the words being used. It is always well to adopt language used by the child to ensure that there is understanding of the task.

Number Conservation. Start with a pile of poker chips (nuts, sticks, coins, etc.) and make two parallel rows of six. Say to the child, "This is your row and this is mine. How many do you have, how many do I have?" If the child does not count correctly, have him try once or twice and then help him. Say, "Now you have six chips and

I have six chips, but I am going to move mine like this." Spread one row out so that it is longer than the other on both sides. "Now do we both have the same number of chips or does one of us have more?"

Preoperational children generally say that the longer row has more, even when they can count both rows of six. A way of assessing how close a child is to concrete operations is to ask, "Suppose I put my chips back as they were before, would we both have the same number of chips then?" Children who say that both will be the same when the chips are returned to the starting point, but not as they are now, are at a transitional state. Such children could benefit from transformational exercises—seeing, evaluating, and manipulating materials that change in form and appearance while remaining constant in other respects. Children who are not transitional need practice in classifying and in seriating all sorts of materials.

Length Conservation. A slightly more consolidated sense of concrete operations is manifested by children who demonstrate the conservation of length. This task, like the others, can be administered with many different materials. I often use two unsharpened pencils because they are readily available and are familiar. But two equal-sized dowels, or rulers, or pens could serve equally well. Place the two pencils parallel on the table and ask:

"Are both pencils the same length? Are they both equally long?"

After the child agrees that both pencils are equally long, say, "Now I am going to move one of them like this," at which point push one pencil slightly ahead of the other. "Now are both pencils still equally long, or is one longer than the other?"

Children who say that one pencil is longer have not yet attained length conservation. Because length conservation follows number conservation by about a year, children will have number concepts before they have numerical length concepts. It would seem, then, that measuring that involves the transport of constant units is more difficult than counting and simple arithmetic. Measuring activities might be delayed until children demonstrate the conservation of length.

Right and Left. The understanding of relational concepts moves from the absolute to the relative. Children begin by thinking of relations, such as left and right, as properties of things analogous to color and form. It is only in middle childhood that children come to appreciate the true relational character, a property that exists *between* rather than within things, of concepts such as right and left. The progress of the child's understanding of right and left during the elementary school years is a good index of her progress in concrete operations generally.

The simplest right-left task can be carried out by simply standing or sitting opposite the child and asking the following questions:

"Show me your right hand and your left hand." Sometimes a child may not know which is his or her right and left, but still understand relations. So, even if the child is "wrong," ask him or her to point to your right and left hands. If the child judges correctly, make the task a little more difficult by crossing your arms in one direction and then in another. A child who lacks an understanding of relations such as right and left is preoperational and needs experiences of putting things "on top of," "inside," "behind," "beside," one another.

Even children who know their own right and left hands, and can correctly judge the right and left of an adult standing opposite them, may not have a fully developed relational concept. Usually this does not appear until about ages seven or eight. To assess this more advanced stage of concrete operations you need three small but different objects. I have used a comb, a coin, a pencil, a pen, a stick, a hair ribbon, a ruler, and so on. Put three objects in a row on the table and (supposing the objects are a penny, a comb, and a pencil) ask:

Is the penny on the right or on the left of the comb?

Is the pencil on the right or the left of the comb?

Is the comb on the right or on the left of the pencil?

Is the comb on the right or on the left of the pen?

Even though a child may correctly judge the relations of the penny and the pencil, he or she still may not comprehend the simultaneous relations of the comb. To understand the comb questions, the child must grasp that it can be *both* on the right of the penny *and* on the left of the comb, and that is more difficult than deciding which side is left and which is right. The introduction of complex relational tasks, such as number lines, might well wait until the child has attained true relations of right and left.

Combinations. The last task to be described is useful in assessing children who are moving into formal operations. As with the proverbs, it is revealing because responses at all age levels are qualitatively rich. For materials you require four differently colored objects such as marking pens, poker chips, plastic blocks, or toys. Place the four differently colored objects on the table and say, "I want you to put these four colors together in as many different ways as possible taking them one, two, three, and four at a time. See, I can put the blue and the green together, or the blue and the red and so on. See how many different ways you can put them together."

Children at the concrete operational level will often move the objects around as they call out the possible combinations but they often miss or forget to name some of the combinations. Young people who are more advanced in formal operations will name the combinations while just looking at the materials but without manipulating them. They also make few if any errors.

These are a few simple tasks for assessing the cognitive level of children and adolescents. It has to be emphasized that these are rough measures that need to be tested out against the child's actual performance. Sometimes a child who shows operativity on the tasks will have difficulty with concrete operational curriculum material while other children who have no trouble with the instructional materials have trouble with the assessment tasks. But for most children the tasks do reveal where they stand vis-à-vis the curriculum, and provision should be made for offering instructional materials that roughly approximate the child's level of cognitive development.

ACHIEVEMENT TESTING AND GRADING

Any discussion of developmental assessment would not be complete without some reference to achievement testing and grading. From the point of view of a developmental approach to education, which insists that children be active participants in reconstructing knowledge, tests and grading are at the very least a hindrance to the educational process. Piaget (1970), who is usually quite unemotional in his discussion of educational matters, is most emphatic in his discussion of testing:

> Everything has been said about the value of scholastic examinations, and yet this veritable plague on education at all levels continues to poison—such terminology is not too strong here—normal relations between the teacher and the student by jeopardizing for both parties the joy in work as well as mutual confidence. The two basic faults of the examination are that generally it does not give objective results, and it becomes, fatally, an end in itself (for even admission examinations are always, first of all final examinations: the admission examination for high school becomes an end for primary education, etc.).
>
> The school examination is not objective, first because it contains an element of chance, but mostly because it depends upon memory more than on the constructive capabilities of the student. (As if he were condemned never to use his books once he was out of school!) Anyone can confirm how little the grading that results from examinations corresponds to the final

useful work of people in life.* The school examination
becomes an end in itself because it dominates the teacher's
concerns, instead of fostering his natural role as one who
stimulates consciences and minds and he directs all of the
work of the students toward the artificial result which is
success in final tests, instead of calling attention to the
student's real activities and personality [pp. 73–74].

In short, for Piaget, standardized examinations are educationally
harmful, because of the reverberating effect they have on educational practice. Tests, which measure primarily figurative learning,
encourage figurative (involving adult direction and memory) methods in the classroom in order to prepare the children for the tests.
In a very real sense tests, which were meant as an appendage of
education, have become preeminent. The tail now wags the dog.

Piaget is not opposed to assessment in principle. The procedures
outlined in the previous section are witness to that. But developmental assessment is objective (in the sense that there is little room
left for chance in the determination of the child's responses) and
assesses operative and connotative learning as well as figurative
attainments. Finally, developmental assessment, in which the
teacher shows interest in and respect for the child's productions,
strengthens rather than weakens the student-teacher relationship.

In Piaget's view, developmental assessment is a continual process
that records the actual work children do during the year. A
collection of the child's work, a folder containing some of her
writing, some of his work in math, and science, etc. is much more
meaningful than a grade. Keeping such a record, and making
decisions about what samples of work are to be contained in it, is a
valuable learning experience in itself. The same cannot be said for
taking tests. In short, *documentation* rather than examination is
consistent with the educational philosophy of the active classroom.

If examinations are harmful to the educational process and not

---

* A recent article by McClelland (1973) documents how little grades and IQs
correlate or predict vocational success.

terribly useful prognostic instruments, why do they continue to be used? The answer is, I believe, that examinations serve social and political purposes and are useful in getting money and in winning votes. It is in the American way of education, if something is not going well, to pour in more money or to make it a campaign issue. Ironically, the school system that is doing poorly on tests is likely to get more money than one that is doing well. If tests and test results could be removed from the social-political arena, they could quickly be removed from schools as well. At some point society must discover that bad education does not really make good politics.

VIII
CURRICULUM ANALYSIS

"The intellectual and moral structures of the child are not the same as ours; consequently the new methods of education make every effort to present the subject matter to be taught in forms assimilable to children of different ages in accordance with their mental structure and the various stages of development."   J. PIAGET

In the broadest sense a curriculum can be said to be a set of priorities as to what skills, concepts, and facts children are to acquire at what time and in which order. The classroom teacher, however, is not faced with one set of priorities, but rather with three. In addition to the *school* curriculum, mandated by society, the teacher must also take account of the *developmental* curriculum (maturational) priorities, and the *personal* curriculum (individual differences) priorities. For the classroom teacher, then, the curriculum presents a problem of balancing and coordinating three sets of priorities. The aim of the present chapter is to suggest some guidelines for the coordination of these sometimes conflicting, sets of demands.

Before proceeding to that discussion, however, the three types of curricula need to be described in more detail. The school curriculum is basically the sequence of math, science, language arts, social studies, manual and fine arts skills, skills concepts, and facts that are mandated by the school system. (It is not my intention here to go into the many and difficult disputes about which components of the school curriculum are more important or which programs—math, social studies, or reading—is the "best." Rather, I would like to suggest guidelines for assessing whether any given curriculum, in whatever field is developmentally appropriate to the children to whom it is being offered.)

The developmental curriculum is essentially the sequence of abilities and concepts that children acquire more or less on their own. Much of Piaget's (1950) work has been devoted to revealing this developmental curriculum in all its breadth and scope. Children acquire concepts of mass, weight, and volume (1941, with Inhelder), of space (1956, with Inhelder), time (1970a), and causality (1974), of geometry (1960), speed, and movement (1946) in ways and in sequences oftentimes different from those which are taught in school. The concepts children acquire on their own are part of their basic adaptive equipment, what they need to get along in the world as living creatures. Such concepts have never been taught in the schools because adults assumed children already had them.

In this regard a cautionary note is in order. There has been a tendency, now that the developmental curriculum has been "discovered," to substitute it for the school curriculum. That is to say, some "Piaget-based" curricula aim at teaching the kinds of concepts (conservation of substance, liquid quantity, and so on) that Piaget has shown most children acquire pretty much on their own as a consequence of their active involvement with the environment. Such substitutions, however well intentioned, are a mistake. The school curriculum is important. It represents man's accumulated knowledge and forms part of the child's cultural heritage. The school curriculum is the prime vehicle for transmitting that heritage. In contrast, what the developmental curriculum provides, as this chapter attempts to clarify, is not a curriculum to be taught but rather a set of *tools for the analysis of the school-curriculum.* Put differently, the developmental curriculum provides criteria for judging whether any given set of curriculum materials is appropriate to the cognitive level of the children to whom it is being presented.

Before turning to some examples of developmental curriculum analysis, a third set of priorities must be mentioned, although they cannot be dealt with in detail here. The third set of priorities, the personal curriculum, has to do with the priorities that each child brings to her schooling as a consequence of his or her own unique talents, abilities, and inclinations. Suggestions about how these personal curriculum priorities can be coordinated with the school curriculum will be given in Chapter IX, where the relation of interest and constructive cognitive activities is discussed. In this chapter we will examine the school curriculum in light of the developmental curriculum.

CURRICULUM ANALYSIS

The analysis of developmental curriculum can go on at different levels and in different directions. For example, one can ask at what age should certain subjects, such as philosophy or geometry, be taught?—a legitimate question for developmental curriculum analysis and a difficult one as well. Bruner (1961) in a well-known statement has argued that "any child can be taught any subject at any age in an intellectually honest way." But there is little agreement as to what is intellectually honest. To a mathematician, a child who is copying forms on a geo-board may not be doing geometry. An educator, on the other hand, may believe that geo-board activities are basic to the grasp of geometric concepts and that the child is doing geometry when she is constructing forms with rubber bands.

It is really not my intention to get into such disputes here, because they are less pedagogical than they are semantic. Whether a geo-board is preparing a child for geometry is less significant than the fact that it is an activity which is interesting and by means of which she is acquiring spatial concepts, whether one calls them geometrical or not. The crucial question is not whether or not a child is learning a particular subject matter, but rather whether or not she is learning. Perhaps an illustration will help to make this distinction clear.

Not long ago I visited an English primary school in a well-known English university town. Most of the children who attended the school were the children of faculty members and were, as one might expect, quite bright and verbal. In the second grade classroom I was shown work the children had done on the London fire of 1666. The children had been read a story about the fire and shown pictures about it. Their task was to write a little essay about it. The essays were exceptional in their clarity, organization, and vocabulary, but they had a monotonous quality—they were essentially restatements of what the children had heard. The essays, despite their high level of competency, were entirely lacking in originality and spontaneity. Moreover, since the material was far beyond the children's level of comprehension, it was not likely that it would be retained.

Several days later I had the occasion to visit a small village school located near an automotive assembly plant. Most of the children who attended this school were the offspring of blue-collar workers or tradespeople in the village. The second-grade children in this group were writing essays too, but of a very different sort. The day before, they had visited a small church, had examined the gravestones in the yard, and made rubbings of some of the stones. The essays written by these children made up, in spontaneity and originality, for the lack of the grammatical and rhetorical finesse, so evident in the essays of children of academics. And this material, tied as it was to the children's own experience, was much more likely to be retained because it could be assimilated to their existing body of knowledge.

Now, from my point of view, the issue raised by these two examples has less to do with the teaching of history than it has to do with the way second-grade children learn. Whether the story of the London fire is called history or fiction is less important than the fact that the historical and geographical concepts presupposed by the story are far beyond the grasp of second-grade children. Again, whether or not a visit to a graveyard is an "historical" experience is less significant than the fact that it was a real and meaningful experience that children could relate to and represent in their own way.

Accordingly, in the present discussion I am not going to get into arguments about what sorts of experiences or lessons should or should not be a part of different disciplines. Rather, I want to take examples of materials in major curriculum domains and examine them from a cognitive developmental point of view. Three facets of curriculum will be examined—instructions, content, and graphic display.

READING

There are any number of reading programs on the market, ranging from psycholinguistic, look-say, to phonic approaches. Many of these programs are well produced and useful in teaching beginning reading. But all could benefit from more careful phrasing of instructions, wiser selection of content, and a better thought-out graphic display.

Instructions. Recently one of the children at the Mt. Hope School came up to my office to do some of the exercises in his phonics work book. He was working at a desk in the corner of the room, and I noticed at one point that he was experiencing difficulty. I went over and had him read the instructions to me. He read, "Color all of the balloons with the long A's red, color all the balloons with the short a's green except those followed by a silent e which should be colored blue." The trouble with this instruction is obvious in that it requires too many operations to be kept in mind simultaneously. The child is expected to keep in mind three different combinations of letters, sounds, and colors. A task which seems concrete, namely, coloring balloons to designate different sounds, has been made enormously complex by the instructions. In this case the young boy could have handled any one of the sound-color combinations with ease, but dealing with all three at once was not possible for him.

Other examples of convoluted instructions will be provided in later sections. In general, however, young elementary-school children have trouble in keeping more than two contingencies in mind at once. For this age group (kindergarten through second grade), it is best to begin with single operation instructions. "Color all the balloons with long A's red." Double operation instructions can be introduced when the children appear bored or unchallenged by the single-operation task. Triple-operation instructions should probably be reserved for older age groups or exceptionally bright children.

Content. The content of beginning readers is almost uniformly dull; "Bill and Will sat on a hill" is not going to win any Newberry awards. This dullness is somewhat excusable since children who are just beginning to learn decoding skills tend to focus on decoding rather than on content. Once children get beyond this point, however, the interest value of the stories *does* make a difference. Most curriculum builders are not good storytellers. It has always puzzled me why curriculum writers do not use stories written by professional storytellers which are published in children's magazines, such as *Jack and Jill* and *Humpty Dumpty.* These magazines have been in existence a long time and they provide a rich repository of good fiction for children that could be incorporated into reading programs.

The advantage of using stories for children written by professional writers is that professional writers understand the craft of storytelling; if they are good, they have an intuitive sense of what is interesting to children. Moreover they know and follow some basic rules about storytelling to children. For example, when reading with an eight- and a nine-year-old child at the Mt. Hope School, I discovered that the heroine of the story, for nine- and ten-year-old children, was only six. Any writer for children would know that the hero or heroine must be a year or two older than the children to whom the story is addressed. It is these little "tricks of the trade" which the professional storyteller knows but which are generally not known to the curriculum writers. Paradoxically, stories written by children are interesting to them and to other youngsters, and promote interest in reading (Ashton-Warner, 1963).

It might be argued, however, that the stories in reading books are meant to develop specific decoding and vocabulary skills. While I would not disagree with this contention, I think the order of construction ought to be turned around. Good interesting stories ought to be chosen first, and the vocabulary and decoding exercises built around them, not the reverse. Interesting stories involve children in reading and make skill learning a natural concomitant. With artificial, dull stories neither the story nor the learning has much interest.

Similar considerations hold for reading material for older children too. That is to say, the first and most important criterion in choosing literature should be its literary quality, not its teaching value. Points about grammar, paragraphing, and so on can be made with many different kinds of material. Of course literary quality is in part a matter of taste, and there should be sufficient flexibility in the choice of materials to satisfy young people with different interests and orientations. Some of the articles in *Popular Mechanics* are, on examination, quite well written. The delicate task is always to elaborate young people's own interests by providing quality material for them to pursue on their own.

Graphic Representation. We know least about the role of graphics in the learning process. And yet, even what is known, and seems obvious, is too often neglected in the production of curriculum materials. I have seen books for beginning readers in which the print was incredibly small and the words cramped together. The accompanying pictures were often complicated and overly detailed. Certainly a major principle of graphics for young elementary-school children is that print be of decent size, clear and uncrowded, and that pictures be simple and direct.

There is another point about graphic representation that should be made. Children use pictures as contextual cues to word recognition and meaning. The closer the picture approximates the story being told, the more helpful it is. There is nothing more frustrating to a child, or to an adult for that matter, than a picture that does not coincide with the story. This is particularly true about crucial elements of the story. If there is a bicycle in the picture, there should be one in the story. And if a child is said to have red hair, then the child in the picture should have red hair.

The value of making the drawings relate to the text in a direct way is clearly evident in the popularity of the Dr. Seuss books. Part of the fun of such books as *The Cat in the Hat* and *To Think That I Saw It on Mulberry Street* is the fact that the pictures are so distinctively unique to the story, indeed, they could go with no other story. That, by the way, is not a bad criterion for assessing the cognitive value of pictures that accompany texts.

MATHEMATICS

Piaget's work has perhaps had more impact in the domain of mathematics than in any other curriculum area. The "new math" was, in part at least, inspired by his findings. And the late Max Beberman, prime mover in the writing of the "new math," was familiar with Piaget's writings. Yet the new math curricula were not always successful. In execution they suffered from the usual defects in instructions, in content, and in graphic materials. The examples below are taken from several different contemporary math curricula.

Instructions. Instructions in mathematics should in most cases present no problems, since all they need do is instruct the child as to what operations are to be employed. Yet, rather than do this simply and directly, many texts resort to metaphors that are more likely to confuse than to help children. In one math series an instruction reads: "Write the number sentence"; and later: "Make each number sentence true." In both cases all that needed to be said was: "Find the sums and the products." Talk of an equation as a sentence is a metaphor that children, who may not know what a verbal sentence is, are not likely to comprehend.

In another series the metaphor is a "computing machine" that multiplies or adds with constants. Yet it is easier for children to grasp simple constants than to understand a computing machine. Instructions such as "multiply every number by five" or "add five to each number" is all the child needs. Metaphors and analogies, which play such an important part in adult learning, are confusing to children. The use of unnecessary metaphors in instructions for children is one of the most pervasive instructional errors across all curricular domains.

In this regard, a personal example is instructive because it demonstrates how difficult it is—even for a child psychologist—to keep the child's perspective in mind. My eight-year-old son Ricky and I were out sailing one day when he asked how the wind made the sailboat move. I began explaining that the wind pushed the sail but that the lead keel kept the boat from moving in the same direction as the wind. It got a little complicated and I realized how difficult it is to explain vectors to a child. So, I resorted to analogy. I told Ricky to think of his movable practice frame (against which he throws balls and from which they bounce back so he can practice catching) and how the frame moved when he threw the ball at it. I told him to think of the ball as the wind and the frame as the sail. At this point he stopped me and said: "Dad, please don't take this personally, but that is a terrible way to explain sailing to a kid. I understood it better when you were talking about the keel and the sails!"

Content. One of the points that Piaget makes again and again with respect to mathematics is the importance of the child's working with manipulative materials and not just with symbols. And it is true that more and more elementary classrooms are equipped with geo-boards, chip trading games, blocks, and so on. But often these materials are not used, or at least not used in the way that would help children acquire basic mathematical concepts. Frequently, neither the curriculum builders nor teachers know, or take sufficient account of, how children spontaneously form mathematical concepts.

In examining American mathematics books I found exactly what Piaget (1973) describes below:

> Experiments that we have been able to carry out on the development of mathematical and physical ideas have demonstrated that one of the basic causes of passivity in children in such fields, instead of the free development of intellectual activity they should provide, is due to the insufficient dissociation that is maintained between questions of logic and numerical and metric questions. In a problem of velocities, for example, the student must simultaneously manage reasoning concerning the distances covered and the lengths utilized, and carry out a computation with the numbers that express these quantities. While the logical structures of the problem is not solidly assured, the numerical considerations remain without meaning, and on the contrary, they obscure the system of relationships between each element. Since the problem rests precisely on these numbers, the child often tries all sorts of computations by gropingly applying the procedures that he knows, which has the effect of blocking his reasoning powers [pp. 99–100].

In math curricula, as in reading, the logical abilities required by the child are taken for granted, and only the math concepts or facts are presumed to be what the child needs to learn. Hence even the manipulative materials are misused, if they are tied up from the beginning with numerical rather than with strictly logical problems. The child needs a basis in logic to acquire mathematics, and this basis is not present from the start, but must be developed. It is to the development of logical abilities, rather than to the acquisition of "math facts" that elementary, and advanced, math instruction should be directed.

Some examples of the confounding of the logical and mathematical operations may help to make this discussion more concrete. One area where this confounding is quite clear is in the matter of coins. One first grade text asks children to "Find the value of each coin collection," and below this instruction are pictures such as three pennies and a nickel, four pennies and two nickels, and so on. The child is asked to write down the total in a box.

Consider for a moment only the logical problem that is involved. A nickel is the class of five pennies, but it is really not five pennies, it is a single coin. So a nickel is both like five pennies and also different. Nickels, dimes, and quarters are thus higher-order units, much as a foot is a higher-order unit of inches. Such higher-order units are complex cognitive constructions. Hence a child must know something of higher-order classifications if she is truly to understand coins. Such logical understanding should precede mathematical exercises about coins. To be sure, children may solve some coin problems, but in a rote way and without true understanding—much as children can compute geographical distances (such as the distance between two states or two planets) without really understanding the units or distances that are involved.

Just one other example of a confusion of the logical and the mathematical will be given. In a section of a math book entitled "Find the Differences" there are boxes with lobsters and seahorses, shells and starfish, fish and turtles, snails and crabs. From a reasoning point of view, this task is much more difficult than if all the animals for a given problem were of the same kind. For example, in the box with two lobsters and eight seahorses the equation to be solved is $10 - 8 = $. But what does the 10 stand for? The 10 stands for the combined class of lobsters and seahorses—crustaceans. To make sense out of the problem, therefore, the child has to form a higher-order classification that may be beyond his powers. So again she has to resort to rote procedures if she does not have the logic.

Many more examples could be given, but these may suffice to illustrate how logical and mathematical issues are sometimes confounded in elementary math curricula. The value of manipulative materials can also be undermined if logical problems are confounded with mathematical ones. The use of differently colored Cusenaire rods confounds the logical and the mathematical. That is, the child has to grasp that white stands for the "class of all ones," red for the "class of all twos," and so on, at the same time that he or she is dealing with mathematical issues. Using rods of different unit lengths but of all one color eliminates the difficulty. The introduction of color, which seems to simplify matters from an adult point of view, often complicates them from the child's point of view.*

Graphic Presentation. Some of the difficulties described above have to do with graphics as much as they do with content. Pictures of lobsters and crabs do not really help the child form a higher-order classification. In graphic presentation the errors are the same as in the symbolic domain, namely, a failure to take sufficient account of the logical problems entailed in the graphic materials.

Consider the graphic display used to illustrate the inequality signs. The artist chose to identify the "greater" sign with a mouth, so that the more numerous figures were always the ones being "eaten." But such logic defies children's logic and their common sense notions: that the bigger set should "eat" the smaller one. It is a minor matter, but by going against the child's expectations the picture makes learning the direction of the inequality signs more, rather than less, difficult. And the use of different animals, or simply different-colored animals, again adds a needless logical difficulty to the mathematical problem.

We encountered a different sort of graphic display problem at the

---

* On the other hand, those well trained in the use of the Cusenaire rods can help children avoid such confusions. Unfortunately only a small percentage of teachers who use the rods are trained in their utilization.

Mt. Hope School which nonetheless resulted from a failure to appreciate the logical components of the task. Children were dealing with a work book in which several of the same problems were displayed on the same page in both a horizontal and in a vertical arrangement, for example, $3 + \square = 10$ and $\begin{array}{r} 3 \\ + \square \\ \hline 10 \end{array}$. Some of the children who succeeded with the problem in the horizontal arrangement made errors when it was in the vertical arrangement. In the vertical arrangement they solved the problem like this $\begin{array}{r} 3 \\ + \boxed{13} \\ \hline 10 \end{array}$.

I believe that the reason the children made the error was that the vertical problem is logically more difficult than the horizontal one. Whether in the vertical or the horizontal direction, the problem requires a "hidden subtraction," of three from ten, so the child has to perform a subtraction before the addition will hold. In the case of the vertical arrangement, however, other operations are called for. The child must mentally transform the plus sign so that it applies to the box and must translate a single line as an equals sign. Because of these additional logical operations called forth by the vertical arrangement, the children "forgot" the hidden subtraction and performed the simple operation of addition.

I am not suggesting that vertical arrangements not be used. I am suggesting that the logical difficulties inherent in different arrangements be acknowledged and used with intelligence and forethought. For example, had all of the problems on the page been arranged in the vertical manner, the children would not have had to make the shift from the vertical orientation, and the difficulty could have been lessened. Certainly even switching formats on a page may be useful, if it is done intentionally and with an understanding of the logical difficulties it poses. Without such knowledge the difficulties posed by the graphic presentation could be attributed to dullness or "learning difficulty" on the part of the child. If we want to challenge children intellectually, we should know what it is we are doing and why we are doing it.

A major thrust of the curriculum movement of the 1960s was to construct new science and social science curricula at the elementary and secondary levels. In many cases those building the new curricula were well informed not only about their discipline but also about child development. And some curriculum developers have tried to use Piaget as a guide for the construction of their subject-matter. Many of our contemporary science curricula are the most child-development-centered programs we have in elementary education.

Even these new curricula, however, suffer from the same problems that were revealed in the areas of reading and math. Often the difficulty stems from too great an emphasis upon the conceptual content of the lessons and too little concern with the logical structures of the task the child is being set. In analyzing some illustrative science lessons we will again approach them from the standpoint of instructions, content, and graphic presentation. And, again, I do not mean to single out any particular science curriculum for criticism, but to select examples to represent errors that can be found in most programs.

Instructions. In one elementary science series that contains several really fine units there are some rather glaring lapses. On one page there is a picture of a large and a small soccer ball and a large and a small rubber ball, which could be the same size but at different distances or of different sizes at the same distance. There were no cues for the child to make the discrimination. The questions, for both pairs of balls, were:

Are the balls the same?
Are they the same size?

Which looks nearer?
How can you tell?

The problem with these instructions is their ambiguity on the one hand, and their contradictory implications on the other. The question as to whether the balls are the same could be answered in the affirmative if the child thought the balls were the same in size but that one was farther away than the other, or that they were both soccer balls. There is no way to tell from the question what meaning was intended. In the same way a negative response could have meant that the balls were not the same in size or in type. The meaning of the question and of the child's responses is ambiguous.

The next three questions are inappropriate for a different reason: the constraints they place on child thought. Presumably science education should encourage operative thinking and not close the child's options, but allow him to come to his own conclusions. The thrust of the exercises is for the child to go against his perceptual judgments and to say that the balls are the same size and that the big one looks nearer because it is bigger. The drawings are such that there is no real way to know whether the balls are the same size but a different distance, or different sizes at the same distance. To be "right" the child has to say things he believes to be wrong, and without any data that would substantiate the desired response.

Additional examples of ambiguous and overly directive instructions could be given but another set from the same series will be presented to illustrate the kind of instructions that are straightforward and that facilitate active exploration and operative thought.

A magnet can move some objects but not others.

List the objects your magnet will move.

List the objects your magnet will not move.

Content. In many ways the poor instructions cited in the preceding discussion were a matter of inappropriate content. The use of size-distance relationships is simply the wrong way to teach children about "near" and "far." Measurement, which the unit brings in later, is much closer to the child's level of understanding. The trouble with size-distance relationships (usually taught in introductory psychology courses) is that they require formal-operational thought to be understood. That objects look smaller when they are far away is primarily a psychological matter and has to do with the operation of the visual system.

To be sure, children can easily discriminate between near and far objects in their environment. But they cannot understand how they make these discriminations. The problem with the lesson near–far was that it was not really aimed at helping children recognize near–far things, but rather at giving them some "understanding" of why they were able to make the discrimination. This sort of lesson fails to distinguish between what Piaget calls *practical* as opposed to *reflective* intelligence.

A child has many skills which he or she uses effectively but cannot understand or reconstruct in a verbal or conceptual way. Piaget (1974a), for example, had children at different age levels build a house of playing cards. They were then asked to describe what they had done (i.e., "I put this card here, balanced it with this card," etc.). It was only toward late childhood that young children could describe their motor behavior correctly. The child's perception of near–far objects, like building a house of cards, is a matter of practical intelligence. It does not become part of reflective intelligence until the young person can grasp the psychology of vision, which is not until middle adolescence at best.

Graphic Presentation. It seems to me that science illustrations should be simple and direct. Many of the illustrations in the new science curricula are of this sort and nicely complement the text. But sometimes the graphics go beyond what makes good sense. For example, in one book there is a picture of the earth with children standing at different places on it and holding balls. The questions have to do with the directions in which the ball will fall. A final caption at the end of all the questions reads, "The earth pulls on all objects."

What is wrong with the illustration is that it presents the child with an impossible metaphor. The lesson about gravity is interfered with by the graphics which require a level of cognitive sophistication far beyond the grasp of most elementary-school children. They can give the right answer to be sure, and this might seem to justify the use of such illustrations. But the child answers on the basis of what he or she knows rather than what he or she sees, and the illustration, far from being instructive, is merely confusing.

These few examples from science curricula illustrate once again how easy it is to slip into an adult perspective and to assume that the child's conceptual reality is comparable to our own. In the realm of science education this often appears as a confusion of practical and reflective intelligence. Lessons on size-distance and gravity go awry when exercises assume that reflective concepts can be taught by demonstration as if they were practical concepts. The result is that such lessons merely confuse children about practical skills at which they are already quite competent.*

As far as science goes, the elementary school period is a great time for observation, classification, and recording. But it is not a good time for learning experimental methods and general theoretical principles that are only fully understood at the formal operational level. Learning to observe carefully how plants grow and leaves unfold, learning to identify the different species and subspecies of plants and animals is valuable training for young people that paves the way for more experimental and reflective approaches to science in adolescence. What we must constantly guard against in the teaching of science, and of the other subjects, is the introduction of abstract adult conceptions as if they could be learned by simple perceptual discrimination.

* Teaching "grammar" in the early grades repeats the same error.

SOCIAL STUDIES CURRICULA

Contemporary social studies curricula for the elementary school are perhaps the worst violators of the rule that instructional content be suited to the children's level of conceptual understanding. When I read that first grade children are being taught the continents, explorer routes, and the different cultures of the world, I cringe. The concepts involved in such topics are so far removed from young children's experience and comprehension that they have no alternative but to learn figuratively. How can children, in any meaningful way, reconstruct the continents, or explorer routes, out of their own experience? Such concepts are much too abstract for first grade children to learn operatively. This does not mean that the social sciences cannot be taught at the early grades, only that what is taught be in "chunks" small enough for grade school children to digest.

Instructions. The major problem with social studies instructions, which are usually questions to be answered, is that they frequently involve concepts far beyond children's comprehension. For example, in a first-grade book in the section on communities children are asked: "What religions do people have?" This is just below a more concrete question: "What food do they eat?" It is really not until adolescence (Elkind, 1961, 1962, 1963) that children understand what religion is about (because it involves the concept of belief, a formal operational concept) so the question has to be empty. Again the same sort of criticism could be made of the following question: "Why do people need recreation?" The question is much too general for first-grade children. Each concept—"people," "need," and "recreation"—is a broad concept that children do not grasp fully. To ask that they begin to put them together in causal ways is asking much too much.

Content. A good deal of the content of the elementary social studies curriculum is simply too abstract, too removed from the child's own experience to be of much lasting value. A personal example may illustrate what I mean. Our middle son came home one day pleased that he was learning about the planets. He did indeed learn their names, relative sizes, and distances from the sun. But I was sure that this was figurative learning and that he had no operative understanding of what he had learned. I checked a few months later and he had forgotten everything but the name of a planet or two.

One of the units that appears in almost all of the elementary social science curricula has to do with the globe, continents, our country, and so on. I really have no objection to globes because they can be turned and thus allow the child in some way to relate, in an intuitive way, to the notion of the earth as a sphere. But for children in the early grades, learning about oceans and continents and land masses is much like learning about the planets—it is figurative rather than operative and the knowledge will not be retained.

To demonstrate the difference between figurative and operative learning of social studies curricula, I carried out a little experiment. A group of second-grade children had learned the names of the states. In particular they had learned to recognize New York State and some of the cities in it and the surrounding states. But I discovered something interesting when I began to ask questions about distances. Rochester is about 300 miles from New York City, but only about 100 miles from Erie, Pennsylvania, and about 60 miles (across Lake Ontario) from Canada. But the children were sure that any two cities in New York State were closer together than any two cities in adjacent states!

This is clearly a boundary problem. In other chapters I have talked about the difficulty children have in understanding that one and the same person, or number, or letter, can belong to two different classes or be in two different relations at the same time. Maps present boundary problems of the same kind. Children have difficulty grasping that one and the same boundary can belong to two different states. Despite the maps, children conceive of states as existing in a kind of geographical limbo, where every city in the state is closer to every other city in the state than to any city outside the state.

I could go on with countless illustrations but that is perhaps unnecessary. I do believe that social studies can be meaningfully taught at the elementary school level. At the Bank Street Schools in New York, for example, there is a regular progression in social studies content. Until the age of seven or eight the focus is upon "here and now" aspects of the immediate social environment. For the somewhat older children the topic is still New York but they then study older New York by visiting graveyards, old buildings and other examples of the past. Only after the age of nine or ten do the children deal with topics which are both spatially and temporally distant from them.

Graphic Presentation. One of the predominant features of social science curricula is the use of graphics to illustrate concepts. But what is striking are the many levels of symbolization, from a child getting his hair cut, to pictures of Eskimos, to aerial photographs of cities and perspective photos of city streets. It is rather amusing, in a way, that these graphics take for granted that children can deal with the near-far symbolization that the science lesson is trying to teach them! But the near-far issue is not the problem with the photographs. To really relate to them children need to tie them to their own experience. How much more meaningful and exciting the photographs would be if they were of the child's city, the child's street, or the child's school.

The trouble with pictures of Eskimos or Chinese is that they are idealizations that have little to do with reality. A child who sees happy, smiling Eskimo children may construct fantasies that have nothing to do with the hardships of Eskimo life. American children also get the feeling that only America is modern and that all the rest of the world is still quite primitive. Partly this is because we depict foreign peoples in terms of what is colorful rather than what is going on at the present time. A product of this type of education, I still remember, on my first trip to Europe as a young man, how surprised I was to find elevators and other "modern" conveniences. What impressions children do get of foreign places from social studies materials are thus likely to lead to erroneous assumptions and reconstructions.

I want to emphasize, again, my belief that social studies can be taught at the elementary school level. What is required is that we look at the world from the child's perspective as well as our own. Once we do this we can find many objects, experiences, and events that bridge the two perspectives. Field trips of all sorts, to farms, museums, concerts, planetariums, and so on provide the kinds of experience that make for a solid foundation in social studies.

THE ARTS

Teaching the arts in schools presents many of the same problems of the other curricula. In fact, the arts are often taught more poorly because teachers, on the whole, know less about them than about other subjects. As in the other curricular domains, problems often arise because the tasks are too complex for the children to cope with in a competent, successful way.

Drawing and painting are cases in point. From the preschool years through the early elementary grades drawing seems to evolve naturally in children. At first they begin with scribbles but then they quickly move to drawing shapes. Children are first and foremost interested in drawing shapes and forms that are pleasing. When children begin to draw forms that resemble horses, people, and animals, they are not really trying to depict what they see but rather what they know or feel about them. Much as the young child creates new words to express his unique conceptions, so he creates new forms to re-present his own unique perceptions.

"Often, however, the child's spontaneous art collides head-on with the typical formulas adults have passed down from one generation to another. Watchful and well-meaning teachers who coax young children to draw real life objects are not being helpful; indeed their efforts may stifle the pride, the pleasure, the confidence so necessary to the growth of the creative spirit" (Kellogg and O'Dell, 1967, p. 17). In art, therefore, the imposition of adult standards and demands can actually inhibit and block further development. "Most children, however, lose interest in drawing after the first few years of school because they are not given this chance to develop freely" (p. 17).

This is not to say that the teacher has no part to play in art instruction, for he does. Drawing is a connotative skill and the teacher can provide help by providing materials (paints, easels, etc.) and the time and opportunity to draw and paint them too. The teacher can help children with the mechanics of holding pencils, mixing paints, and so on. But the content and manner of execution have to be left to the children themselves.

As in the case of art, children's creative verbal expression has to be encouraged without undue direction. Asking children to write rhymed poetry, for example, blocks free expression, puts severe restraints on the child's already limited vocabulary. On the other hand, having children write their own stories, free verse, or descriptive passages (about what the children see or have seen) often yields aesthetically pleasing work. And when they write in this way children learn both how to express their feelings and to communicate with others. Below are pieces of writing done by one of the Mt. Hope School students:

Lies

I took a flying carpet to school, the school
bus flew up to space.
I saw a dinosaur knock down Xerox Square.
I saw a martian come out of a flying saucer in my backyard.
My garbage can blasted off like a rocket ship.
I saw a sea monster pop out of the Barge Canal.
I was in New York City and I saw Godzilla knock down the
Empire State Building.

Red

It reminds me of fire engines.
It reminds me of green because green people are on Mars,
and Mars is red.
And Mars reminds me of Jupiter and Jupiter has a red spot
that can fit four earths!
The red lights and balls on the Christmas tree and
the fourth of July, the red firecrackers.

EUGENE CLANCY

Drama is another domain where children show spontaneous interest and development. In the early years the sense of drama can be seen in children when they play "house" or "grown-up." Mimicry, of adults and of other children, and mime are also quite natural and spontaneous to children even if they are sometimes put to less than noble ends. As in the case of drawing and writing, the child's dramatic impulse should not be stifled by too much adult direction, memorization of parts and so on. First let children express what they hear, see, and feel with their bodies and expressions. "Let's be cats" or "let's be lions" is all the stage direction children need to begin with.

Closely related to drama is movement. In recent years there have been some truly creative programs for children in movement and gymnastics. In these domains as in the others, I have already described, children can really do graceful, appealing work if their natural spontaneity can be encouraged. But this encouragement is more than putting on a record and telling the children to dance, it involves setting a mood and a theme for which the music and the movement are a natural accompaniment.

The last area I will deal with is music, which paradoxically has some of the best curricula for children but it is often provided outside of the schools. Playing an instrument (as opposed to composing or directing) is basically a sensorimotor skill. As such it is an artistic skill that children can master, with more or less proficiency, at an early age. The Suzuki system, where young children are taught to play the violin by ear, is the prime example. Young children in the Suzuki program can play quite acceptable violin concerti at four years of age. But the teaching is accomplished by imitation and not by reading music. Reading music is taught much later.

Learning to play an instrument can thus be taught, at least initially, as a figurative skill. Later, when the child begins to read music and to write some of his or her own songs, it becomes an operative skill as well. Finally, during adolescence when young people get into composition and theory, it also becomes a connotative skill.

Music, then, provides a good model of a domain where the sequence of skills taught closely parallels the Piagetian stages of development. It is not surprising, therefore, that music education is the most successfully taught of the art forms. More people probably play instruments well than write well, paint, or draw well. What is distressing about good music education is that most of it is done privately, outside the school. There is, in the school, little provision for group instruction, much less for private lessons, and little money for instruments. Music education in the schools often amounts to little more than music *appreciation.*

Music provides a domain in which there is a curriculum nicely suited to the child's cognitive and physical capacities. The variety of instruments, moreover, can accommodate a variety of individual differences in interests and talents. The sense of competence a child gains in learning to play an instrument, the sense of cooperation that comes in playing with others, and the sense of satisfaction that music itself provides, all speak to the importance of music education. To be sure, not all children are musically inclined, but no special aptitude is required to play some instruments in an acceptable if not an inspired fashion. How regrettable it is that the one curriculum most suited to the child, the music curriculum, is not sufficiently emphasized in our public schools. In my opinion music education should become an important part of the elementary school curriculum, with financial provision for instruments and small group lessons.

IX
THE ACTIVE CLASSROOM

> "As for those new methods of education that have had the most durable success, and which without doubt constitute the foundation of tomorrow's active school, they all more or less draw their inspiration from a doctrine of the golden mean, allowing room both for internal structural maturation and also for the influences of experience and of the social and physical environment."
>
> J. PIAGET

All of the preceding chapters have, in their own way, been leading up to this one; namely, the implications of Piagetian psychology for classroom practice. Piaget (1970b) himself, when describing schools and classrooms that he believes exemplify a developmental approach, prefers the term "active" to describe them, and that is why the term is used here. Very simply, an active classroom or an active school is one in which there is a great deal of operative and connotative, as well as figurative, learning taking place. This chapter will describe ways of facilitating these three modes of learning: through provisioning, grouping, the teacher's role, classroom rhythms, and discipline.

PROVISIONING

Provisioning has to do with arranging and outfitting a classroom so that it encourages figurative, operative, and connotative learning on the part of the children. In this discussion of provisioning, I will rely rather heavily upon my observations of some informal British primary schools. To my mind, the provisioning in the most exemplary of these schools represents a concrete embodiment of what Piaget suggests is an appropriate environment for active participation on the part of children.

As far as general arrangements go, a classroom outfitted with child-sized tables and chairs is to be preferred to rows of desks. Having a number of movable desks in the classroom is, nonetheless, valuable because some children need or prefer the security and structure a single desk can afford. The advantages of tables and chairs over desks are many, but the most important is the facilitation of small-group interaction. Such interaction, as we shall see in the discussion of discipline at the end of the chapter, is a very important part of a classroom organized along Piagetian lines. Tables also facilitate teacher mobility and the flexible grouping that will be described later. Last, but not least, tables give children large and comfortable work areas.

With respect to actual materials, these should be selected with an eye to encouraging all three modes of learning. Figurative materials might include math and reading workbooks and even dittoed exercise sheets (preferably screened according to the principles of curriculum analysis described in the preceding chapter). Operative materials might include such materials as geoboards, chip trading, attribute blocks, and materials that the children themselves have brought in such as shells, pine cones, leaves, and stones. Connotative materials would include everything from paints to linoleum blocks. Moreover, connotative learning can also be encouraged by attractive displays, flower arrangements, sculptures, antiques, and paintings that lend grace and interest to a classroom.

Some materials actually promote all three types of learning. Plants and animals, for example, are aesthetically pleasing and can serve as starting points for pieces of descriptive writing or line drawings. They can also serve operative learning if children do such things as measure them periodically and chart growth as a function of time. Plants and animals can also aid figurative learning by furthering vocabulary (terms naming, and relating to, animals) and aiding discriminations (say between male and female hamsters). Plants and animals also provide opportunities for small-group interactions around shared responsibilities—caring for the plants and animals—which can be beneficial to mental growth and personal discipline.

One feature of some of the well-provisioned classrooms that I observed was a place set aside as a "quiet corner" and provided with a bit of carpet, some soft pillows, a record player, and some books. Such quiet corners allow children to be alone when they need to be or simply to take a break from an ongoing activity that is very demanding or that is becoming a bore. In this regard it is well to recall that, as Piaget says, children are more like adults in their modes of functioning than in their mental structures. Children get bored, tired, and need to stretch their legs occasionally no less than adults do. The provision of a quiet corner addresses this facet of child functioning.

Another aspect of provisioning has to do with the children's own work. Many teachers who run active classrooms like to leave space in the room to fill up with the children's work as the year progresses. In one school I visited children were allowed to choose from examples of their own work and to display their choices. The children, of course, did not have to display any of their work if they did not choose to. This practice, it seemed to me, was a nice way of fostering the child's aesthetic sense.

A final aspect of provisioning should receive special mention. This has to do with reflecting the regional environment in the school. I recall visiting a school in Montana where outside the windows were mountains, vari-colored rocks, wild flowers, fossils, and so on. But none of these were in evidence within the classroom. Some aspects of the immediate surroundings of a school should be brought indoors to make the school more continuous with the environment. Sometimes it can be the ethnic environment that is reflected in the school. In Denver, for example, the Del Pueblo School has mostly Mexican-American children and the motif is

Spanish throughout, including large wall murals in warm tones and displays of basketry, weaving, and pottery. It is a school in which young Mexican-Americans can feel at home. And for ghetto children, bringing aspects of the country into the city can also be helpful. Apples for cider, grapes for jelly, and peanuts for peanut butter, help bring the country environment into the city.

Provisioning a classroom, therefore, should be done with the encouragement of figurative, operative, and connotative learning in mind. In my view, a classroom should be a continuation of the natural environment and of the home environment rather than be starkly separated from these. Out of doors and at home the child learns operatively and connotatively, and these modes of learning are most encouraged when the classroom provides examples of the richness and variety of the natural and cultural worlds that exist outside the school.

Provisioning classrooms at the secondary level should follow the principle of making the school environment continuous with rather than separate from the outside world. But whereas children need the natural world brought within the school to exercise and develop their abilities, young adolescents need the social world brought into the school. Pictures of current adolescent idols, as well as those of contemporary political and literary figures, can be displayed. Young adolescents can also appreciate abstract art and sculpture, and displays of this sort of work can be made available too. At this level, classrooms are generally more specialized, and displays should reflect something of the subject matter. Photographs of Paris, some tools of wine making, and so on could be in a room where French is taught. Displays at this level should provoke curiosity, expand vocabulary, and satisfy young people's aesthetic sense.

FLEXIBLE GROUPING

One of the ongoing controversies in education has to do with ability grouping, grouping children within a classroom according to levels of academic attainment. I do not want to go into all of the psychological pros and cons here, but instead would like to approach the problem from the standpoint of Piaget's psychology. Piaget (1950) distinguishes between "vertical" and "horizontal" *décalage*, or separations. Vertical *décalage* has to do with qualitative differences in mental ability. The difference between children at the level of concrete and at the operations level of formal operations is an example of a vertical *décalage*. Horizontal *décalage* has to do with differences in the age of attainment of various concepts at a certain level of mental ability. On average, children discover the conservation of number a year before they discover the conservation of length, although both require only concrete operations. This is a horizontal *décalage*.

Within elementary classrooms, therefore, there is the possibility of two kinds of groupings—those separating children at different levels of cognitive *development* (vertical *décalage*) and those separating children at different levels of cognitive *attainment* (horizontal *décalage*). Clearly, the vertical separation is more crucial than the horizontal, because it presupposes providing curriculum materials at two quite different levels, for example, using classification and seriation work for preoperational children and number games and "math facts" for concrete-operational children. Horizontal grouping is often a matter of convenience in the grouping of materials and a way of preventing boredom among the more rapid learners.

Many of the arguments against such "ability" grouping are based on the negative psychological effects such grouping can have on children's self-concepts. A child in the slow group (whether vertical or horizontal) is stigmatized to himself and to his parents. And children in the advanced groups can get puffed up about themselves and lord it over slower children without regard for their feelings. Children function emotionally like adults in negative as well as in positive ways.

But grouping, which seems to be essential to the effective working of large groups of children, need not have negative effects.

First of all children grow and change rapidly and at different rates. At the Mt. Hope School the groups are constantly changing as some children surge ahead while others march along at a steady pace. Moreover, by making the groups small and increasing their number, the gradations become less distinct and there is more concern with the work at hand than with the level of grouping. But the main point is that the grouping is flexible and that group composition is always changing in response to individual patterns of growth and learning.

One form of flexible grouping that makes good psychological sense, and has been successful in the British primary schools and worked well in many American elementary schools, is vertical age grouping. In England, for example, many primary classes include five-, six- and seven-year-olds, while at the older age levels, eight- and nine-year-olds and ten- and eleven-year-olds are combined. Particularly at the younger age levels such vertical age grouping has distinct advantages. One of these is that it capitalizes upon the attachment dynamism described earlier (Chapter VI). When children have the same teacher for three years, strong bonds of attachment are formed that facilitate the child's learning in order to please and to reward the teacher. In addition, children get to feel that the classroom is *their* room and not the private possession of the teacher.

In addition, vertical grouping also facilitates the "age dynamism" discussed in Chapter VI. Younger children can model their behavior after that of the older children and be encouraged to read and write with the facility of the older children. The older children, in turn, can take pride in their accomplishments as they see how far they have come in just a few years. Similar benefits, although perhaps less powerful, are to be derived from vertical grouping at the older age levels. From the social motivational standpoint, therefore, vertical grouping makes good sense.

It also makes good sense from the point of view of cognitive development. Piaget (1948) argues that one of the important dynamics of mental growth is peer interaction. Such interaction is particularly potent when the children are close to one another in cognitive levels. Some recent research (Botvin and Murray, 1975) has shown that when children are close together in cognitive levels the children who are behind copy and learn from the children who are more advanced. A child who does not have conservation of weight may attain it from working with or observing a child who does.

Of course it could be argued that in some same-age classes there is already a tremendous spread of ability, perhaps of four or five years, and that vertical age grouping only compounds the grouping difficulties. In fact, however, the range of variability for three combined age groups is not much greater than it is for one. The reason is, of course, that the lower range of abilities among the older children is covered by the lower age ranges in the group, just as the higher range of abilities for young children is covered by the older groups. Vertical grouping also facilitates the utilization of many small groups, and this avoids some of the stigma of ability grouping.

Some other advantages of vertical age grouping should be mentioned, not the least of which is continuity within the group. Each year some children leave and some new children enter, but at least half of the group remains for at least another year and these remaining children are familiar with the classroom, the teacher, and the classroom routine. This group of veterans makes the incorporation of new children into a cohesive group much easier than if all the children were new from the very start. In England, some schools enter children on their birthdays rather than on a fixed starting day, and this, too, makes their incorporation into the group easier. In developmental terms, assimilation of the child into the group and accommodation of the group to the child is easier if there is an existing group than if the group itself needs to be formed from scratch.

THE TEACHER'S ROLE

The most general characteristics of the teacher of a truly active classroom are *flexibility* and *mobility*. Flexibility is all-important because the proportion of teacher direction has to vary depending upon whether the children are engaged in figurative, operative, or connotative learning. In addition the teacher has to be flexible in the sense of shifting priorities, from the school to the developmental or to the personal curriculum when circumstances demand. Mobility is important, because to observe children at their work and to be available for assistance and counsel the teacher must be moving among them and not sitting at the head of the room. The teacher in the active classroom moves to the children rather than the children moving to the teacher.

Obviously, flexibility and mobility are not the only attributes required of the teacher in the active classroom. An understanding of children, a mastering of curricula, skill at assessment, and caring for and commitment to children are also part of the ideal package. But in this section I want to focus on the teacher's role in instruction and to look a bit closer at the flexibility and mobility that are required to encourage the kind of active learning prescribed by a developmental approach to education.

Flexibility. The extent of teacher direction in children's learning has been a matter of continual debate. On the one hand the traditionalists argue that the teacher should play a major role in directing children's learning. In such a view the teacher decides which material the child is to learn, when he is to learn it, and how he is to learn it. Programmed learning is a good example of teacher- or authority-directed learning, in which all pupil options have been decided in advance by the curriculum.

At the other extreme is the almost total lack of teacher guidance and direction, such as the "Messing About" suggested by Hawkins (1971):

> There is a time [in elementary education] much greater in amount than commonly allowed, which should be devoted to

free and unguided exploratory work (call it play if you like, I call it work). Children are given materials and equipment—things—and are allowed to construct, test, probe and experiment without superimposed questions or instruction. I call this phase "Messing About". . . . In some jargon, this kind of situation is called "unstructured" which is misleading; some doubters call it chaotic which it can never be. "Unstructured" is misleading because there is always a kind of structure to what is presented in a class [p. 60].

From a developmental point of view, both approaches have their place in an active classroom so long as they do not dominate it. When children are engaged in figurative learning, for example, it is appropriate for the teacher to assume a relatively more directive role than, say, when children are engaged in operative or connotative learning. In helping children with phonics or with writing or with arithmetic computation, which are primarily figurative skills (although based upon logical abilities), the teacher needs to provide direction and modeling. The same is true for the use of cutting tools, the handling of animals, and so on. There are many kinds of information the teacher must convey directly which would not be practical—or might even be dangerous—for the child to discover by himself or herself.

In the case of operative learning, however, the teacher must play a much less directive part. Operative learning occurs when children discover concepts through their own active exploration of materials. The guidance and encouragement of operative learning may be said to be one of the more difficult of the teacher's tasks. It involves a most delicate balance between teacher and child direction that is perhaps best exemplified in Piaget's (1951a) semiclinical interview procedure:

MART (9;5): "How did the sun begin?—*I don't know, it's not possible to say.*—"You are right there, but we can guess. Has there always been a sun?"—*No. It's the electricity which has always been growing more and more.*"—Where does this electricity come from?"—*From under the earth, from water.*"—What is electricity?"

—*It's the current.* "Can a current of water make electricity?"—
Yes."—What is this current made of?"—*It's made of steam.*
(Steam, electricity and current seem to him to be all the same
thing.) "How did the electricity make the sun?"—*It is current
which has escaped.* "How has it grown?"—*It's the air which has
stretched, the electricity has been made bigger by the air.*

SCHM (8;8): "How did the sun begin?"—*With fire, it's a ball of
fire which gives light.*—"Where does the fire come from?"—*From
the clouds.*—"How does that happen?"—*It's electricity in the
clouds.*—"Do you think that somebody made the sun?"—*No, it
came all alone.* "The sun is alive and conscious." [p. 278]

Note that in this example, the examiner begins with a leading
question (teacher direction, but then follows up the child's answer
(child direction) with a question designed to get the child to
elaborate his response (teacher direction). In the same way I once
brought some of my wine-making equipment to the Mt. Hope
School (teacher direction), but the children were concerned not
with making wine, but with how the press and crusher worked
(children direction), so we began talking about how wheels and
levers work (teacher direction) until the children decided they
would like to see the crusher in action (child direction).

Operative learning, the acquisition of concepts by reasoning and
induction from actual experiences with materials and things, is
neither totally child-directed nor totally teacher-directed but involves a flexible interchange of leadership. It was the lack of such a
flexible interchange between teacher and child to which Piaget
(1970b) objected in his visit to Susan Isaacs's famed "Malting House
School."

And indeed, in the little Malting House School in Cambridge, Mrs. Isaacs and her collaborators did in fact abstain
rigorously from all adult intervention, on the theory that it is
precisely adult instruction and its clumsy mistakes that prevent children from working. What they did do was to present
their pupils with what amounted to a genuine, fully-equipped
laboratory so that they could then be left to organize their
experiments themselves. The children, ranging from three to

eight years in age, had the greatest possible number of raw materials and instruments at their disposal: test tubes, boiling tubes, Bunsen burners, etc., not to mention all the apparatus for natural history study. The results were by no means without interest; the children, even at that early age, did not remain inactive in this environment so well equipped for research, but undertook all sorts of manipulations that were evidently of passionate interest to them; they were really learning to observe and to reason as they observed, both individually and in common. But the impression that my visit to this astonishing experimental school made upon me was twofold. On the one hand, even these exceptionally favorable circumstances were insufficient to erase the various features of the child's mental structure. . . . On the other hand, some form of systematization applied by the adult would perhaps not have been wholly harmful to the pupils. Needless to say, in order to draw any conclusion it would have been necessary to pursue the experiment up until the end of the subjects' secondary studies; but it is highly possible that the result would have demonstrated, to a greater degree than these particular educationalists would wish, the necessity for a rational, deductive activity to give a meaning to scientific experiment, and the necessity also, in order to establish such a reasoning activity in the child, for a surrounding social structure entailing not merely cooperation among the children but also cooperation with adults [pp. 168–69].

Practice in giving the Piagetian tests such as those described in Chapter VII is thus helpful in guiding operative learning. Such learning can be initiated by something that is brought into a classroom, such as a telescope, a plant, an animal, or an antique beer mug. Obviously whatever material one starts with exercises a certain amount of direction. But children still have plenty of leeway to pursue the subject from their own perspective. The teacher then follows their lead and helps them to elaborate questions and suggests ways of finding answers. In a very real sense, operative learning involves the Socratic method and is exciting and challenging for both teacher and learner.

In connotative learning the teacher exercises less direction and the children exercise more. When children have enjoyed an operative activity observation and discussion about pine cones and wild flowers, say, it is appropriate for them to be allowed to re-present their experience in their own way—verbally, graphically, or otherwise to engage in connotative learning. Figurative learning provides the tools for such expression while operative learning provides the content. The teacher provides children the opportunity, the time, and materials. But the teacher also provides *standards*. The teacher's most important role in connotative learning is to help children do work of the quality that they are really capable of doing.

In this connection some observations I made when visiting informal schools in England are relevant. In one classroom the children were working on linoleum blocks. One young man had done his carelessly and the teacher suggested that he do it over because "you can do better work than this." In another classroom the children were writing stories. One girl had finished her story and asked the teacher to read it, which he did. The teacher read it and said it was excellent, but noted that there was much crossing out of words and cramped writing. He suggested that she copy it over carefully so that (if she chose) it could be displayed for visitors to see. In connotative learning the teacher is far from passive, he is active in a different way than he would be in figurative learning.

Flexibility, then, is the keynote for the teacher in the active classroom. Sometimes he will assume much direction, sometimes little. And the nature of that direction will itself be different, depending upon the kind of learning. In figurative learning the teacher often serves as a model for imitation, while in operative learning he is a colleague in an ongoing exploration. But in connotative learning the teacher is a critic, challenging the child to do his best work. *Model, colleague, critic*—these are the major roles the teacher must play in the improvisational theater that is the active classroom.

There is another kind of flexibility that is required of the teacher in the active classroom and this is the readiness to shift curriculum priorities as the situation demands. For example, soon after the Mt. Hope School opened there was a theft. A young man came in and took the secretary's purse from her desk. One of the teachers saw the young man leave the building and gave chase, while the secretary called the police. It was a case of overkill and soon there were four police cars, with lights twirling and radios blaring, in the parking lot. The young man was caught and led, handcuffed, into one of the police cars. There was questioning by detectives, fingerprint taking, and much more before the police contingent left.

Fortunately the children were inside and heard but did not see much of the commotion. The teachers told them what had happened, and that the young man had been caught. Not surprisingly the children were very excited by the whole episode and too agitated to continue working on their reading and math. The teachers wisely decided to allow the children to draw pictures of the thief, and the police cars, or to write stories about the event. "Working through" the excitement of the theft was a personal curriculum priority that in this case had to take precedence over the school curriculum. Other, more pleasant occasions—like the visit of an important person to the school or community—may also require a modification of priorities.

Mobility. In an active classroom, where children work in small groups or alone, the teacher has to move about observing and interacting. Teacher mobility is not only essential to facilitate small groups and individual work, it is also essential to the spirit of the classroom. A teacher who is mobile, who does not sit at the head of the class all day, suggests a very different kind of authority than one who does. Children after the age of six or seven know adults are fallible and do not have all the answers. Teachers who assume that they have all the answers and that they have nothing to learn appear pompous and ridiculous to children who have no real respect for their authority.

On the other hand, the mobile teacher, the one who works alongside children and who learns with them, communicates a very different kind of authority. It is an authority of method, not of content, of how to approach problems and to find solutions, not one of providing answers. Children can accept the authority of method because it is demonstrable—the teacher can show them how. But the authority of content is always arguable, can be challenged and debated. When a teacher says, "Columbus discovered America," a child may mutter under her breath, "My father said Leif Ericson did."

The mobile teacher, who moves among children, of necessity communicates a different spirit than the teacher who sits in front of them. It is a cooperative spirit, one of working together toward common goals buttressed by mutual respect and consideration. This cooperative, democratic spirit is difficult if not impossible to achieve if the teacher sits at the front of the classroom and receives children at his desk. This physical arrangement automatically makes the teacher the higher authority. Teacher mobility, therefore, in many different ways, communicates the cooperative democratic spirit of the active classroom.

Before closing this section it is important to note the changes in teacher role occasioned by different stages of cognitive development. At the preschool level, when children lack concrete operations, formal instruction or figurative learning is inappropriate because children cannot follow rules very well. So at the preschool level the emphasis has to be on operative learning and on connotative learning wherein the teacher plays a limited directive role. Figurative learning in the preschool child is generally limited to learning to label such things as forms, colors, and letters.

In the elementary school, once children have attained concrete operations, figurative learning, particularly of the sight vocabulary aspects of reading and the mechanical (handwriting) aspects of writing and math, is appropriate. In the early grades perhaps as much time needs to be given to this type of learning as to the operative and connotative modes. After the tool skills have been mastered, more weight can be given to operative and connotative learning, say in science and in social studies, and figurative learning can be continued in giving children additional skills in the practical arts, printing, painting, weaving, etc.

With adolescence, and the advent of formal operations, learning modes become more differentiated in coordination with the subject matter and ways of teaching, i.e., teachers teaching only one subject. In effect, different teachers become specialists in subjects wherein one or another learning mode predominates. At the junior and senior high school levels of education, figurative learning is represented by teachers in the manual arts (wood shop, machine shop) and languages (French, Latin). Operative learning is represented by teachers of social studies and science (usually physics, biology, and chemistry), whereas connotative learning is represented by teachers of literature and of the fine arts.

In describing contemporary American education in cognitive developmental terms I am not advocating the status quo. There is, at a very general level, a rough correspondence between school structure and cognitive development and it would be surprising if this were not so. But the extent to which the different disciplines are in fact taught—figuratively, operatively, or connotatively—is probably far from desirable. At the high school level both science and literature may be taught figuratively even though the structure of the disciplines cries out for operative and connotative approaches. So what would seem possible in principle, the provision of all three types of learning for each and every subject at the high school level, may not occur in fact because of a preference for and adherence to figurative learning.

THE RHYTHM OF THE SCHOOL DAY

In *The Psychology of Intelligence*, Piaget (1950) talks about biological rhythms, such as hunger and thirst, as predecessors of the functioning of intelligence itself: "Rhythm, regulations and 'grouping' thus constitute the three phases of the developmental mechanism which connects intelligence with the morphogenetic potentialities of life itself" (p. 173). What Piaget suggests is that there may be a waxing and waning of assimilative and accommodative activities with a balancing equilibration as an end point.

It is probably reading too much into Piaget to say that he suggests some such rhythm for the school day. And yet a rhythm of this sort would certainly be consistent with the theory and seems a useful starting point for discussing the patterning of the school day. Such an approach suggests that the school day should provide opportunities for figurative learning (accommodation), for operative learning (assimilation), and for connotative learning (equilibration). When such activities should appear in the school day is perhaps less important than that they should occur.

One thing is clear, however, and it is implicit in Piaget's statement, that we are all, adults as well as children, rhythmic creatures. We seem to function best if there is a regular pattern or schedule to our activities. Routines or schedules are like concepts, once you have them they operate automatically and save one the trouble of accommodating anew to each novel situation. Instead of reacting "what is that?" we can say "that's another fingagubub" and be done with it. Schedules and routines, if they are not too rigid, free us to devote all our energies to the task at hand.

What routine or schedule the school day follows is probably less important than that there be some routine or schedule. Even the so-called "integrated" or "unbroken" day followed in the informal British primary schools has a pattern. There is, for example, a break at midday for lunch and there is a quiet time for gathering together and hearing a story at the end of the day. And the children, though free to choose their own activities, often build up regular patterns of work on their own.

Some sort of schedule or routine is thus important not only because it is economical with respect to time, but because it corresponds to a rhythmicity which is part of our organismic nature. At the Mt. Hope School we have a routine which suits our children and our needs, but certainly is not a model for all schools. I describe it here because it grows out of our experience, but I recognize that we have a richness of adults and that a single teacher responsible for thirty children may not be able to use it as a model. For many teachers work of all kinds may have to be distributed throughout the day.

One observation, which may not be novel but yet seems important for classroom scheduling, is that most children are at their brightest in the morning. The morning hours are the ones in which the most productive work gets done. We use the mornings primarily for work in academic skills, which are the most difficult because they involve figurative, operative, and connotative learning. Learning to read, for example, involves perceptual recognition of individual letters (figurative learning), the combination of one sound with multiple letters and multiple letters with one sound (operative learning), and the connection of printed words with concepts and objects (connotative learning). A similar kind of analysis could be made for math.

So we start the day with a circle meeting to plan for the day, to hear any news the children wish to communicate, and to make any special announcements about future events. Then the children break into small groups for work in math and reading. At noon they have an hour to eat their lunch, to play games, or to go out of doors when the weather is nice. The afternoons are given over to excursions to farms, to the library, to the zoo; or to gym, art, music, or science activities. Discussions about displays, such as the pine cones collected earlier, often take place in the afternoons. At the end of the day the children get together as a group to hear a story or to listen to records.

The positioning of art, music, and science in the afternoon does not mean that we regard these as of less value than the other subjects. Rather we believe that the first few years of schooling are crucial for the attainment of tool skills and that the child's most productive hours should be devoted to them. Active inquiry into science and social studies requires tool skills as a basis. At the later grade levels, after the tool skills have been mastered, science, literature, social studies, art, and music can begin to share the "golden" hours of the morning.

In general, then, some sort of schedule or rhythm for the school day is essential. But routines and schedules should be flexible enough to bend for special events, such as parties and visiting dignitaries. And schedules should be responsive to children's needs, to extraordinary growth patterns. And it should be remembered too, that while regular routines are comfortable, breaks in routine are invigorating. A schedule should always be the teacher's servant, never the master.

DISCIPLINE

Probably the most pervasive and difficult issue in running a classroom is the matter of discipline. Before I attempt to describe the sort of discipline that would be present in an active classroom, some general discussion is necessary. Although Piaget does not often talk about affective issues, when he does it is usually around the matter of discipline and respect. Accordingly, a brief review of Piaget's position regarding discipline in general might be useful before describing how it might be instituted in practice.

From a developmental perspective, discipline is not a unitary phenomenon but one that undergoes transformations with age and the development of cognitive abilities. In young, preoperational children, discipline is largely external, and children behave in socially appropriate ways for fear of punishment from adults or in order to win adult approval. After the age of six or seven and the advent of concrete operations, discipline remains external but is now exercised by two agencies, adults on the one hand and the peer group on the other. It is only in adolescence that discipline becomes truly internal in the sense that the young person behaves in socially appropriate ways to satisfy himself as well as out of respect for others. It is for this reason that Piaget says that it is only in adolescence that a young person has a "true" personality.

This general development from external to internal discipline comes about, according to Piaget (1948), as a consequence of the child's progressive understanding of rules on the one hand, and the evolution of feelings of respect on the other. Discipline, from this standpoint, is at once cognitive and affective, involving as it does the subordination of personal impulses and desires to the control of rules at first laid down from without, but eventually from within. In discussing the evolution of discipline, then, we can first look at the development of the child's understanding of rules and then at his evolving feelings of respect.

In his book *The Moral Judgment of the Child* (1948), Piaget suggests that the understanding of rules evolves in a series of stages related to age. Among preschool children, rules are seen as part of physical reality and are believed to have existed forever and to be immutable. During the concrete operational stage children come to see rules as man-made and changeable. Then, with adolescence and the attainment of formal operations, higher-order ethical and moral rules are constructed which are believed to hold for all mankind but which may not be obeyed by all.

Coincident with this development is the evolution of respect. In his writings on this subject Piaget leans heavily on the work of Bovet (1926). Bovet argued that, in the young child, rules are obeyed largely out of respect for adults. For Bovet, respect is a complex emotion involving a combination of love and fear. In young children, according to Bovet, respect is *unilateral* inasmuch as it constrains the child to obey adults but not the reverse (except in pathological cases where children dominate parents by the use of tantrums and so on). Adults may respect children but in another way—i.e., through love and fear for their immediate and future well-being. But it is not a respect that entails following the commands of the child. This period of unilateral respect coincides with the belief that rules are fixed and immutable.

During childhood proper, after children attain concrete operations, a new form of respect emerges. This form of respect grows out of the concrete operational child's new-found ability to relate to peers in meaningful ways. Thanks to his egocentrism, the preoperational child cannot take the point of view of others when it is different from his own. Two young children thus talk *at* rather than *to* one another. For example, two children in a sandbox were heard to carry on the following conversation:

"My mommy is going to buy me some new shoes, red ones!"

"This block is too big, I need a small one."

"My Mommy is going to buy me a new coat too!"

But once a child has concrete operations, he can put himself in another child's position and see things from his perspective. This is crucial to meaningful conversation that requires both parties to follow the other's train of thought as well as his own.

Out of this new mode of communication among peers emerges a new form of respect, *mutual respect*. Like unilateral respect, mutual respect involves a combination of positive and negative emotions. The positive emotion is that of "liking" one's age mates and enjoying their company. The negative emotion is fear of being disliked, rejected, or made fun of by peers. Unlike unilateral respect, mutual respect puts children on an equal plane with one another. It goes along with the understanding that rules are people-made and changeable. At this stage children often make up their own rules (of a game) and follow them with considerable exactitude.

Although neither Piaget nor Bovet discusses it directly, it seems to me that their work suggests that a new form of respect emerges in adolescence with the attainment of formal operations. This is *self-respect.* Like the other forms of respect, self-respect also grows out of a combination of love and fear, this time directed toward the self. It is a new form of respect because only in adolescence, thanks to formal operations, can young people develop a sense of themselves as a totality, putting together into some working whole all the diverse and contradictory things that they know about themselves. Self-respect waits upon what Erikson (1950) calls a "sense of ego identity."

Self-respect involves a love for one's positive qualities and a fear that one will not have the will power to follow courses of action, to obey rules, that one has committed oneself to. Self-respect thus coincides with conception of rules as *ideas* that one can understand and try to live up to because they have been incorporated into the self. A failure to live up to rules and commitments incorporated into the self damages its integrity. Hence, in adolescence self-respect becomes a powerful motive for obedience to social norms.

From a developmental point of view, self-respect, which is the basis for principled social life, grows out of mutual respect. The concern about acceptance and rejection by peers gets transformed, in adolescence, into concern about acceptance and rejection of the self. The importance of the peer group in this transformation was stressed by Sullivan (1953) in his concept of "chumship." Sullivan believed that it was through close chumships, formed in late childhood, that young people were able to elaborate their self-concepts and to establish principled modes of interaction and true intimacy in adult life.

At each stage of development then, discipline involves a relation between rules on the one hand, and respect on the other. What mediates obedience to rules is a *sense of obligation,* the interface between rules and respect. But the feeling of obligation occurs only in relation to someone the child respects, toward whom he or she feels both love and fear. In *To Understand Is To Invent* (1973) Piaget writes:

> The small child does not feel obligated to obey an order from a brother whom he loves, or from a stranger whom he

only fears, while orders from the mother or father make him obligated and this continues to be felt even if the child disobeys. This first type of relationship (obligation based on unilateral respect) assuredly the earliest in the formation of clinical sentiments, is capable besides of remaining at work during the entire childhood, and to outweight all others, depending on the type of ethical education adopted [p. 115].

Piaget argues that unilateral respect is insufficient to provide children with a moral and ethical rudder in later childhood and adolescence:

While it is unilateral, this initial type of respect is, above all, a factor of dependency. Doubtless the child discovers in growing up that the adult subjects himself—or at least endeavors to subject himself without always being able to do so in fact—to the orders that he gives. The rule is thus sooner or later felt to be superior to those he respects. On the other hand, the child one day experiences a multiplicity of instructions, sometimes contradictory, and finds himself in the position of having to make choices and establish hierarchies. But without a source of outside ethical behavior other than unilateral respect alone, he will remain what he was at the beginning—an instrument submissive to ready-made rules, and to rules whose origin remains external to the subject accepting them [p. 116].

During the concrete-operational period and the formation of mutual respect, a different feeling of obligation emerges. This obligation is different in that at this level children, in Piaget's words, "participate in the elaboration of the rule that obligates them." Piaget argues that this new mode of obligation imposes upon children not just obedience to the rules, but also to the *method* of forming rules. That is, the child begins to feel obligated to construct or elaborate rules by "coordinating the points of view of others with his or her own."

From Piaget's standpoint the problem of moral or ethical education, the attainment of a sense of obligation or discipline by the child, is directly parallel to the problem of education generally. That is to say, whether it is a sense of obligation or understanding of mathematics, the question is whether it is best learned by being imposed from without or constructed by the child in the course of his own efforts. Piaget writes:

> Education, founded on authority and only unilateral respect, has the same handicaps from the ethical standpoint as from the intellectual standpoint. Instead of leading the individual to work out the rules and the discipline that will obligate him or to work with others to alter them, it imposes a system of ready-made and immediately categorical imperatives on him. In the same way that a contradiction exists in adhering to an intellectual truth from outside (without having rediscovered and verified it) so it can be asked whether there does not exist some moral inconstancy in recognizing a duty without having come to it by an independent method [p. 118].

What one might add to Piaget's description is that in adolescence the sense of obligation is directed not toward persons, nor to the method of arriving at rules, but rather to the idea of obligation itself, that is to say, to a sense of *duty*. In adolescence young people feel obliged to honor their commitments, in the general sense, whether these obligations are to other persons or to rules or to the methods of their formation. The mutual respect and involvement in rule-making in childhood thus give rise, in adolescence, to a higher-order sense of obligation, the sense of duty, that is the motive behind much ethical and moral behavior.

The implications of these developmental considerations for classroom practice seem to be clear and unambiguous. Classrooms permitting group decision-making, with regard to rules and punishments for transgression, are more beneficial to psychological growth than classrooms where the rules are laid down from without. Children who are not allowed to participate in constructing some of the rules governing their own behavior are in the same position as children who are not permitted to reconstruct actively the concepts they are learning.

> In other words, just as a pupil can recite his lessons without understanding them and can substitute verbalism for rational activity, so a child obeying is sometimes a spirit subjugated to an external conformism, but does not understand the real meaning or facts surrounding the rules he obeys, or the possibility of adapting them or making new ones in different circumstances [p. 119].

For Piaget an active classroom has children who are involved not only in reconstructing reality but also in working out their own disciplines, where the sense of obligation comes from having been involved in the formulation of the rules and not from the authority of the teacher. In active classrooms, matters of property rights, of one child disturbing another, of keeping materials in good working order and the classroom reasonably neat can be matters for the group to deal with and to regulate.

It is important, too, that children not only be allowed to make some classroom rules but that they be allowed to change them as circumstances demand. A danger that has to be avoided in allowing children to make rules is the adult's tendency to codify and make permanent that which is transient for children. It must be remembered that it is the very process of making rules cooperatively that fosters mutual respect and obligation. Frequent repetition of the process is thus developmentally healthy and should not be prevented out of some sense of "you made the rules and you have to stick to them." Remaking the rules is part of the learning process.

Closely related to the matter of permitting the children to originate some (but certainly not all!) classroom rules is the matter of punishment. When children have a part in making the rules and in designating the consequences of breaking them, the result is far different from the adult making the rules, deciding on the punishment, and meting it out. When children break rules they themselves have made and accept the consequences they themselves have established, confidence in themselves is supported at the same time as is confidence in the system of rules. In contrast, arbitrary rules and punishments are "degrading to the person who administers them and whose principle is felt to be totally unjust by the child" (p. 124).

In conclusion, then, from a developmental perspective, discipline is not something separate from active education but is an integral part of it. If discipline is to be more than figurative, tacked on from outside without comprehension or commitment, then children have to be involved in the construction of at least some of the rules that regulate classroom life. Establishing and re-establishing rules is thus another very important activity in which children are encouraged to rediscover and reconstruct reality. Social reality, no less than physical reality, must be reconstructed by the child if it is to lead to true discipline based on respect for others in general and respect for one's self in particular.

CONCLUSION

In this book I have tried to present a systematic child development approach to education. The approach is systematic in that I attempted to derive principles of classroom practice from more general principles of child growth and development. The question I wish to deal with in this conclusion is the chance such a child development approach has of being accepted by American education. It is difficult to play the prophet and I have no special claim to clairvoyance. All that I can really do is to describe some of the social events and forces that seem conducive to the acceptance of the orientation described here and some that would appear to work against its becoming a major theme in American education. I am not going to attempt to be exhaustive or detailed, my aim is simply to highlight some diverse trends in American society and what they may imply for the kind of educational philosophy that has been described in this book.

It appears that America is currently overproducing teachers and that this trend will continue for some time into the future. That is unfortunate for the many young people who wish to move into the educational profession. But it does have the positive consequence that school systems can be much more selective in choosing from among the best-trained and qualified applicants. Obviously, any change will take place slowly because of tenure, but overall I see the quality of teachers and of teaching improving over the years. And I believe that concerned, dedicated, and bright teachers have always gravitated, intuitively or consciously, toward a child-development orientation in their teaching. So my hope is that a child-development orientation in the schools will slowly increase along with the improvement in the quality of teachers and of teaching.

Second, I believe that the impact of Piaget's work and theory will begin to be felt in more extensive and more significant ways than heretofore. When Piaget first became known on these shores, there was a great deal of conjecture about what his work meant for education. Much of the new curricula of the sixties was presumably guided by Piaget's work. But some of this work was based on a rather superficial reading of Piaget, and many of the more important educational implications of his work, such as curriculum analysis, rather than curriculum construction, were overlooked.

It appears that this situation is slowly changing and that there is emerging a new generation of psychologists and educators who have a deeper and more comprehensive understanding of what Piaget is all about. As this group increases in size, its influence upon teacher training, research, and administration will increase as well. The process is a slow one, but that is not unusual in science. Between the discovery of knowledge and its application in meaningful ways there is always considerable time lag. This is particularly true in social science, where new ideas have to overcome embedded attitudes and prejudices. Darwin's theory about the evolution of the species is a case in point. Piaget's revolutionary theories about the origins of human knowing take time to be assimilated and to be applied. I very much hope that this book will be part of a "second stage" in the application of Piaget's work to education which is broader and deeper than the work done during the first stage.

A third positive sign with respect to the future of a child-development orientation for education is at once more personal and more general. In my travels about the country talking to educational groups I am sustained by the many teachers who tell me or who write me to say how meaningful to them were the child-development concepts I presented. The concepts did not really tell them anything they did not know already. But the concepts did help them to organize their experience and to get new insights by looking at classroom behavior from a child-development perspective. I suppose my greatest hope for the future of a child-development orientation in education is the promise it holds for teachers. Once teachers learn about the work of Piaget it is really impossible for them ever to see children in quite the same way as before.

If there are positive signs favoring the gradual acceptance of a child-development orientation in education, there are negative ones as well. Children and education remain the scapegoats of the political system. If black children are not achieving in the schools it is the schools' fault, never mind the prejudices that exist outside the school and which discourage black children from making the effort needed to do well at academic work. And if America falls behind Russia in some technical field, let's get more science into the schools. Never mind the lack of foresight in political planning or the lack of government support for a particular area of research. *When the government or the society gets sick, children take the medicine.* It is hard to predict what new ailments will next afflict the local or the federal government, but the medicine is not likely to be child-development oriented. I see the political exploitation of children and education to be the single most serious hindrance to the establishment of a truly child-centered educational system in this country.

There are other hindrances as well. The extreme competitiveness of our society constantly works hardships on children and militates against the acceptance of a child-development orientation. When I hear parents bragging about how they are teaching their young preschool children to read, I have the impulse to shake them. It is parent need and not child need that dictates such teaching. Parents feel a pleasant sense of superiority when their children can do something the neighbors' children cannot. Never mind that the early-reading child is bored to death in kindergarten and is often a social isolate. And parents also push for curriculum content that is prestigious without regard for whether it makes any sense to the children. Only in America could a third-grader say, as one young man told me recently, "I have already had nuclear fission." The need to push children educationally, to satisfy parental pride—which is blind to the child's level of development and to his or her best interests—is a continuing hindrance to child-development-oriented education. It is important to add, however, that it is far from being entirely the parents' fault. Many parents have been persuaded by professionals and by the media that children will suffer if they are not taught academic skills early in life.

There is a last hindrance which, unfortunately, is to be found in educational personnel themselves. While it appears in different forms and guises, the theme is basically the same: "You can't beat the system so why try." When I speak to teachers many tell me that when they went into education they really had high ideals and wanted to set up exemplary classrooms. But their principals and supervisors frustrated them at every turn, imposing unwanted curricula, restricting purchases of new materials, and demanding excessive paper work. I listen and I know that much of what they say is true.

When I speak to principals they often tell me about their plans and their hopes for the school when they arrived, how they wanted a model school in which children were happy and learning and where parents were welcome. But it turned out that the teachers were not very cooperative. They rejected curriculum suggestions and were always asking for more money and privileges. Parents were quick to criticize but were slow to praise what was happening in the school. So, sadly, the principals had to give up some of their high hopes. I listen and I know that much of what they say is true.

And when I speak to superintendents they too tell me about the plans they had for the system, how they sometimes left better paying jobs and nicer communities because they thought the new job was a challenge and that they could really bring about change. They wanted to upgrade the academic achievement of the schools, introduce innovative programs that could be national models, and so on. But realities hit hard. The school board was full of conservatives who blocked initiatives in almost every direction. School principals were often too set in their ways to modify their schools and programs and parents were interested in getting children into college and not in the quality of education the children were receiving. I listen and I know that much of what they say is true.

Bringing about change in education is not easy, it never has been and it never will be. But I don't think we should give up; if I did I would never have bothered writing this book. Change in education will come slowly, by evolution and not by revolution. In this regard, I suppose, I have become a Christopher. I believe that each of us can light one little candle. A teacher might put a bit of rug in the room and create a quiet corner. A principal might introduce a coffee hour when she or he and the teachers could relax and socialize. And the superintendent might get the board members to visit a school and to see what is really going on. Little things, but they mean a lot. If each of us lights one little candle perhaps we can significantly brighten the lives of children in our schools.

APPENDIX

Some Questions and Answers

In some ways writing a book is like preparing a lecture. Both the writer and the lecturer choose the material they plan to present and decide when and how they will deliver it. The lecturer, however, has one advantage over the writer, namely, that he has immediate feedback from his audience. He can determine by their posture and movements whether the members of the audience are raptly attentive or profoundly bored. The lecturer can, if he is observant, adapt his message to his audience. But he has an added advantage as well—he can respond to questions. In so doing he deals with issues foremost in his listeners' minds but which may have been far removed from his own.

In this Appendix I would like to usurp the prerogatives of the lecturer and to answer some of the questions readers might possibly ask. These questions have not been made up out of whole cloth, but are some of the questions most frequently asked when I have presented some of the ideas given here at educational conferences and workshops. Some of these questions might have been answered in the text, but such incorporation would have been strained. On the other hand, taken together, the questions and answers have a kind of wholeness that justifies bringing them together here.

Q: You have emphasized the importance of teaching children at their own level. I wonder if there is not an inherent danger in such an approach. Isn't it possible to know too much about children? Perhaps by dealing with children at their level we rob children of some of the complexity and ambiguity that is essential to cognitive growth.

250

A: I believe that there is considerable truth in what you say and that we would never want to deprive children of the difficulty of confronting words and concepts that are beyond their level of comprehension. But that is impossible to do in any case. Children in our society are bombarded on every side with adult words and concepts, on television and on radio, on billboards, and in magazines and newspapers. The child's experience in school is but a small part of his total experience. It is just for that reason that the school should be a conceptual haven where the materials, concepts, and language are at the child's level. At school he should learn that he can master *some* concepts and *some* vocabulary and hence develop the confidence that he will later master concepts and words he does not understand.

The danger you suggest, that children will be deprived of the stimulation of having to deal with more complex language and concepts, would only be serious if we lived in a totally child-centered society. The likelihood of that happening is, in my opinion, remote. The opposite danger, of not having settings where children can operate at their own level of language and comprehension, seems much more real and much more frightening. That is why I advocate child-centeredness at home and at school, but not for the society as a whole.

Q: While we are talking about child-centeredness, how can you be sure that you really do appreciate the child's point of view? Could not your ideas about how the child sees the world be another "externalization?" How can you be sure you know what the child is thinking?

A: The point is a good one but reflects a misunderstanding that I have obviously contributed to. The child's point of view, no less than the adult's, is not a passive, fixed standpoint, but an ongoing, changing one. Any ideas that we have about the child's point of view have to be seen as guesses, as educated hypotheses about what is going on inside his head. To test out the guesses we have to talk with children and observe their behavior. We can check our guesses against this data and have to accept their truth or falseness with a certain degree of confidence, but never with complete certainty.

I suppose I am saying that we have to approach understanding the child's point of view in the same way that we approach the problem of taking another adult's point of view—through discussion and trial and check. We cannot be any more certain about another adult's point of view than about the child's. The real issue is to appreciate that the child's view may be different than our own and that we have to work every bit as hard to appreciate it as we do to appreciate the point of view of an adult. The aim of trying to look at the child's point of view is to help adults overcome their assumption that the child's perspective is the same as their own. While we appreciate that this is true for other adults, we do not believe it is true for children; it is a form of adult egocentrism.

We can never be sure we really do have the child's viewpoint, but that is less important than the fact that we make the effort to understand it. Children appreciate an adult's effort to understand them which communicates both liking and respect. Even though the effort does not fully succeed at the cognitive level, it does succeed at the affective level. So, perhaps we can never fully appreciate the child's point of view, but trying to appreciate that point of view is well worth the effort.

Q: What sort of education would you advocate for teachers?

A: My problem with this question is the disparity between a description of what I would like to be the case and what is actually happening in teacher-training. So let me speak to the ideal and then try to touch base with reality. First of all, I think advancement to teacher-training should involve selection, that not everyone who wants to should go into teacher-training. At the Mt. Hope School we carefully screen students before they are allowed to participate in the practicum course in which they work in the school. We try to screen out young people who want to get into the program for the wrong reasons, in most cases those "wrong" reasons are personal and highly idiosyncratic—like wanting to convert children to a particular ideology. In every profession, in every trade, there is a selection process; I believe there should be one in education too.

Please understand, I am well aware of the many dangers inherent in trying to set up criteria for selecting people to enter teacher-training. On the other hand, I believe that the dangers of not selecting are even greater. Some people, and they may be fine and outstanding individuals, should never set foot in a classroom. The most important criterion for a teacher is that he or she like and enjoy children. We find that students who have baby sat, worked in summer camps, done volunteer tutoring, and so on make our best students. Their interest in children was sufficient for them to seek out experiences with young people on their own. Other qualities that we look for are patience, openness and flexibility, and a sense of humor. These are not the only criteria, but they are very important ones.

As far as training itself goes, I believe that teachers should be, first and foremost, *child-development specialists*. That is to say, they should be thoroughly grounded in research and theory in child development and should themselves have experience in conducting investigations. (By the way, I believe psychologists who wish to do research on educational issues should have training as teachers.) Such training should involve extensive experiences in observing and in talking to children such as those described in the chapter on assessment (Chapter VII).

There are many reasons for training teachers as child development specialists. First of all, a scientific orientation of openness, of questioning, of appreciation for how much there is to know and how little we really know is a healthy one. It is an attitude we want to instill in children, and if teachers model it in their own behavior, a major share of the task will have been done. Second, a thorough understanding of children, as I have tried to suggest in this book, can become a basis for assessment, curriculum analysis, and classroom practice. Child development provides a conceptual and data base for teaching, so that it can be grounded in science *as well as* art. I certainly would not want to take the art out of teaching; I would like to get a little science in.

Training teachers as child-development specialists has other benefits as well. For one thing, it can give teachers a greater sense of professionalism, a sense that they have knowledge and skills that parents and administrators do not have. With this sense of professionalism, teachers can stand up to pressures they regard as injurious to children on scientific grounds. They can read the scientific literature and support their arguments with research evidence. We will only move toward a true science of education if teachers have a scientific orientation and if educational researchers have a genuine appreciation of what teaching in a classroom is all about.

I know much teacher-training is, in fact, far from this ideal. But teachers can acquire expertise in child development in other ways; evening-school courses, in-service workshops and so on. Of course not all courses in child development speak to educational issues. One of my aims in the present book is to come a little closer to the ideal I suggested above in that I have tried to show, in a systematic way, how Piagetian child psychology provides a comprehensive educational philosophy and practice.

Q: You have talked a lot about stages and the ages at which certain mental abilities usually appear. Is it possible to accelerate children, to get them, say, to concrete operations earlier? Wouldn't that be beneficial?

A: The question you raise is a familiar one and Piaget has encountered it so often in this country that he has dubbed it, "the American Question." The question has many different facets and I cannot touch on all of them here. First, and perhaps most important, Piaget's stages are stages of *development*. Human development involves maturation as well as experience and probably has an optimal rate for full growth and realization. Would we, even if we could, accelerate the average age of menarche to eight or nine for most girls?

The point is that when we talk about development we are talking about the child as a physical, social, and intellectual totality in which the social and the intellectual as well as the emotional and physical are in constant interaction. To talk about accelerating concrete operations is a little like talking about accelerating menarche in the sense that it assumes that the functions or abilities in question exist in a vacuum apart from the rest of the child. But they do not. As I have tried to show, particularly in the chapter on understanding the child, each stage of development involves an elaborate system of conceptions that relate to physical and emotional growth as well as to experience.

To be sure, it is possible to get children to improve in certain cognitive operations as a function of training. Piaget's coworkers have demonstrated this in a recent series of studies (Inhelder, Sinclair, and Bovet, 1974). But in those studies as in the one conducted by myself and my colleagues (Elkind, Koegler, and Go, 1962) the effects of training were always relative to the child's level of cognitive development. As a result of training the relative differences between children stay the same, but they all move up a bit.

But such training, and all training studies, touch only a limited portion of the child's intellectual world. The real problem with acceleration is that it is impossible to accelerate the child as a whole. And because intellectual development is in synchronization with other aspects of development, acceleration of cognitive development alone would be maladaptive. Consider the bright child who is emotionally immature and the problems one has in placing such a child in a classroom. Or think of the emotionally mature child who is slow in developing. Again, asynchrones in development present nothing but problems for teachers and parents, let alone the child. So the desire to accelerate children intellectually ignores the totality of the growth process and risks, if it is successful, the danger of producing developmental asynchrones detrimental to the young person.

Q: What about language and mental growth?

A: Again, this is a complex and a difficult issue. I can only give you what I believe to be Piaget's position and one with which I am in agreement. For Piaget, language emerges out of general intelligence but eventually becomes a mental system in its own right. In the beginning, therefore, the structures of language are limited by the structures of intelligence. There is considerable recent literature which supports this contention (cf. Brown, 1973; Bloom, 1975). A study by Sinclair-de Zevart (1969) illustrates this dependence. She found that preoperational children used words like "big" and "little" to describe three-dimensional objects. Concrete-operational children described the same objects as "tall" and "thin" or "wide and low." Training the young children in the use of dimensional terms had little effect, and they still did not use their description of objects.

So, in the early years, thought determines many aspects of language. As children grow older, the relationships shift. Although there is not a great deal of evidence on the matter, it could well be the case that a certain level of language proficiency is essential for the attainment of formal operations. The deaf, for example, are proficient in concrete operations but show some deficiencies in formal-operational thought. The blind, in contrast, show deficiencies in concrete-operational thought but are proficient in formal-operational thought (Furth, 1966).

A final point: Although the operative aspects of language are closely related to the child's level of cognitive development, the figurative aspects are not. Children acquire many more words than they understand. The young child's facility in language is often deceptive in that often he or she appears to know much more than he or she really understands. One has to be cautious, then, in taking a young child's language as a gauge of understanding. When young children ask about sex, for example, they are usually talking about the physical differences between men and women, not the physical interactions that unite them.

Q: You, and presumably Piaget, speak to the "average" child, to norms of growth and development. But no individual child is ever average; individual differences are what teachers must deal with not with averages. Haven't you, and Piaget too, avoided the central problem of the classroom teacher, the individual child in his or her uniqueness?

A: I would have to say that I agree with the premises of this question but not with the conclusion. It is certainly true that the educational philosophy that has been presented in this book is a developmental, and hence a normative one. And it is also true that no individual child is average and that a teacher must deal with individual differences. But the conclusion from these premises, that a normative approach says nothing about individual differences, does not follow. Let me explain.

First, with respect to individual differences we have to ask how such differences are to be understood. At least two different approaches have been taken to answering this question. One approach is quantitative and the other is qualitative. When, for example, we speak of individual differences in intelligence, we mean that individuals can be arrayed along a measurable contin-uum or dimension by means of tests. Another approach is qualitative and suggests that individuals can be grouped in a set of more or less distinct categories such as "impulsive or reflective" or "field independent vs. field dependent" or "first-born" or "only child" or "middle child."

My point is that whether we approach individual differences quantitatively, or qualitatively, we still approach such differences from the standpoint of norms, either dimensions or generalized descriptions of certain "types" of individuals. No child can be described in isolation from norms of one sort or another and even "uniqueness" is defined relative to other individuals since it is a quality or set of qualities that the individual does not share with others. But to know that he or she does not share them one must know not only the individual, but many other individuals as well.

So individual differences cannot be dealt with independently of norms. The real question, in approaching individual differences, is what set of norms shall we use? In this book, the emphasis has been upon the use of developmental norms and of assessing children with respect to their attainment of concrete or formal operations. Because these are "deep" rather than "surface" structures and because—thanks to Piaget—they are so well understood, knowing where a particular child is on this developmental continuum has direct and, I believe, important educational implications. The chapter on curriculum analysis was devoted to demonstrating how a knowledge of the developmental level of the child could be used to analyze and to select appropriate curriculum materials.

As to individual uniqueness, I know of no other psychologist who has spoken to this issue more eloquently than Piaget. The central question of Piaget's epistemology is "how does anything new come about?" He has not provided a complete answer to the question, but he has described the processes—assimilation, accommodation, and equilibration—that participate in the process. And perhaps that is all one can do, for if one could predict or deliberately bring about the new, it would not really be new. There is, of necessity, therefore, a certain indeterminancy in human creativity.

A final word, the use of developmental norms in assessing individual differences has an advantage over other norms. Most children, with the exception of the severely retarded, attain concrete operations. Hence, they are capable of learning the basic academic tool skills. If they are not acquiring these tool skills, despite having concrete operations, then we must look to our educational materials and practices and not to the child. The advantage, it seems to me, of the use of developmental norms in assessing individual differences is that, in accounting for school failure, the onus falls on the school program and not on the child.

Q: In this book you have spoken primarily to elementary education. How does this educational philosophy apply at secondary and higher levels of education?

A: Some of the principles outlined in the book, particularly in the chapters on learning and motivation, are, from my point of view, appropriate at all levels of education. For example, at the University of Rochester I run a practicum course for undergraduates. They must commit themselves to the course for a full year and during the year they spend at least a day a week in a school setting. They are required to keep a diary and to attend a weekly seminar in which they discuss their work with the children. In the seminar they are also helped to acquire observational and instructional skills.

In this practicum the students are given the opportunity to interact with children in a school setting which fosters operative learning. They are also introduced to new concepts and terms (such as operative and figurative learning) and they are given an opportunity—in the seminar and in their diaries—to re-present their experience or to tie up their concepts with their new-found terms and with their own language. Hence connotative learning is encouraged as well. In short, I believe that at all educational levels and in all curricular domains, education will be most effective if all three learning modes are encouraged.

It is also true, however, that the relative priorities given to one or another of the three curricula (described in Chapter VIII) should probably be altered. That is to say, during periods of rapid physical and intellectual growth, during the preschool and again during the early adolescent years, the developmental curriculum has to be accorded particular attention. These are periods when intellectual structures (concrete operations and formal operations respectively) are in the process of formation and in which there is a great deal of stimulus-nutriment-seeking activity. Therefore, provisioning at these levels of education is particularly important. Young children need materials of all sorts, blocks, forms, buttons, and so on, to classify and seriate. Young adolescents need issues to argue, projects to undertake collectively, and curricular materials at the formal operational level (such as algebra, history, and metaphorical literature) to whet their new intellectual abilities. At the preschool and early adolescent levels, well-provisioned classrooms, replete with diverse materials providing exercise for emerging cognitive skills, are essential from a developmental perspective.

During the elementary-school years, particularly the middle ones, and the middle years of secondary education, more emphasis can be placed on the school curriculum as such. At the elementary-school level this involves the tool skills of reading and mathematics. At the high-school level it may mean training in the tool skills of science, mechanics, fine arts, and so on. For those going on to college, the tool skills will be different from those going directly to work, but in either case it is the school curriculum rather than the developmental curriculum that comes into prominence.

At all levels of education, however, and regardless of content, the results will be most satisfactory for the children and for the school, if operative and connotative learning and not just figurative learning are encouraged and given an opportunity to occur.

Q: In your brief discussion of tests and grading you suggested that they were negative in their effects upon children. I agree with that. But I and most other teachers I know about are still required to give tests. Saying that tests are not helpful to children, however, is not very helpful to teachers. What can we do about it?

A: Yes, you are quite correct. In this book I have spoken in terms of the ideal, what education would be like in the best of all possible worlds (Piagetian, of course!). But I am well aware of the realities and we are forced to give tests at the Mt. Hope School. Under the circumstances we have adopted the old saw "if you can't beat them, join them." Before you say that such capitulation is in complete contradiction to everything I have advocated thus far, please let me explain.

I don't like tests and I believe, as Piaget does, that they distort the whole educational process. But they are a fact of life and continue to be taken seriously by parents, administrators, and politicians. Under the circumstances it seems very important that we get children to take tests operatively rather than figuratively. Tests are foreign to children, the language is strange and so too is the format and the whole climate of "testing." Consequently, children often respond to tests on the basis of figurative cues and fail to look at the tasks from an operative standpoint. As a consequence they do not do as well as they might.

What we do at the Mt. Hope School is to prepare the children for taking the tests and prepare the teachers for administering and scoring them. With respect to the children this means: talking about tests and testing, providing samples of previous tests that children can work on at their speed so that they can become familiar with the language and format under nonstressful conditions, and simulation of testing procedures and instructions. Such preparation is in no way loading the deck in favor of the children. Most tests presuppose just such preparation and assume that the children are competent test-takers. But test-taking is a learned skill, not an intuitive one. Children need help to learn to do it well. By preparing children to take tests, by making them more sophisticated test-takers, we are actually conforming to the rules of good testing.

As far as teacher preparation goes, this means, first of all, reading the tests over ahead of time both with respect to content and instructions. If there are clear-cut ambiguities in the instructions (looked at from the standpoint of curriculum analysis described earlier), the teacher should correct them. The point of the examination is to get the best possible performance from the children, and they should not be handicapped by poorly thought-out instructions. In addition to having the children do a number of practice runs, it is also important to tell them in advance and several times when the "for real" testing is to happen. To give children the best chance possible, the tests should be given first thing in the morning, never late in the afternoon. And tests should be scored carefully— with so much riding on them it makes little sense to treat them carelessly no matter how much we dislike them.

At present, tests seem to be a way of life in most school systems and in all likelihood this will continue to be the case. But some of the negative effects of testing can be lessened if we take testing seriously, as everyone else seems to do, and prepare ourselves and the children much in advance. With such preparation and by testing under optimum circumstances, children can attack tests operatively as challenges to their intelligence and not of their memory skills. So long as test scores play such an important part in American education, children should be given every opportunity to perform on them at their very best.

BIBLIOGRAPHY

Ainsworth, M. D. S. Object relations, dependency and attachment. *Child Development*, 1969, *40.* 969–1025.

Ashton-Warner, S. *Teacher.* New York: Simon & Schuster, 1963.

Baldwin, J. M. *Thought and things* (Vols. 1 & 2). New York: Macmillan, 1906.

Bartlett, F. C. *Remembering.* Cambridge, England: Cambridge University Press, 1932.

Benedict, R. *Patterns of culture.* Boston: Houghton Mifflin, 1934.

Berlyne, D. *Conflict, arousal and curiosity.* New York: McGraw-Hill, 1960.

Binet, A. *L'Etude experimentale de l'intelligence.* Paris: Schleicher Feres, 1903.

Bloom, L. Language development. In F. D. Horowitz (Ed.) *Review of Child Development Research* (Vol. 4). Chicago: University of Chicago Press, 1975, pp. 245–304.

Bolles, R. C. Learning motivation and cognition. In W. K. Estes (Ed.) *Handbook of Learning and Cognition.* New York: Wiley, 1975.

Botvin, G. J., & Murray, F. B. The efficacy of peer modeling and social conflict in the acquisition of conservation. *Child Development,* 1975, *46,* 796–799.

Bovet, P. *The child's religion.* New York: Dutton, 1928.

Bowlby, J. *Separation.* New York: Basic Books, 1973.

Braine, M. D. S. The ontogeny of English phrase structure: The first phase. *Language,* 1963, *39,* 1–13.

Brainerd, C. & Allen, T. Experimental inductions of the conservation of "first order" quantitative invariants. *Psychological Bulletin,* 1971, *75,* 128–144.

Briggs, C., & Elkind, D. Cognitive development in early readers. *Developmental Psychology,* 1973, *9,* 2, 279–280.

Brown, C. *Manchild in the promised land.* New York: Macmillan, 1965.

Brown, R. *A first language.* Cambridge, Massachusetts: Harvard University Press, 1973.

Bruner, J. S. *The process of education.* Cambridge, Massachusetts: Harvard University Press, 1961.

Burgess. E. W. (Ed.) *Personality and the social group.* Chicago: University of Chicago Press, 1929.

Burtt, H. E. An experimental study of early childhood memory. *Journal of Genetic Psychology,* 1932, *40,* 287–295.

Burtt, H. E. A further study of early childhood memory. *Journal of Genetic Psychology,* 1937, *50,* 187–192.

Burtt, H. E. An experimental study of early childhood memory: Final report. *Journal of Genetic Psychology,* 1941, *58,* 435–439.

Chomsky, N. *Syntactic structures.* The Hague: Mouton, 1957.

Claparéde, E. *Le Developpement mental.* Neuchâtel: Delachaux et Niestle-S.A., 1951. (First edition 1906.)

Cremin, L. A. *The transformation of the school.* New York: Vintage, 1961.

Darwin, C. *The origin of the species.* Oxford: Oxford University Press, 1956 (sixth edition).

Deci, E. L. *Intrinsic motivation.* New York: Plenum, 1975.

Dewey, J. *Experience and education.* New York: Macmillan, 1938.

Dewey, J. *The child and the curriculum, the school and society.* Chicago: University of Chicago Press, 1957 (first published in 1900 and 1902).

Dewey, J., & Dewey, E. *Schools of tomorrow* (with an Introduction by Wlliam Brockman). New York: Dutton, 1962 (first published 1915).

Dowdeswell, W. H. *The mechanisms of evolution.* New York: Harper & Row, 1962.

Durkin, D. *Children who read early.* New York: Teachers College Press, 1966.

Elkind, D. The development of quantitative thinking. *Journal of Genetic Psychology,* 1961, *98,* 37–46.

Elkind, D. The child's conception of his religious denomination I: The Jewish child. *Journal of Genetic Psychology,* 1961, *99,* 209–223.

Elkind, D. The child's conception of his religious denomination II: The Catholic child. *Journal of Genetic Psychology,* 1962, *101,* 185–193.

Elkind, D. The child's conception of his religious denomination III: The Protestant child. *Journal of Genetic Psychology,* 1963, *103,* 201–304.

Elkind, D. Discrimination, seriation, and numeration of size differences in young children. *Journal of Genetic Psychology,* 1964. *104,* 275–296.

Elkind, D. Preschool education: Enrichment or instruction? *Childhood Education,* 1969, *45,* 321–327.

Elkind, D. Perceptual development in children. *American Scientist,* 1975, *63,* 5, 533–541. (a)

Elkind, D. We can teach reading better. *Today's Education,* 1975, *64,* 4, 34–38. (b)

Elkind, D., Koegler, R., & Go, E. Effects of perceptual training at three-age levels. *Science,* 1962, *137,* 3532, 755–756.

Elkind, D., & Weiss, J. Studies in perceptual development III: Perceptual exploration. *Child Development*, 1967, *38*, 553–561.

Erikson, E. H. *Childhood and society*. New York: Norton, 1950.

Fantz, R. Visual perception from birth as shown by pattern selectivity. *Annals of New York Academy of Science*, 1965, *118*, 793–814.

Featherstone, J. *An introduction: Informal schools in Britain today*. New York: Citation Press, 1971.

Froebel, F. *The education of man*. New York: D. Appleton & Co., 1893.

Freud, S. *The ego and id*. London: Hogarth, 1927.

Freud, S. The dynamics of the transference. In J. Strachey (Ed.) *Collected papers: Sigmund Freud* (Vol. 2), London: Hogarth Press, 1953. (a)

Freud, S. Screen memories. In J. Strachey (Ed.) *Collected papers: Sigmund Freud* (Vol. 5). London: Hogarth Press, 1953. (b)

Furth, H. G. Thinking without language: Psychological implications of deafness. New York: Free Press, 1966.

Gelman, R. Conservation acquisition: A problem of learning to attend to relevant attributes. *Journal of Experimental Child Psychology*, 1967, *7*, 167–187.

Gesell, A. *Studies in Child Development*. New York: Harper, 1948.

Gibson, E. J., & Levin, H. *The psychology of reading*. Cambridge, Massachusetts: The M.I.T. Press, 1975.

Glucksberg, S., Krauss, R., & Higgins, E. T. The development of referential communication skills. In F. D. Horowitz (Ed.) *Review of Child Development Research* (Vol. 4), 1975, pp. 305–341.

Goffman, E. *Behavior in public places*. Glencoe, Illinois: The Free Press, 1963.

Goodnow, J. Problems in research on culture and thought. In D. Elkind & J. H. Flavell (Eds.) *Studies in Cognitive Development: Essays in Honor of Jean Piaget*. New York; Oxford University Press, 1969, pp. 439–464.

Green, J. A. *The educational ideas of Pestalozzi*. New York: Greenwood, 1914.

Groos, K. *The play of man*. New York: Appleton Century Co., 1914.

Hall, G. S. The contents of children's minds on entering schools. *Pedagogical Seminary*, 1891, *1*, 139–173.

Hartmann, H. Ego psychology and the problem of adaptation. In D. Rapaport (Ed.) *Organization and Pathology of Thought*. New York: Columbia University Press, 1951.

Hawkins, D. Messing about in science. In C. H. Rathbone, *Open Education*. New York: Citation Press, 1971, 58–70.

Herndon, J. *The way it spozed to be*. New York: Simon & Schuster, 1968.

Holt, J. *How children fail*. New York: Pitman, 1964.

Hutchins, P. *The surprise party*. New York: Macmillan, 1969.

Inhelder, B. *Le diagnostic du raisonnement chez les debiles mentaux*. Neuchâtel: Delachaux et Niestlé, 1943.

Inhelder, B., Sinclair, H., & Bovet, M. *Apprentissage et structure de la connaissance*. Paris: Presses Universitaires de France, 1974.

Isaacs, N. *Some aspects of Piaget's work*. London: Froebel Society, 1959.

Itard, J. M. G. *The wild boy of Aveyron*. New York: Appleton-Century-Crofts, 1962.

Jensen, A. How much can we boost IQ and scholastic achievement? *Harvard Educational Review*, 1969, pp. 1–123.

Jourard, S., & Lasakew, P. Who does what to whom? *Human Behavior*, July 1973, 54–55.

Kellogg, R., & O'Dell, S. *The psychology of children's art*. New York: Random House, 1967.

Kilpatrick, W. H. *The Montessori system examined*. Boston: Houghton Mifflin Co., 1914.

King, E. M., & Friesen, D. T. Children who read in kindergarten. *The Alberta Journal of Educational Research*, 1972, *XVIII*, 147–161.

Klein, G. Peremptory ideation: Structure and force in motivated ideas. In R. R. Holt (Ed.) *Motives and Thought: Psychoanalytic Essays in Honor of David Rapaport*. New York: International Universities Press, 1967, pp. 78–128.

Koffka, K. *Principles of Gestalt psychology*. New York: Harcourt Brace, 1935.

Kohl, H. *36 children*. New York: New American Library, 1967.

Köhler, W. *Gestalt psychology*. New York: Liveright, 1947.

Kraus, R. *Whose mouse are you?* New York: Macmillan, 1970.

Kugelmass, S., & Lieblich, A. Perceptual exploration in Israeli children. *Child Development*, 1970, *41*, 1125–1132.

Lévi-Strauss, C. *Structural anthropology*. New York: Basic Books, 1963.

Lévi-Strauss, C. *Elementary structures of kinship* (edited by R. Von Sturmer). Boston: Beacon, 1969.

Lewin, K. *Principles of topological psychology*. New York: McGraw-Hill, 1936.

Livesley, W. J., & Bromley, D. B. *Person perception in childhood and adolescence*. New York: Wiley, 1973.

McClelland, D. C. Testing for competence rather than for intelligence. *American Psychologist*, 1973, *28*, 1–14.

McGaugh, J. L., Weinberger, N. M., & Whalen, R. E. (Eds.) *Psychobiology: The biological basis of behavior*. San Francisco: W. H. Freeman, 1966.

Mead, G. H. *Mind, self, and society*. C. Morris (Ed.) Chicago: University of Chicago Press, 1934.

Mehler, J., & Bever, T. G. Cognitive capacity of very young children. *Science*, 1967, *158*, 141–142.

Miller, G. A. The magical number seven, plus or minus two: Some limits on our capacity for processing information. *Psychological Review*, 1956, *63*, 81–97.

Mills, C. W. *The sociological imagination*. New York: Oxford University Press, 1959.

Montessori, M. *The Montessori method*. New York: Schocken, 1964 (first printed in 1912).

Montessori, M. *Spontaneous activity in education*. Cambridge, Massachusetts: Robert Bentley, Inc., 1964.

Opie, I., & Opie, P. *The lore and language of school children*. London: Oxford University Press, 1960.

Peel, E. A. *The pupil's thinking*. London: Oldbourne, 1960.

Piaget, J. *Recherche*. Paris: Edition la Concorde, 1918.

Piaget, J. Correlation entre la rapartition verticale des mollesques du valars et les indices de variations specifiques. *Revue susisse de zoologie*, 1920–21, *28*, 125–133.

Piaget, J. *Les notions du mouvement et de la vitesse chez l'enfant*. Paris: Presses Universitaires de France, 1946.

Piaget, J. *The moral judgment of the child*. New York: The Free Press, 1948.

Piaget, J. *The psychology of intelligence*. London: Routledge & Kegan Paul, 1950.

Piaget, J. *The child's conception of the world*. London: Routledge & Kegan Paul, 1951. (a)

Piaget J. *The judgment and reasoning of the child*. London: Routledge & Kegan Paul, 1951. (b)

Piaget, J. *Play, dreams and imitation in childhood*. New York: Norton, 1951. (c)

Piaget, J. *The language and thought of the child*. London: Routledge & Kegan Paul, 1952. (a)

Piaget, J. *The origins of intelligence in children*. New York: International Universities Press, 1952. (b)

Piaget, J. *The construction of reality in the child*. New York: Basic Books, 1954.

Piaget, J. *The child's conception of geometry*. London: Routledge & Kegan Paul, 1960.

Piaget, J. Cognitive development in children: Development and learning. *Journal of Research in Science Teaching*, 1964, *2*, 176–186.

Piaget, J. *The mechanisms of perception*. New York: Basic Books, 1969.

Piaget, J. *The child's conception of time*. New York: Basic Books, 1970. (a)

Piaget, J. *Science of education and the psychology of the child*. New York: Orion, 1970. (b)

Piaget, J. *Structuralism*. New York: Basic Books, 1970. (c)

Piaget, J. *Biology and knowledge*. Chicago: University of Chicago Press, 1971.

Piaget, J. *To understand is to invent*. New York: Grossman, 1973.

Piaget, J. *La prise de conscience.* Paris: Presses Universitaires de France, 1974. (a)

Piaget, J. *Understanding causality.* New York: Norton, 1974. (b)

Piaget, J., & Inhelder, B. *Le developpement des quantites chez l'enfant.* Paris: Delachaux & Niestle, 1941.

Piaget, J., & Inhelder, B. *La genese de l'idie de hasard chez l'enfant.* Paris: Presses Universitaires de France, 1951.

Piaget, J., & Inhelder, B. *The child's conception of space.* London: Routledge & Kegan Paul, 1956.

Piaget, J., & Inhelder, B. *The psychology of the child.* New York: Basic Books, 1969.

Piaget, J., & Inhelder, B. *Mental imagery in the child.* New York: Basic Books, 1971.

Piaget, J., & Inhelder, B. *Memory and intelligence.* London: Routledge & Kegan Paul, 1973.

Piaget, J., & Szeminska, A. *The child's conception of number.* New York: Humanities Press, 1952.

Preyer, W. *L'ame de l'enfant.* Paris: Felix Alcau, 1887.

Rapaport, D. The autonomy of the ego. *Bulletin of the Menninger Clinic,* 1951, *15,* 113–123.

Redl, F., & Wattenberg, W. W. *Mental hygiene in teaching.* New York: Harcourt Brace Jovanovich, 1953 (2nd edition).

Rotter, J. B. *Social learning and clinical psychology.* New York: Prentice-Hall, 1954.

Rousseau, J. J. *Emile.* New York: E. P. Dutton, 1955. (Translated by Barbara Foxley.)

Russell, B. *A history of western philosophy.* New York: Simon & Schuster, 1945.

Sameroff, A. J., & Chandler, M. J. Reproductive risk and the continuum of caretaking causality. In F. D. Horowitz (Ed.) *Review of Child Development Research* (Vol. 4). Chicago: University of Chicago Press, 1975, 187–244.

Schafer, R. Ideals, the ego ideal, and the ideal self. In R. R. Holt (Ed.) *Motives and thought: Psychoanalytic essays in honor of David Rapaport.* New York: International Universities Press, 1967, 129–174.

Seguin, E. *Idiocy and its treatment by the physiological method.* New York: Teacher's College, Columbia University, 1907.

Shinn, M. W. *Biography of a baby.* Boston: Houghton Mifflin, 1900.

Sinclair-deZwart, H. Developmental psycholinguistics. In D. Elkind & J. H. Flavell (Eds.) *Studies in cognitive development: Essays in honor of Jean Piaget.* New York: Oxford University Press, 1969, 315–336.

Silberman, C. E. *Crises in the classroom.* New York: Random House, 1970.

Skinner, B. F. *The behavior of organisms.* New York: Appleton-Century-Crofts, 1938.

Slobin, D. I. *Psycholinguistics.* Glenview, Illinois: Scott Foresman, 1971.

Spencer, H. *The principles of psychology* (Vol. 2). New York: Appleton, 1896.

Strauss, C. L. *Structural anthropology.* New York: Basic Books, 1963, p. 21.

Strauss, C. L. *Elementary structures of kinship.* Boston: Beacon, 1969.

Sullivan, H. S. *The interpersonal theory of psychiatry.* New York: Norton, 1953.

Tolkien, J. R. R. *The hobbit.* New York: Ballantine, 1966 (first printed in 1937), 183–184.

Waelder, R. The psychoanalytic theory of play. *Psychoanalytic Quarterly,* 1933 2, 208–224.

Wallon, H. *Origines de la pensee chez l'enfant.* Paris: Universitaires de France, 1947.

Watson, J. B. *Psychological care of infant and child.* New York: Norton, 1928.

Weir, M. W. Development changes in problem-solving strategies. *Psychological Review,* 1964, *71,* 473–490.

Wertheimer, M. *Productive thinking.* New York: Harper & Row, 1945.

Wiener, N. *Cybernetics.* New York: Wiley, 1948.

Wilson, E. O. *Sociobiology: The new synthesis.* Cambridge, Massachusetts: Belknap Press of Harvard University, 1975.

INDEX